P9-DEZ-077

SERVICE WITH A SMILE

Ronelle Ingram

Edited by:
Rebecca A. Kanan

Published by:
Asay Publishing Company
420 N. Range Line Road, Ste. 19
Joplin, MO 64801
1-800-825-9633 or 1-417-781-9317 (for all other company products)
1-417-781-0427 (Fax)
http://www.asaypub.com

Additional books may be ordered on the Asay Publishing website at:
http://www.asaypub.com/newbookstore

Author:
Ronelle Ingram, P.O. Box 50041, Irvine, CA 92619
email: ronellei@msn.com

Edited by: Rebecca A. Kanan, Asay Publishing Company
Cover Designed by: Brenda Tidd, Asay Publishing Company
Photography by: Anamaria Brandt, Tustin, CA

Printed by: Johnson Printing Service, Dallas, TX

ISBN 1-58156-093-1

This book is dedicated to:

Fargo	**CADE**	**Rán**
Past	**Present**	**Future**

Table of Contents

Preface

"Sometimes A Career Will Find You"

By Ronelle Ingram

Growing up in the 1950s/60s, I never envisioned myself as a copier technician. Horse trainer or lawyer were my spoken career choices. Actually, all I wanted to do was make enough money to be able to support my love of showing horses. Much to my parents' disdain, after graduating from UCLA, I became a horse trainer. After two years of living my dream of having people pay me to ride their horses, I figured out that this was very hard work. The joy of riding my own horse, too, was diminishing.

So, I dusted off my college diploma and went in search of a job. It was 1972. The women's liberation movement was gaining momentum. Somehow, I wound up at Savin. In retrospect, I was duped into taking a job in their service department. They told me they wanted to integrate women into their field service department. New age thinking? No. The goal was to get cute girls into the customers' offices to sell service agreements under the guise of being a tech.

By the time I figured out their program, I had become a pretty good copier tech. Because I had a "man's job," I was making more money than a traditional woman's job would pay. I was able to support my horse habit. After two years, I left Savin to work as the service manager of a newly-formed Mita dealership. Actually, I was the entire service department as well as receptionist, warehouse person, and sales representative. The company grew and prospered. Over the years, I have changed companies. I have hired, trained, and managed hundreds of field service technicians. I have learned many lessons the hard way, and I can recognize failure as well as success.

From the very beginning, the companies belonged to NOMDA (National Office Machine Dealer's Association) and I was sent off to the FIX service manager's seminars. FIX provides its attendees with a written guideline of how to manage a service department. FIX also introduced me to the world of NOMDA and later BTA (Business Technology Association). For the past twenty years, I have been a NOMDA/BTA instructor. I have taught dozens of different programs throughout the years. I have spoken in 49 of the United States, in Canada, Europe, and Australia. I have taught the FIX seminar more than 100 times to more than 3,500 service managers and company owners over the past twenty years.

As a FIX instructor, I was often being interviewed and quoted in business magazines. I was approached to write one article for Solutions magazine in 1993. Then, I was asked to write another and another. In 1996, I began writing my "Service With a Smile" column for Asay Publishing Network's RS&R (Repair, Service, and Remarketing) News. Over time, I added *ImageSource* and *ENX Magazine* to my monthly writing schedule. Along the way, I have written for more than a dozen other publications.

I must admit, I enjoy speaking more than writing. But each one does seem to feed the need for the other. I have been forced to stay ahead of the learning curve. I have always tried to practice what I preach. Better yet, I have shared with my readers my daily trials and tribulations of running a service department. My ongoing teaching of FIX and other service management programs has enabled me to learn from other service professionals all over America and many parts of the world.

I have traveled over a million airline miles, met thousands of people, and learned something new on each occasion. My articles have been a way to share with the industry a bit of the knowledge I have gained along the way.

None of this would have been possible without the help of Bob Geschwender, who has worked with me for the past 25 years. Bob has allowed me the professional and personal freedom to use all my vacation time to speak and write. He has also continually provided me with ideas and topics that I have turned into articles and seminars.

My thanks also to Rebecca Kanan, who integrated over 100 computer files into an organized grouping—this book—representing about 10 years of my writing. Special thanks to Roger Asay, whose encouragement allowed this book to happen. Also thanks to Marc Spring, Susan Neimes, Brent Hoskins, Enieda Lewsjeski, and Neal McChristy, who have all corrected my spelling, laughed at my grammatical errors, and always given me a new deadline to meet.

Through the years, I have always tried to stay true to my goal in life—to give back more than I receive. I have always tried to share the knowledge I have gained, through whatever means. The office machines industry has been very good to me personally and professionally. Each day that I go to work, I actually do approach my career in service with a smile.

Editor's Introduction

For as many years as Ronelle Ingram has been writing, she has amassed a large and faithful following. Readers have come to anticipate her pithy and down-to-the-bone honest advice about managing service and sales, both in small companies and large corporations dealing with office machines and equipment. An untiring speaker and author, Ingram has delighted audiences and readers, among them dealers, technicians, and managers, by offering serious, practical ideas—with a smile.

Drawing upon the success of Ronelle Ingram's articles that have been published throughout the office machines industry for more than a decade, Asay Publishing Network decided to pursue the publication of Ingram's collected articles. Included are selections from among her writings for *ImageSource* Magazine, *ENX* Magazine, and Repair, Service, and Remarketing News, which have appeared in print form and on the Internet in e-form. Her scattered monthly products have been reaped, winnowed, and harvested to create this book.

Each one of these sections can be used independently as a study guide for your next company, service, or sales meeting. Each chapter or section can be a personal reminder of a better way to accomplish a needed result. They can also help you to help others create profit and prosperity in their personal and professional life. As Ingram often says, "Good people make good employees."

In the following pages, the reader will find advice about managing efficiently; overseeing sales and service matters; dealing with personnel, particularly technicians; drafting maintenance and other agreements, along with handling technological changes and costs associated with them; and continuing to grow personally and professionally through self-actuated learning. While timeless in nature, the advice also pinpoints moments and people in the industry's history that have captured the essence of success.

Rebecca A. Kanan,
Editor

Chapter 1

The Business of Being In Business

Efficiency

The Business Card: Your Easiest Advertisement

The business card can be as powerful a repair tool as the screwdriver, updated software, vacuum, or digital meter to the working-service professional. Easily the most under-utilized tool carried by a service technician is the business card.

Most service departments can learn a lesson from the marketing side of their company. Sales people seem to require a re-order of business cards on a regular basis. When techs are asked to produce their business cards, they often struggle to find a chemical-soaked box of unopened cards at the bottom of their "car stock/miscellaneous" box.

The presentation of a business card to customers is a ritual of professional behavior in our society. Upon visiting a customer for the first time, the effective technician will present his or her card to the receptionist. This conveniently announces the tech's name and the company represented. The moment of first impression becomes a professional, positive interaction.

Upon an initial meeting with the key operator, the tech should again present the business card and verbally acknowledge the key operator's name.

I am constantly asked, "How can we get our technicians be part of the active marketing staff of our company?" The simple use of a business card is the cost-effective, non-threatening, proactive tool for successful on going and future sales.

Pick a Card, Any Card

The customer's selection of "their buyer of choice" is sometimes a matter of convenience. Your chance of making a sale today is increased each time a customer has the opportunity to touch your company's name and telephone number. I send a "thank you" note and my business card to every new customer I interact with on the telephone. My business card is included with every correspondence that leaves my office, be it, to customer, dealer, or vendor.

High employee morale and excellent customer relations go hand in hand. If you want your techs to act in a professional, pro-customer manner, treat them as professionals. All technicians must be issued business cards. Whenever a promotion is made, new business cards should be issued. Techs should be required to carry business cards in their tool case, service vehicle, and on their person (wallet, purse or pocket).

At a recent service meeting, I had a surprise drawing that required technicians to deposit their business card "in the hat." Much to my pleasure, 30 techs had a business card in their wallet. The other two quickly went to their tool case in their car to retrieve a business card.

I continually stress the need for service techs to have their business cards in a convenient location for ease of availability. Try doing a reality check of your own service reps. As an owner or service manager, randomly ask your technical staff for a business card. If they cannot give you, their boss, a business card within 15 seconds, they probably are not dispersing the company's mini-advertising billboard to your potential customers.

Be All That You Can Be

Take a little time to rethink the title that is designated on the card. Service tech or technical field engineer--which is worth $100 per billable hour? Master field engineer, senior technical supervisor, manager of customer retention, client satisfaction supervisor, digital connection specialist. . . s-t-r-e-t-c-h the limits of creativeness.

The business card can become your company's most cost-effective advertising medium. Today's business cards have e-mail addresses, photographs, maps to simplify finding the local office, advertising of new products, lamination, printing on both sides, convenient tent folding, dual or triple-color, holographs, perforated edges. The list goes on and on. If you perceive yourself as a creative, aggressive business, make sure you business cards reflect your conception.

Once your field staff is conditioned to carry their business cards, stretch their comfort level of use. Cards are to be given to friends, family members, business associates, church members, and neighbors, and posted on the local neighborhood bulletin boards.

I was recently called by a local restaurant manager seeking information on purchasing a new piece of equipment. At the end of the conversation, I said, "How did you hear about our company?"

"I saw your business card in our monthly-drawing fishbowl," the customer said. As it turned out, I did not win the free lunch, but this restaurant is now our customer, thanks to my business card.

Any time you attend a professional meeting, have your business cards ready for sharing. This shows any potential customer or joint vendor company that you are prepared. Any business person who doesn't have enough foresight or customer savvy to have a clean, unwrinkled business card to share is probably not the type of company where you would want to do business.

Advertising, self-pride, professionalism . . . the business card is the right tool for the job.

Driving Service Department Profits

It's an age-old quandary for businesses: company cars or per-mile reimbursements? While company owners and field personnel will always debate this issue, there is, in the end, no right or wrong answer.

Although company cars are a wonderful benefit for any employee, they are, nevertheless, a costly enterprise for a business. Costs extend far beyond the initial price of the vehicle, ongoing fuel charges, and maintenance. Once a company begins providing vehicles, a fleet car manager is necessary and an enormous amount of time for record keeping is required to optimize the investment. In addition, you become responsible for all the daily situations that come with the ownership or lease of these vehicles.

Using Company Cars

Whenever a car breaks down, it becomes your responsibility to have another employee pick up the stranded technician; get the car towed; arrange and pay for the repair; provide a replacement vehicle; and chauffeur the tech around until you can provide that person with a working mode of transportation. While attending to transportation problems, the tech is being paid for little more than sitting around and waiting.

Many companies that supply vehicles restrict non-company-related use. Those that do permit personal use usually assess a set cost per month that must be paid by the employee. When an employee pays for evening and weekend use, companies must be very specific about who else is eligible to drive the company-owned vehicle.

Employee-Owned Vehicles

There are creative ways to pay for employee-owned cars, with mileage reimbursement rates actually structured around desirable work habits. If the goal is to have techs drive late-model, well-running vehicles, you can pay for performance. Cars that are less than three years old can earn an employee a penny or two bonus per mile over the base rate. On the other hand, a staff member with a vehicle three to five years old would receive a lesser amount per mile, and so on.

Paying per-mile reimbursement is typically more cost effective than spending time monitoring a fleet, even if the fleet is merely a single car. Basically, an allowance eliminates the headaches of vehicle repair costs and up-keep.

In addition, when continual breakdowns are negatively affecting a tech's attendance, mileage compensation can be reduced. The mathematical logic is sound. When an employee-owned car is not in running condition during regular work hours, paying a lesser percentage of the cost of the vehicle is appropriate. During any month that field-working time is missed due to car trouble, the per-mile reimbursement rate is reduced for the entire month.

Reimbursement Restrictions

In times of record-high gas prices, acknowledgement of the situation is necessary. It is important that management shows sensitivity to the plight of employees who use their personal vehicles in their work. A temporary increase of a penny or two per mile, or a creative reimbursement program, may be worth the cost if it improves employee morale.

The Internal Revenue Service has very specific rules about employee mileage reimbursement and use of company-owned vehicles. If you pay a flat monthly rate, the money must be treated as taxable income. (The owner of the vehicle may take deductions at the end of the year on their personal income tax.) An employee cannot be reimbursed for driving to or from work or for their first call (if it is closer than the office). When the company-owned car is driven to work, those miles must be considered taxable income. Yes, it is an involved issue, but information is available on the IRS's Web site: www.irs.gov

Travel Time Charges

Once you decide how your company is going to provide transportation for your field technicians, you must establish a way for your company to be reimbursed for the time and expense of traveling to a customer's location.

Charging a set travel cost, which some companies add to their hourly service rate, is a common practice. Typical charges of $5 to $110 for travel are seen. By increasing the base service rate to include the cost of travel, issues of travel charges are instantly eliminated. Using the wording, "priority response $25," may be more acceptable than, "travel charge $25." Some companies believe separating the labor rate from the travel rate makes their service charge appear more competitive in their marketplace.

Every dealership must establish guidelines to deal with the travel and car issues in their own way. The key to dealing with travel expenses is to be aware of the various issues when establishing your company's policies. Do not be afraid to periodically review and change the way you are paying mileage or charging for travel time. A company car is a privilege, not a right.

Establish written policies. Review and change them as needed, and be fair. Monitor the use of company cars. Review the expense reports before payment. Establish appropriate business practices. Treat the company car or mileage reimbursement as any other ongoing business expense. Use monetary reasoning rather than emotions.

Ten Service Department Travel Points to Consider

1. Is the customer billed for travel on the return call?
2. If a customer requests a service call and the office is closed upon the tech's arrival, do you charge for travel only?
3. Is a minimum service-call rate charged?
4. If a customer is outside your regular service area, will you service them for an additional travel charge?
5. Should you charge by the mile or by the hour?
6. Should the starting point be your office or the location of the last service call?
7. If your sales staff sells outside a designated area, should the customer be penalized with a higher travel charge?
8. Will you establish travel zone charges with varying rates for different areas, and will zone charges be extended to different rates on your service agreements?
9. For those of us who service in areas that require payment for parking, who pays that cost, and is the customer assessed the cost of parking?
10. Should service agreement rates vary if parking costs $10 per hour, and can you require a customer to validate parking or pay the additional cost?

"My Car was Stolen . . ."

"I've been in an accident. My car's been totaled. I'm lucky to be alive."

"It's gone. I parked right in front of my own house. I'm waiting for the police now."

How do we deal with the technician whose personally-owned vehicle is stolen or damaged? While listening to the personal tale of hardship, I have to bite my tongue so as not to blurt out, "What about our parts?"

Who pays for the loss? Does the per-mile paid by the employer for mileage reimbursement cover the cost of privately purchased comprehensive insurance to cover the cost of up to $10,000 of employer-owned parts and equipment? What about the time it takes to inventory the lost parts, order, and reorganize all the new pieces?

Should the liability of the lost items vary depending on whose fault the accident or theft is? After a tech has his or her car stolen, does the employer present a bill for $7,000 while the tech is trying to negotiate a down payment for a replacement vehicle?

If the vehicle is company owned, what personal responsibility does the technician have for the company's lost possessions?

Most service managers have had to deal with the dilemma of a stolen, damaged, or missing car, tool case, parts, beeper, cell phone, or laptop computer. An ounce of prevention is worth much finger pointing and shuffling of blame.

I put together a program of self-insurance for my techs. I brought the idea before the group as a whole at a routine service meeting. I asked for their input. Was it fair to the company? To them? Where does personal responsibility end and company responsibility take over?

No Chasing the Horse if the Barn is Locked

I passed around the following form: I asked my 35 techs to look into how much coverage their homeowners, renters, or auto insurance provides them. I said, "We will revisit the question in one month. Think it over. It will be your decision."

At the end of the service meeting, 23 techs handed me their already-signed form, agreeing to take the one-cent reduction in mileage reimbursement. I was pleased with their sense of responsibility and fairness toward the company. The following month we again discussed the program. Thirty-four of 35 techs signed on.

Although I never did implement this program, I am hopeful the additional focus on personal responsibility for company property will be its own insurance policy against any future loss. By locking the barn door in advance, I won't have to chase the horse.

Car Stock Insurance Program

You are financially responsible for the safekeeping and return of all company parts, supplies, tools, manuals and other equipment issued to you. The company is offering to self-insure (including the deductible) any loss* of any issued parts, supplies, tools, manuals and equipment for a one cent per mile reduction in your expense reimbursement. **The average car stock inventory is valued in the $10,000 range.**

If you choose **not** to take advantage of the company issued insurance, **you are completely responsible to repay the full cost of any company owned and issued parts, supplies, tools, manuals and other equipment that is lost or damaged.** Any normal working hours spent on the recovery, replacement, reorganization or follow-up on lost or stolen parts will be taken as sick, vacation, or non-paid time basis.

For those who choose not to take advantage of the company insuring our property, make sure you check with your homeowners, renters or car insurance to see if you have coverage for company owned equipment stored in your personal car or in your home.

As a reminder, anyone using a vehicle that does not completely protect (camper shell, locking compartment etc.) all company owned parts, supplies, tools, manuals, and equipment will have their mileage auto reimbursement decreased by a penny per mile until such protection is provided. Anything that is lost or stolen from the unprotected area is the responsibility of the technician.

Our goal is not to present any undue burden on any employee; rather, we are trying to close the barn door before the horses escape. Part of your responsibility as an employee is to protect company property.

When you park your car, be aware of the capital investment that is stored in your vehicle. Part of your per mile reimbursement should be allotted for your insurance coverage.

Would you park your car in an unlighted alley at 3:00 AM if there were seventy $100 bills on the dashboard for all to see? Think before you park. Do not leave CD's, leather jackets, laptop computers, vacuums, tool cases, wallet, beeper or garage door opener in open view. A baby blanket and a well-chewed teddy bear is better deterrent to theft than a copy of GQ or Sports Illustrated covering the corner of a fancy multi-drawer parts box.

*Police report, insurance claims report, photos or other verifying material must be presented to verify loss or damage.

Personal Inventory Sheet

Total cost of parts from inventory $ ______________________________

Tool Case $ ________ Tools $ ______________ Vacuum $ __________

Manuals $ __________ Meter $ ______________ SurTest $ __________

Supplies $ __________ Other $ ______________ Map Books $________

Total Estimate of car stock inventory $____________________________

****

I ________________________________ hereby authorize the company to reduce my mileage expense rate by one cent per mile. This one cent per mile reduction will constitute full payment of company sponsored insurance to cover any loss* or damage* to any company owned parts, supplies, equipment, tools or manuals.

Signed ____

Print ___________________________ Date ______________________

*Police report, insurance claims report, photos or other verifying material must be presented to verify loss or damage.

****

I ________________________________ do **not** choose to take part in the company sponsor insurance program covering the cost of parts, supplies, tools, manuals and other equipment. **I take complete financial responsibility for the full wholesale cost of all company issued parts, supplies, manuals, tools and other equipment. I understand I will be completely responsible for the full repayment of all cost related to the lost or damage of any company owned parts, tools, manuals, supplies and equipment assigned to me.**

Signed ____

Print ___________________________ Date ______________________

Maintenance Agreement Disclaimer

The service manager's basic mindset is to look consistently for potential areas of concern. Better to be pessimistic and prepared than optimistic and surprised.

A service manager's job is to anticipate the worst scenario, have a contingency plan, and diligently work to never let anyone find out how prepared we are for potential disaster.

In Monopoly, the "Get Out of Jail Free" card is highly coveted. This card has the ability to get you out of unforeseen future problems. It's a mini-insurance policy for your well-being. A well-written maintenance agreement can allow you this same sort of protection from future disaster.

The Wear of Time

As office equipment gets older, it costs more to service. You're more vulnerable. Older equipment fails easier. It's harder to find parts. Metal fatigue increases.

As personnel leave, fewer employees are trained on older equipment. Those who are trained are your senior--and highest paid--employees.

Quality service departments that replace parts proactively and perform complete preventive maintenance procedures and installations of all factory recommended modifications, can easily keep equipment working for many years.

However, a vulnerable time in the life of a customer's loyalty is the fifth- or sixth-year renewal of their servicing agreement. There is a fine line between pricing a maintenance agreement high enough to provide a reasonable expectation for profit, yet low enough to insure the customer will continue to do business with you.

The customers realize that the need for new equipment is quickly approaching. Our goal is to solidify their loyalty while protecting our company from the potential liability of covering old equipment under a new maintenance agreement. This potential for vulnerability can be shifted in your favor.

Federal regulations require office-equipment manufacturers to stock parts for five years after the last date of manufacture. We, as servicing dealers, can use this limitation to our own advantage.

For the past several years, I have used this disclaimer notice on all maintenance agreements offered on older equipment (five-plus years):

> **DISCLAIMER:** Due to the age of this equipment, if (ABC Co.) cannot acquire parts and/or adequately repair this piece of equipment, the maintenance agreement may be canceled. A prorated credit will be applied to your account.

We had a self-inking stamp made that fit in a blank area of our current maintenance-agreement form. We print up our monthly MA renewal forms as usual. During the pre-mailing check-over, we stamp the disclaimer on all equipment five years and older. We make sure NOT to stamp any older equipment we have recently sold as refurbished during the past three years.

Fore-Warned is Fore-Armed

It really is a win-win sort of agreement. The dealer will continue to care for the equipment as long as it is economically profitable. When the time comes that parts and/or repair is no longer practical, a credit (not a refund) toward future purchases will be given.

First-time receivers of this disclaimer stamped on their MA will sometimes call with concern. Our office staff is trained to explain to the questioning caller that service will continue as usual.

We are simply informing them, in advance, of the future potential of parts being a little harder to obtain. They are reassured that we and the manufacturer will try to retain access to all the commonly needed parts. Additionally, as older equipment is traded, we keep a few machines in reserve as a source for non-consumable replacement parts.

In effect, we are telling them: Everything will be done to optimize the continued well-being of your current equipment. The time is coming for you to think about budgeting for new equipment. Be warned in advance, if your equipment does require non-consumable parts, they may be replaced with previously-used parts.

As the years go by, you can continue to stamp the disclaimer statement on each successive year's maintenance agreement. When the time comes that you can't adequately repair the equipment, you have warned the customer in advance. In many cases, the customer calls us to apologize for dragging out the life of the machine for so long. They know they have been warned. The inevitable has finally happened.

Anticipate Aging

Because equipment ages, dealers need to prepare for a professional, positive transition from old to new. The dealer gains credibility by proactively informing the customer, in advance, of potential extended down-time.

You can keep the pricing at a level where you can make money or morally (legally) bail out of the maintenance agreement while keeping the customer's full payment. This "credit" can easily be used as the initial payment for a lease on new equipment. This is a great selling technique that can put your customer into new equipment from your company without any additional, immediate payment.

By consistently using the disclaimer stamp, you have earned the right to diplomatically say, "I told you so," and remove all embarrassment from not being able to acquire parts or adequately repair old equipment. You can continue to generate revenue from older equipment while limiting your liability. Using the disclaimer stamp can be as lucrative to your service department as the "Get Out of Jail Free" card is to your Monopoly game.

Short Term Rentals

One of the strengths of the small office-equipment entrepreneur is the ability to provide equipment and services that the "big guys" cannot offer. One of the industry's most lucrative areas of business has become the short-term rental. If you are already shaking your head and thinking "We don't do short term rentals (too much hassle for too little return)," you need to keep reading.

What are you doing with all of those analog copiers that are being returned? Many of us still have a few in our showrooms. Three-year-old segment 2, 3, and 4, low meter count analog copiers can be purchased off lease-returns starting at $100. The industry has turned their back on analog. In the rush to digital, we forget that many of our customers care more about getting a cheap copy than they care about the copier.

Over 50 percent of our short-term rentals turn into long-term rentals or purchases (leases). The same dealer who refuses to be paid for a two-week rental, quickly agrees to do a free two-week trial. Historically, more rentals turn into sales than do free no-obligation demos. Most copier dealerships have a piece of equipment that can be economically made usable for a one-month rental.

Most dealerships have long tenured analog technicians who have not made the transition to digital equipment. Therefore, it is becoming increasingly difficult for the dealerships to find enough analog work to keep those techs busy, much less pay for themselves. The ability to provide equipment on an immediate short-term basis can produce additional revenue, keep your senior technicians working, and set your company apart from other local dealers.

Forming a Short Term Rental Program

Have a short-term rental form ready to be filled in, faxed, or e-mailed, and make sure there is a space for:

-- All equipment being rented (specify accessories including the need for a stand)
-- Cost of the equipment
-- Separate lines for cost of the delivery and pick-up
-- Minimum length of rental
-- Value of the equipment
-- Total due upon delivery
-- Method of payment

All random rental requests should be connected to a pre-designated person with a pre-determined back-up. The random caller requesting short-term rental information must not be sent to a voice mail. These callers are usually calling from the Yellow Pages of the phone book or multiple Web sites. It is not unusual for the same caller to contact me two or three times within 30 minutes. They are getting confused as they work down the list of copier company advertisements.

A knowledgeable, prepared employee must be available to respond immediately. When unexpected needs occur, the customer is ready and willing to pay extra for their instant needs to be fulfilled. A customer who is calling around will often hang up without leaving a message. Even worse, some other company will have made the deal before anyone from your company gets the chance to call back.

Assign Roles

The ideal in-house person should be someone who knows the instant availability of equipment. All short-term rental requests and "can you deliver it today" callers are automatically transferred to me, because I have a grasp of what equipment is (or can be made) ready for instant delivery. If it is a current customer calling, I usually have a working knowledge of their history, pay record, and overall needs and restrictions (stairs, limited work hours, space or electrical irregularities).

All service managers know that from time to time they must get a "loaner" machine ready to take to a customer whose equipment is down and who is demanding, "Fix it today or get me a loaner." Service managers can always hustle and get a machine to a customer in a hurry. This same mentality can be used for becoming proactive in providing rental equipment on very short notice.

Confirm Basics With Callers

Once I am connected to the caller requesting short-term rental information, I quickly establish the actual need. If the caller is not a current customer, I quickly (within the first two minutes) and professionally explain the delivery and pick-up charges with a base rental rate. Our standard one-month rate is charged whether they keep the equipment four hours or 30 days.

Next, I confirm that the delivery location is within our servicing area. I also ask if there are stairs or any other special delivery circumstances. Then, I give a price range of $400 to $900, depending on copier size, copies needed, delivery and pick-up dates, and length of time needed.

The $400 to $900 response instantly gets rid of 25 percent of the non-customer callers. The other 75 percent of the callers are excited to find someone who is willing to provide a short-term rental at any cost.

Once the approximate cost is established, I start asking questions concerning specific needs, anticipated volume, space availability, accessories, etc. Many people think they need a high-speed copier that can make 10,000 copies in one or two days. When I explain the need for special electrical outlets and a huge amount of space, they usually determine that a mid-size copier will accommodate their needs.

Generally speaking, people who say they will make thousands of copies usually do not. People who say "a couple hundred," actually make a few thousand. You can be very creative with base cost and overage charges. Very often, the overage charge on copies is greater than the base rental rate. People who try to think "cheap" understate the amount of copies they plan to make. Big profits can be made by pricing a low base rate with higher overage charges.

New customers are required to pay for delivery, pick-up, and first and last month's rental by credit card or upon delivery. The rental agreement must be faxed back signed before any preparation is started. When the customer pressures me by asking, "How quickly can you deliver?" I respond by saying, "Within 24 hours of the rental agreement being signed and faxed back to me." Established customers can be billed net 10 days for the total cost of delivery, pick-up, first and last month's rental charges. Our average short-term rental generates a $1,000 initial billing.

Typical Rental Charges

Small, 12-15 copies-per-minute, cost $75 each for delivery and pick-up; $95 for the base rental (includes 500 copies overages at 3.5 cent per copy, as well as service and supplies). Mid-size, 30-45 copies-per-minute, cost $230 for delivery, $230 for pickup, and $310 base (includes 5,000 copies and overages at 2.5 cents per copy). It is very important to state the hours that service is provided. Many people requiring a special event weekend rental think you will provide service 24/7.

I know of no other way to earn $500 to $1,000 on a piece of un-sellable analog equipment that is taking up space in my warehouse or showroom. We have a few long-time repeat short-term rental customers who we allow to pick-up and return the small rented copiers. One local car dealer rents a small tabletop copier every three months to use at a tent sale.

Now, for the most important part of this short-term rental program. We have found that over half of the short-term rentals we installed are extended into longer rentals. Our average one-month rental turns into a seven-month rental and 25 percent of our short-term rentals turn into sales.

If new equipment is purchased, all rented equipment comes with an automatic 50 percent credit on the first three months of the rental. Any rental that is kept for one year is picked up at no charge. Any rental kept for two years is credited back to the original delivery charge.

When a chargeable service call reveals a piece of equipment that is either too costly to repair or parts are no longer available, the customer is offered a short-term rental. The cost of the first hour of service is credited toward the rental. Later, if the customer buys the equipment, 50 percent of the first three months of the rental are credited back.

Make Opportunities

Remember that the secret is to set up a system that commits the customer to continue to do business with you. Once you have a little bit of their money (commitment), continue to treat the customer fairly and you will have the opportunity to earn much more.

The entire process can start with the positive answer to the question, "Do you do short-term rentals?" Plan ahead. Teach your receptionist to divert all short-term rental questions to a designated in-house employee that knows the condition of all available machines. Learn to use those analog techs to generate additional revenue. Take advantage of those seemingly worthless analog trade-ins. Provide a product that the bigger companies are refusing to offer.

Short-term rentals can provide long-term profits to your company. Instant need, relatively low cost, and next day delivery can make a profitable sale happen before the competition even knows there is an opportunity.

Beat the Competition With MSDS

Material safety data sheets–MSDS–are requested by our customers on a regular basis. The callers are relieved when I quickly acknowledge the availability of and my familiarity with the needed information. I ask for their fax number and the make and model of equipment we are servicing. The entire process is handled professionally in less than 60 seconds.

Very often, customers who request copies of the MSDS forms will share their previous frustration when they have tried to obtain the forms from other vendors. "It's refreshing to deal with a company that knows what it is doing."

The customers are reassured that the company they do business with is knowledgeable, well-managed, ecologically responsible, and adheres to federal requirements.

MSDS: Can you or your staff handle a request as efficiently?

By now, many of you are saying: "Why are you telling me this? I am a copier, fax, laser printer, or typewriter dealer. The only potentially dangerous thing in our company is an upset customer. We don't sell anything that's hazardous."

That is not the way our friends at OSHA look at things. Glass cleaner, lubricant, plastic surface cleaner, grease, canned air, much more so toner, developer, and all types of photoconductive drums, fall into the list of products requiring material safety data sheets.

Let me share a story from another company who learned the hard way.

Costly Example

"You just made your company $5,000." I looked up in surprise. A fellow service manager from a neighboring company was standing in my office. He had by-passed the receptionist and come up the back stairs directly into my office.

I replied with a smile, "I hope I did make my company $5,000 today, but what are you referring to?" He pointed to a stack of material safety data sheets that were on the corner of my desk. I had just received them in the mail from our primary manufacturer.

"What do those MSDS sheets have to do with making $5,000?" I queried.

"My company had become a little too casual about responding to customer's requests for the MSDS sheets. To make a long and costly story short," the visiting service manager continued, "a non-customer, located out of our selling area, allegedly made several calls requesting material safety data sheets on some of the products we sell. Each time the sales rep took down the information needed to send them a copy of the MSDS, it became apparent that the information was on a 10-year copier that was out of our territory. Evidently, no one followed through with sending the information.

"According to the customer's complaint, their requests were ignored. Unbeknownst to us, as an authorized dealer, we are required to provide this information to anyone (even if the requestor is not our customer or in our selling area). Evidently, the manufacturer's computerized pre-recorded sales-information-forwarding-system gave this hospital clerk (located over 200 miles from us) our number as the local authorized dealer."

"Fast forward fourteen months. An OSHA agent shows up at our door. She inspects everything. We have all the MSDS on file for her to inspect. But that was not good enough. Before she leaves, after inspecting everything for a couple of days, we get cited and fined over $5,000 for a variety of miniscule infractions.

"We had a company meeting to reemphasize the importance of taking requests for MSDS sheets seriously. We have a new company policy. A mere whisper of a customer's request for material safety data sheets is responded to instantly. We send any customer anything that is requested."

After lunch, I took a new look at the MSDS issue. I pulled out an information sheet and reviewed a five-inch stack of MSDS I had in my file.

The U.S. Department of Labor's Occupational Safety and Health Administration, better known as OSHA, has mandated that material safety data sheets be supplied to anyone who buys or sells any chemical-based product that may be hazardous to the environment or human health.

Classifications Differ

Most MSDS are listed on OSHA's form No. 29 CFR 1910.1200. The Hazard Communication Standards are divided into Health, Fire and Reactivity ratings. They allow five hazard ratings: 0 = insignificant, 1 = slight, 2 = moderate, 3 = high, and 4 = extreme.

Products fall into different groupings of information, depending on the product. For toner and ink, for instance, the sheets list 16 different information sections for each item. These sections include: composition and ingredients, hazard identification, first aid and fire fighting measures, handling and storage, stability, reactivity, toxicity, disposal, and transport specifications. Making the issue more complex is the fact that all MSDS expire every three years.

When our local fire department arrives for our first semiannual fire safety check, they always ask to see our MSDS. This information becomes vital when a fire occurs in a warehousing area. Knowledge of the chemical makeup of certain environmentally hazardous material is a life or death situation to the firefighters.

Some fire departments require dual copies of the sheets to be kept off-site. This is a backup to protect the information in case of a fire that consumes the record-keeping area as well as the actual location of the hazardous material. Other fire districts require the data sheets to be filed directly with the fire department for immediate access before dispatching the firefighters to a potentially hazardous fire location.

Value-added Possibilities

Rather than looking at these sheets as another vexing government infringement on your company's right to do business, consider the value-added selling possibilities.

The next time you are in a very competitive deal, talk smart rather than dropping your price. Offer to provide, as an added value to the sale, customized material safety data sheets for the newly purchased equipment.

Tell the customers that the forms will be provided at no additional cost in duplicate, one for the master files and one to be placed near the new equipment. Explain that this will alleviate the necessity of wasting any of their valuable time tracking down the forms in the future. As a knowledgeable sales professional, you can reassure your purchasers that the manufacturer of their soon-to-be-purchased equipment has taken every measure to ensure the health and safety of their employees.

On several occasions, purchasing agents have asked me to assist them in writing bids for their upcoming copier and fax purchases. I always make sure I mention the need for submitting material safety data sheets for all equipment bids. It's just one more way to frustrate other would-be bidders, as well as underscoring my personal dedication to the ongoing health of our current clients.

Having a speaking knowledge of and immediate access to material safety data sheets on your products is an easy way to stay one step ahead of the competition. If you do not already have these sheets for the products you sell and use, contact your vendors and ask them to mail you original hard-copies (these look much better when used in a sales proposal and fax more readably).

You can follow the rules and be one step ahead of the competition by maintaining an up-to-date library of all the material safety data sheets on the products you sell and use.

Are You Getting Confirmations?

Airlines, hotels and car rental agents all use confirmation codes when making reservations to track follow-up inquiries. As a consumer, I always ask for the reservation number before completing a request for future service.

This confirmation number gives me a sense of security. I know the computer has a record of my service request. Nothing against the human touch, but in today's business world, the computer's memory overrides a nameless reservation clerk's friendly reassurance.

Having easy access to my confirmation number has enabled me to get that last seat on the airplane, receive the unlimited miles discount on the car rental, and secure that upgraded hotel room the clerk knows nothing about.

As a service manager, I have wrestled with the customer who insists they called two days ago, and have yet to see our technical rep. I have no record of their service request. Deep in my heart, I know this customer did not call two days ago. But my service staff is taking the brunt of their faulty memory or they may simply by lying to get to the top of my response list.

I have also dealt with the charge-call customer who insists they have canceled their service call after the service technician arrives at their office. In both cases, it is a no-win situation for the servicing dealer. Arguing with a customer who's lying to you to get special treatment will get you nowhere.

Using Confirmation Numbers

Every incoming service call to my service department is given a "confirmation number" before the caller hangs up. It's value-added, tangible reassurance for our customers and self-protection for my busy dispatchers.

Any time anyone calls to cancel an already placed service call, a cancellation number is given. We use the original confirmation number with the initials of our employee who takes the cancellation call. This helps keep everyone honest and attentive.

Just as our customers have reasonable expectations of the service we provide them, we subtly let our customers know they, too, have responsibilities in this servicing relationship. The use of the confirmation number is greatly appreciated by our regular customers. It also puts those "iffy fringe" customers on notice that we are a professional business organization that prides itself in the work we do.

Tracking Paperwork

These confirmation numbers also allow us to track incoming paper work from our field technicians. The confirmation number cross-references all received paper work.

The majority of my techs only come into the office once every two weeks. The techs know they are held responsible for turning in paper work on every service call that has been assigned to them.

After implementing a tracking program, you will be amazed at how many service orders do not make it back into your office on a timely basis. If you do your invoicing (and reconciliation of parts) off hard copies that are turned in by the tech, you are losing money without a tracking system. The sooner you can get your invoice into the customer's accounts-payable department, the sooner you will have this money in your company's bank account.

At this point, some of you may be asking, "Where do you get these confirmation numbers?" If you are on a computerized dispatch system, the computer automatically assigns some type of number to each new work order. If you still dispatch by hand, simply assign each newly taken call with today's date and number--1211 and 1212 would be the first and second calls taken on December 1.

Why It's Required

Let me take a moment to clarify why I "require every caller to be given a confirmation number."

To make this program effective, each dispatcher must always offer to give the customer a confirmation number. Change is difficult--even such a small change as ending each service call's request with a confirmation number. You as the decision-maker must do whatever is necessary to get your employees to buy into this program.

Your dispatcher's job will become easier when they start ending each call with "your confirmation number is. . . . Thank You." Disconnect the call. The confirmation number gives a professional finality to the conversation. Closing with the confirmation number eliminates the need for the enviable questions of "When will the tech be out?"

It's Win-Win

Consistently using the confirmation number eliminates a great deal of stress for the customer and the employee. Service dispatch can quickly locate all the needed information when the customer proudly recites his or her conformation number. At no additional cost, the confirmation number creates added value.

When a sales person places a call for a customer, give the number to the sales representative. Follow up with a call to the end user reassuring them a service call has been placed on their behalf. Confirm the problem, state the hours of equipment availability, and give them their confirmation number.

This is a win-win situation. Customers love being reassured. Your service department establishes a reputation for being conscientious and very proactive. In no time at all, the confirmation number becomes as reassuring as Pavlov's bell.

The confirmation number helps to keep everyone honest and accountable. Having the dispatcher, customer, and technician use the confirmation number is a true win-win situation. For no additional cost, you can reap the benefits of accuracy and accountability.

The Break-In: How Secure is Your Business?

You can expect, the longer you are in business, that you will be sued, you will have an IRS audit, and your company will be burglarized. Being sued and audited are painful to the owner and senior management. Having your company robbed or burglarized can be emotionally traumatizing to your entire staff.

Personal safety of all employees is the responsibility of everyone in your company. Being robbed during the day or burglarized at night can have both monetary and emotional consequences.

After a burglary, money must be spent to replace the stolen goods as well as to repair whatever was broken by the burglars to gain access to the interior of your building. Owners or facility managers need to take a second look at what policies and procedures should be changed to make sure nothing like this ever happens again.

Shifting Viewpoints

Take a look at your business from a criminal's point of view. Are you an easy mark?

As winter approaches, darkness becomes an issue. Employees will be arriving and leaving during the dark. Is your parking lot well lit? Do all the external light fixtures work? How far must an employee walk to get to the farthest areas of your parking lot? Will someone be available to walk a lone woman to her car?

What can the casual passerby see from the street during non-daylight hours? Do you keep all the building lights on at night? Are there curtains? Are they normally kept open or closed? Do you have cubicles that protect a direct line of sight from the street? Does the company have a policy regarding turning off lights, monitors, and other office equipment? Does the bookkeeper or payroll clerk stay late the last day of the month?

Do you have a working alarm system? How reliable is it? When is the last time you reviewed the security company's call list in case of an activated alarm? As an owner, do you know who would be called? The police? An employee?

As a manager, whom do you have on the security company's call list? Do you know what responsibility you have if you are called at 9:00 p.m. or 3:00 a.m.? Do the responsible people live within a reasonable distance from the company to be able to respond quickly to the security company's call?

Do you have a silent alarm or an external alarm that blares loudly from externally mounted speakers? Will an electrical blackout activate or turn off the alarm?

How many doors and windows have alarm sensors on them? Where are they located in the building? What does the bookkeeper do when leaving late one night and cannot get the alarm to properly set? What about the service manager who is rushing to pick up a preschool child from day care and cannot get the alarm set?

How many employees have keys to the office? When is the last time the locks were changed? Is there a company procedure for when an employee who has been issued a key leaves your employment? Is "do not duplicate" engraved on the keys?

What Could Be Lost

How would your company deal with personally-owned laptop computers being stolen from your office? Who is responsible for items in an employee's desk: PDAs, the high-tech hand-held calculators, money, tickets to the playoff game, eyeglasses, or other items of worth.

Do you park company owned vehicles overnight in an unsecured parking lot? Is the building next door vacant? Do nearby over-grown trees or shrubbery provide an easy hiding place for illegal activities?

So far I have asked many questions with no answers. Criminals work very hard trying to find an easy place to rob. Criminals will always commit crimes. It is your job to make sure they look somewhere else.

A Simple Written Checklist

-- List the name of alarm company and phone number.
-- Who has alarm codes? Who has authorization to designate a change?
-- At what point will the alarm company notify someone of an unset alarm?
-- At what point do you want the police called?
-- At what point do you want someone on your call list called?
-- How many contacts does the alarm company call if no one can be reached?
-- Once an employee is reached, what is their responsibility?
-- When should and when should not an employee drive to the office to check things out?

- -- Upon notification of an alarm, should an employee enter the building?
- -- Will your local police department charge you for a false alarm?
- -- What is it worth to the company to have the police check for a false or unset alarm at 3:00 am?
- -- Does your company have a written policy on leaving unattended valuables (including laptop computers) in the office?

A systematic approach to the security of your employees, building, and contents is a vital part of good business practices. It is much more cost effective and emotionally less perilous to "lock the door before the horse escapes."

After a burglary, owners or corporate officers will erect parking lot fences, enhance exterior lighting, install new door jams, install door sensors, and reinforce sliding glass doors, roof access hatches, and warehouse overhead doors. Often, the cost of a burglary is minor compared to the cost of updating the security needs of your office.

Take the appropriate time and actions to protect your business and employees from the monetary and emotional damage that can be caused by a break-in.

Crisis Management

We are living in one of the most dynamic eras of change in human history. There are lessons for every business owner and employee to learn from the unprecedented events of the week following Sept. 11, 2001. While the human tragedies cannot be dismissed, I would like to focus on the business lessons that can be learned from many current events.

Preparation and diversification can help individuals and businesses deal with the most unexpected events.

As a small business employee, I spend much of my prospecting time looking for niche markets that provide multiple purchasing opportunities: school districts, city, county, state, national government, aircraft manufacturers, telephone companies, large manufacturing companies . . . the bigger the better. Or so I once thought.

The State of California once provided my employer with over a million dollars in yearly revenue. The County of Orange was renting over 300 pieces of equipment from us. We sold over $1,000,000 of equipment to dot.com companies. A major entertainment corporation leased more than $900,000 in equipment. One Los Angeles law firm a made a five-year deal worth over a million dollars.

In each case, the highs created by the sale were tempered as the years went on. Things didn't work out quite as anticipated. The California State Legislature could not pass a budget and we were paid in promissory vouchers. The County of Orange filed for bankruptcy, owing us over $70,000. The dot.com bubble burst. The major entertainment group merged and new management didn't need the additional office machines. The law firm's senior partner died. The firm split up and they simply stopped paying their bills.

Dealing With Changing Times

When a big deal goes bad, the repercussions can severely impact the entire fiscal stability of a small business. That's where preparation and diversification become vital to ensuring stability and longevity.

I'm not sure if any company's crisis management plan ever before reviewed how to deal with the grounding of all (non-military) airline flights over the United States for one week. However, contingency plans can be made for corporate bank accounts being frozen, computer systems crashing, telephone lines being down, the loss of a CEO, earthquake, flood, and storm damage.

Most companies are so busy taking care of the daily needs of running a business, they fail to make any plans for the possibility of a true crisis occurring. Product tampering, embezzlement, structural damage to a corporate headquarters, death of key personnel, calling of a business loan, major law suits, or bankruptcy of your major vendor, can all cause havoc or ultimate destruction for a business.

A Lesson in Preparation

Crises can provide excellent learning opportunities. Learning from the misfortune of others can be much easier than learning while in the eye of the storm.

Even the smallest company can have a plan for dealing with a crucial situation. Often, the difference between a critical situation and a crisis is how the situation is handled. Speed of appropriate reaction is vital. The need for an immediate response necessitates having a crisis management team in place before a catastrophe happens.

Experts recommend that you have an in-house crisis management team. It should be a multi-disciplinary group that is physiologically ready to handle the worst-case scenario. It is best if the crisis management team has members from the IT (Information Technology) group, human resources, public relations, and fiscal management. You also need someone with leadership, speaking, writing, and motivational skills.

In some smaller companies, this may not be possible. One or two people may have to carry the entire load. Ideally, the IT person is needed to protect your information systems, update your Web page, and monitor and process e-mail communication. Human resources are needed to react immediately to any personal needs of those affected. Information dispersment, to internal and external areas, can be processed by your public relations department. When a crisis happens, money usually plays some sort of key role. The fiscal representative needs to monitor needs versus available resources.

The leader, speaker, writer, and motivator can be one of the previous group or a separate person who brings together all the factors of the crisis management group. As you are reading this, you may have automatically attached a person within your company that fits into each one of these criteria.

There may be a few open positions in your crisis management team, but an imperfect team is better than no team at all. Have a predetermined, designated spokesperson in place. Typically, this falls to the Chief Executive Officer of the company. The real crisis happens when something happens to the CEO. True crisis planning will allow for a backup spokesperson, in the case that the CEO is unable to take over the needed leadership role.

Speaking of Disaster . . .

In times of crisis, the sooner a spokesperson takes on a leadership role of information disseminator, the better. If your CEO is not an accomplished communicator in times of minor crisis, a lesser-positioned person with excellent communication skills is an appropriate substitute.

The crisis team should have one outside, but company-savvy, member. His or her role is to objectively appraise your firm's situation and help orchestrate the company's response.

While the crisis team is hard at work, make sure other people are still managing the day-to-day operations of your company. Do not allow the functioning parts of your business to slide into disrepair while traditional management members are handling the crisis.

The public and your employees will measure and long remember the initial response to any crisis. When a crisis hits, stay calm. Collect the facts. Do not go into hiding. Even if not all pertinent information is available, a leader can say, "I am not sure of the all the facts. We are diligently investigating all the relevant information." A nonspecific answer is better than saying nothing or blurting out an incomplete or incorrect response.

"Tell the truth. Tell it all. Tell it fast." This is an old public relations adage. Make no estimate of dollar damage, injuries, or estimated loss. That is the job of lawyers and insurance companies. Don't make any promises you may not be able to keep in the future.

Throughout the duration of the crisis, keep employees informed of developments and anticipated timetables. Provide a written communication employees can give to concerned customers or vendors. Written facts help to reduce the spread of incorrect information.

Assign an employee to handle any questions or inquiries. Let all employees know there is someone on staff to deal with specific issues arising from the crisis. This helps avert distraction, allowing for concentration on their normal work duties.

Active Alertness

Actively monitor employee, customer, public, and media opinions. Scan newspapers, business journals, Internet coverage, live broadcasts, chat rooms, message boards, etc. Consider hiring a clipping service to keep you abreast of media coverage.

Actively solicit and reward employees for reporting signs of impending crisis, including safety concerns, labor unrest, customer complaints, or other distressing rumors.

Preparing for crisis management is not a one-time exercise. Appropriate preparedness is an ongoing process. It requires strategic planning and simulation. Periodic mock crisis drills can be practiced and re-enacted on a yearly basis. Learning how to deal with the stress and volatility of a crisis situation can be taught ahead of time.

Now is the time to take a look at the sensitive underbelly of your company. Learn how to deal with a crisis situation. A preplanned learning exercise will increase your company's ability to successfully deal with a future catastrophe. Better yet, planning for a crisis may prevent you from ever having to deal with one.

According to the Institute for Crisis Management in Louisville, Kentucky, more than 85% of the business crises studied were visible to corporate management before the impending doom happened. More than three-quarters of these situations could have been averted or lessened, had management taken appropriate actions.

Ask the Simple Questions

Put aside a little time to look around your office and take inventory. What can you pinpoint that is working really well? What can you identify that is not working at all? Now consider how each procedure was originally organized, and ask yourself, "If I was setting up this procedure for the first time, would I arrange it in the same manner?" If the answer is no, the procedure is worth a second look.

Do not accept a certain method merely because it's the way you always did it in the past. That is just a lame excuse for mediocrity. And don't make the excuse that you barely have the time to handle urgent work, let alone rethink a procedure that is working reasonably well.

At some point in your service management career, you should rise above what is urgent and start dealing with what is important. This transformation can change an ordinary service department into the superstar department of a company.

Enlist Help

You can start the transformation process by asking a few simple questions of employees. In your next service department meeting, hand out a single sheet of paper with the question, "What can the service department do to increase profits?"

Have at least five, triple-spaced blank lines on the page following the questions. The multiple lines subconsciously tell the tech that you want detailed information. Do not, however, put a place for the person's name. Explain to your workers that remaining anonymous is acceptable; but if the employee believes he or she has an exceptional idea, then recommend that they put their name on the questionnaire, because there could possibly be a prize for the best idea.

This same kind of simplistic questioning can be done in the shop, warehouse, front office, and sales department. It is a proactive suggestion box. Ask, and you just may receive some great suggestions.

Once you have a couple of intriguing ideas that are worthy of your attention, the questioning can continue. Take nothing for granted. Ask the most basic questions.

Let's start with a universal service situation. How can the service department improve the set-up and delivery of new equipment?

I posed this fundamental question to my tech, shop, and warehouse personnel. I received dozens of different answers. We eventually made three lists. First, we listed the standard process, in chronological order, involved in getting a machine into our customers' hands. Second, we listed the problems, or realities, we typically face on a regular basis. Finally, we made a specific game plan that included when, where, what, how, and who was responsible for making sure the newly identified project was actually managed.

The Entire Project

We decided to view the entire process as a project, because, as most of you know, the "selling the box" mentality is no longer viable. In an industry that is continually evolving, selling a solution involves a great deal more than setting up a single piece of equipment that comes out of one box. So, more than ever, it is important to be organized and prepared for the growing number of challenges that a service department faces.

Below are the lists we established to identify the project that will efficiently improve our service department.

Managing the Project – Expectations:
The Standard Process

____ Make sure showroom or demo has appropriate equipment
____ Sales personnel trained to demo and sell appropriate usage
____ Sales personnel check for product availability
____ Sales double checks compatibility of requested equipment
____ Site survey, including space, drops, and electrical, is completed
____ Signed sales order is passed to procurement
____ Lease is approved
____ Products are ordered
____ Procurement gives ETA of products
____ Products are received by warehouse
____ Warehouse stages products
____ Service staff prepares products for delivery
____ Delivery and installation schedule is arranged with customer
____ Delivery personnel transport products to customer site
____ Service staff installs products
____ Training takes place
____ Customer satisfaction is confirmed
____ Customer signs off on installation
____ Customer is invoiced
____ Customer pays invoice

Managing the Project – Problems and Realities

____ Needed product is back-ordered from manufacturer
____ New sales rep does not know the equipment
____ No memory or network card is ordered
____ Customer signs sales order with wrong equipment
____ Improper pricing was quoted
____ Procurement follows incorrect sales order
____ Wrong products are special ordered
____ ETAs provided by procurement are not accurate
____ Products do not show up according to ETAs
____ No one checks on status of purchase order
____ Partial order is received by warehouse
____ Warehouse misplaces part of the order
____ Service does not follow up on status of procurement
____ Customer is not informed of delivery date
____ Service staff is not told product is delivered
____ Service technician is not qualified for installation
____ Second service technician does know what the first technicians did.
____ Installation takes longer than planned
____ Sales rep is unqualified to train on new equipment
____ Customer does not sign off on installation
____ Customer delays paying the invoice
____ Everyone blames someone else for all the problems

Managing the Project – Service Takes Control

____ One person or department takes control
____ Plan for control of the entire process
____ Project review
____ Resource planning
____ Management information
____ Coordination

____ Communication
____ Evaluation
____ Conflict resolution
____ Understanding
____ Get answers, not excuses
____ Customer satisfaction
____ How managed
____ Have and follow the plan
____ Follow-up
____ Use notebook or project management software
____ Follow-up
____ Detail person
____ Follow-up

Our goal was to establish policies and procedures that will ensure the first list of expectations becomes the standard. The mere fact that we were so easily able to make the second list of realities reflects our familiarity with the real-life problems that most dealers face.

Realistic Planning

By establishing a written list of the right way and the not-so-right way to handle things, we were able to establish and implement realistic procedures to improve our procurement, set-up, delivery, training, and customer satisfaction. This does not happen without planning, ongoing management, and quality control through following up and making redundant checks and balances.

Be a strong enough leader to ask the question, "How would we do this if we were setting up the procedure for the first time." Change is the only constant of successful businesses.

Profitable Parts Management

Parts usage, availability, car stock, and warehouse inventory levels can make or break the profitability of your service department. In some smaller companies, parts management can be the difference between staying in or being driven out of business.

Customers pay for and expect their equipment to be repaired. Just getting a body to a customer's office is not enough. If the repair requires parts that take two weeks to acquire, costs more than the customer is willing to pay, or exceeds what the maintenance agreement will cover, no one will we happy.

Profitable parts acquisition and usage is an art that requires a team effort. There are no hard and fast rules for car stock quantities, inventory turns, usage of "used" parts, air orders, board repairs, using of junk machine parts, in-house parts repair, etc. Each area of appropriate parts usage and acquisition must be approached in an individual way. But there can and should be specific guidelines for each of these measures.

Suggested Guidelines

1. Teach all service personal about the need for smart parts management.

Parts are sometimes replaced because of an extra sensitive customer.

Save the drum the architect insists on being replaced because of a small dot which only shows up when running 11X17 copies. This will be an acceptable replacement, for the rental copier, located in a dirty warehouse environment, that runs 81/2 X 11R. Save that drum. Label it appropriately. Don't be penny wise and dollar foolish. It will not save the company money if a technician has to reschedule a call, drive back to the office, search for the used drum for 45 minutes, and disrupt the office by complaining about the warehouse staff who can't do anything right. When using used parts, make sure the cost to obtain them is not greater than the money saved.

2. Be aware of the "Big Picture"

When a customer is going to replace their copier in 60 days, there is no need to do the 600K preventive maintenance servicing. A simple cleaning and new drum blade will suffice. This same service method holds true for the customer who requests major servicing two days before the current maintenance agreement expires. Wait for the renewal check before you invest in servicing that will last for the next six months.

3. Attach dollar value to your parts.

Giving a small part to a favorite customer is detrimental to everyone involved. Whenever a customer asks me to give them something for free, I politely remind, "You are asking me to steal. Having me fired or put in jail won't help either of us." People have gotten into the habit of asking for something for nothing. By being so blunt in my response, I put my customer on notice of the professional nature of our relationship.

My number one responsibility Monday through Friday, 8 to 5, is to ethically make money for my company. Being on friendly terms with our customers is good business, as long as the friendship doesn't extend into giving your product and profits away.

4. Ask technicians to take regular inventory of car stock.
The greater the frequency of requiring techs to do self car-stock inventory, the fewer parts will be carried. They will quickly return parts they rarely use. They will get their parts more organized. Dealers that require monthly car stock inventories normally reduce car stocks by over 50%.

5. Pre-assign extra time to inventory taking.
When a tech finishes his or her last servicing of the day too late to be dispatched to another call, but before standard quitting time, assign that extra few minutes to working on their inventory. Chances are, they will drive home rather than staying in the last customer's parking lot and counting inventory. When the time arrives for the actual completion of the inventory, you will have already provided enough company designated time to complete the task.

6. Technicians generate money in the field, not the shop.
Requiring techs to report to the office each morning to pick up the needed parts will waste more than $20,000 per tech (base rate of $53 cost of the service hour times 1.5 hours wasted each day) in non-sellable labor hours. That $20,000 can buy a great many parts. You could have one less tech and five times the inventory. Unused labor hours can never be sold again. Inventoried parts can be sold in the future.

7. Emergency part orders and the accompanying costs are good business.
Unused (or never to be used) inventoried parts are much more expensive than the tax-deductible payment for air shipment. It is much easier to ask your customers if they would like to pay an extra $15 to $25 for an overnight air charge than to ask them to pay inflated rates to help offset the cost of your million dollar parts inventory.

8. Obtain replacement parts quickly.

New, used, OEM, aftermarket, manufacturer, wholesaler, picked from your graveyard, repaired, etc., find the part NOW. Don't wait two weeks before you start the search. If it takes five phone calls and 50 minutes to locate a needed exotic part, add the cost of acquiring the part to the wholesale cost of the part. The sooner you quote the customer a price for a part, the better chance you have of keeping their business. The longer the equipment is down, the greater the chance of losing their business. It takes the same amount of time to find a part today, as it will to find that part next week.

9. Require a deposit before special ordering parts.

This is especially true when dealing with a new customer, a client with a history of paying slowly, or cancelled calls.

10. Allow your technicians to be honest.

If a tech breaks a part, allow him or her to return the broken pieces for a new part without a personal cost or reprimand. If you require a tech to lie or steal when an honest mistake is made, you are teaching how to be dishonest in the future.

11. Structure a procedure for techs to easily return unneeded parts to your inventory.

Encourage technicians to return unused parts from PM kits or any other unneeded parts to your main inventory. Make sure these returned parts are reentered into your open inventory system quickly.

12. Pay yourself for creativity.

Let's say a customer needs a main board: wholesale cost $150, retail $300. The simple profit would be $150 (freight, storage, labor to order and receive, etc., will be carried in overhead costs). Strive to achieve the same amount of dollar profit (not percentage) on the used or repaired part that you would have made on the new part. Saving the customer money should not have to cost your company money.

A. Using this formula, the used board taken off the junk machine should be sold for a minimum of $150 (plus whatever time it took to remove the part and test it). A justified retail pricing of a used board can rightfully be $225. This allows for the base profit of $150 (new board mark-up rate), plus splitting the saved amount with the customer. This $75 additional markup also covers the cost of having to acquire the used (or repaired) board. I would offer the customer a new board for $300 or a used board with the same 30 day warranty for $225. I would self-insure the used board.

B. There are exceptions to every rule. In order to get the customer's business, I may realize that the most I can get the customer to pay is $150. In this case, maybe a little profit is better than no business.

C. This same formula holds true when selling non-OEM parts. Do not cut your own profits. Make a conscious effort to work smart. You can save the customer money and retain your actual same dollar amount of profit. Too often, the dealer uses percentage as a mark-up base. Don't allow buying smart to reduce your own profitability.

D. As equipment gets older, manufacturers stop providing replacement parts. Make sure the customer pays for your ingenuity and necessary time spent to locate or repair each component. Artful marketing of used parts can be a revenue enhancer, or it can cut into high profit new parts replacement.

13. Add-on versus markup profit.
Some service managers state they receive 100% profit on their parts. Normally, this means their cost has been doubled. I also hear about 300% markup, which usually means the original listed cost has been tripled. In either case, the percentages are misleading. Two dealers can say they work on 40% margins. Their actual bottom line can be entirely different. A part that cost $100.00 selling with an *add-on* profit of 40% will sell for $140.00. Using *markup* profit calculations of 40% will achieve a price of $167. ($100.00 divided by 60, the reciprocal of 40) The *markup* figure of $167.00 creates an additional $27.00 of profit.

14. Plan ahead.
My maintenance agreement's "fine print" allows me to use new, refurbished, repaired, or any other approved parts for replacement. When selling "not new" parts to a chargeable customer, I always offer them the option of a new or used part. I adjust my pricing to always make sure I make the same amount of profit (cash dollars, not percentage) selling non-new, as I would on a new part.

15. Why put new parts in an old machine?
When suggesting the purchase of a used part, I always remind the customer their equipment is made up of hundreds of used parts. There may be no advantage buying costly new parts for a customer's old equipment (unless it is a consumable product). Resellers often sell new parts because they are easier to attain and stock than used parts.

The creative buying, storing, repairing, and marketing of parts can easily double your overall service profits. Prosperous service departments make the most of the parts portion of their yearly budget. A service department must optimize their inventory, use overnight air orders, stock repaired boards, use the "mark-up" method of pricing, and creatively plan to optimize the profit value of each part used.

Planning for Success

The Business Plan. Five year, three year, one year. Some people believe we should have written, well thought-out, formal plans for the future needs of our companies, our jobs, and our personal lives. Many never get around to actual planning. They are too busy dealing with the emergencies of the minute to plan for the successes of the future.

If you are a non-planner, maybe reading on will help you make the decision to stop thinking about the future and actually do something about being a master of your own fate. I congratulate those who have committed to developing formal business planning and long-term expectation and goals.

Professional, forward thinking entrepreneurs realize that each business, division, and department should have a formal written plan. Planning is the foundation of most successful organizations. A written business plan also allows for our own personal growth. This, in turn, will allow for our own personal success.

How to Begin

How do you actually write a business plan in these changing times? What should be included? If your business plan is completely wrong, but you still make money, are you successful?

I received a telephone call from another copier dealer owner asking me these questions. I smiled as I listened to her dilemma. Thinking back five years, my entire knowledge of the office equipment world has been turned upside down. Past performance is no longer an appropriate gauge for the future.

Almost everything has changed. The way we sell, the way we install, the way we service, how we make a profit, how we buy our wholesale products, the inventory we keep on hand, the magazines we read: everything has changed.

And then there is the Internet--friend or foe. accomplice or competitor. Some customers know more about our products than we do. Others are still running successful businesses without owning a computer.

Many small and large businesses, alike, judge success by monetary gain. If there is money in the checking account to pay the employees, vendors, and yourself, you must be on the right track. Why bother with a formal business plan? "My business plan is to make enough money to pay all the bills."

Looking back five years, I had no idea my major vendor would go bankrupt, merge with a huge conglomerate, change their name, and force me to sell printers.

Five years ago, I thought the big five copier manufacturers would be able to make high-speed (100+ prints per minute) digital copiers. I'm still waiting.

Five years ago, I did not know the analog refurb business would almost vanish.

Five years ago, I did not realize my need for technicians would actually shrink.

Five years ago, I didn't realize all my high-riding tech stocks would drop in price.

Five years ago, IT, NT, IMAC, MCSE, A+, Dot Com and CISCO had little relevance to my day-to-day work.

The business plan I wrote five years ago has turned out to be pretty much worthless. My 3.1 crystal ball did not foresee today's NT world.

Plan for Five, Live for One

However, the time and effort spent on the mechanics of writing a formal business plan were not wasted. It was a great learning tool. I can clearly see the areas of greatest change. The five-year plan has been modified more than a dozen times. Our one-year plans have become relatively accurate.

For instance, looking back, in 2001, Southern California gasoline prices skyrocketed to over $2.00 per gallon. I was forced to revisit my 2001 business plan. The IRS increased their business mileage rate by 10%. Our 2001-budgeted travel allowance was no longer appropriate.

Rather than just raise the mileage rate (taking the additional money out of the general funds), our 2001 Business Plan was adjusted. In order to qualify for the mileage increase, each tech was responsible for turning in one (equipment, service, or supply) lead per week. If his or her lead resulted in a sale, the tech instantly qualified for the increased mileage rate for the balance of our fiscal year.

As a manager, my goal was to reinforce the need to achieve more in order to receive more. Rather than just give the additional mileage money, our 35+ techs were required to do a little more. They would receive something extra, by doing a little more. Any tech that was unable to turn in the necessary lead was given the opportunity to turn in a written explanation for their lack of a lead. This written explanation would then qualify them for the additional mileage payment.

During the first 10 weeks of this program, service employee leads were directly responsible for more than $250,000 of equipment sales. The altering of the business plan paid off.

Even Generalities Will Work

My newest business plan is a little more general. Rather than anticipate "a 10% growth of technical staff," my written plan calls for "an appropriate number of technically competent, service employees." Hopefully, I am learning from my mistakes. Vague generalities of needs may be better than being off by 30%. It is better business to correct or adapt an incorrect multi-year business plan than have no plan at all.

Being responsible for creating a written business plan encourages managers to actually *think* about the big picture. Too often, aggressive, high achieving owners and department managers do not allow time for *thinking.*

Each of us must deal with the need to ponder ideas in their own way. Some people need the solitude of a fishing, camping, horseback, or motorcycle vacation to help clear their minds. Others find golf, walking, driving, reading, and listening to music to be catalyst to thought. Hopefully, you know yourself well enough to realize what activities will allow you to be able to have some *thinking* time.

Thinking Time

You need to allow time for thinking before and after putting your business plan into a formal written structure. Setting aside structured thinking time is often very hard for the workaholic, entrepreneurial types.

Whenever the opportunity arises, I try to ask the successful people I meet, "Exactly how to you go about the creative part of your business?"

Each has a different story to tell. But there is a central theme. Leaders are sponges for other people's ideas. They study the failures they see, as well as the successes. They shuffle, adapt, manipulate, and expand on the knowledge they collect.

Those who continue to grow and succeed are diligent workers. They possess a hunger and thirst for achieving greater goals. They believe in a balance of work and play. Both are done with a zeal for accomplishing a specific goal.

Those who have attained their own comfort level of success usually become complacent. They tend to rest on their laurels of past success. Maintaining the status quo becomes a sufficient quest. Mediocrity can usually sustain a business for five years. During this time, the insightful workers move on to more innovative employers. Many older owners or senior managers start focusing on their own retirement. In either case, you can only coast one way . . . down.

Creativity and Refinement

Forcing yourself to create and refine your business plan is a conscious act of competent management. If your company does not require you to create your own business plan, you can be pro-active. Write a business plan for your department. Extend this act to yourself, children, and entire family unit. Create a family plan. Work out a family budget with your spouse and children.

It is much easier to tell a loved one that a desired luxury is "not in the plan," rather than simply saying "No" to a capricious request.

As for the actual writing of a business plan, there are dozens of software packages, books, college classes, and seminars that will guide you through the process. Your local banker may be the one who actually forces you to sit down and write a formal business plan when you need an extension on your business loan.

Getting started is always the toughest part. List the things your business needs to accomplish to be profitable. Then make a list of what you must do to achieve the items named on the first list. A very general outline is a first step toward a successful business plan. While you are reading the rest of this book, make notes of your thoughts. Tab this article as a reminder. Put it in your "in" box on your desk.

Congratulations. You have already taken the first step toward writing your Business Plan.

Chapter 2

Learning To Play Well With Others

Sales And Service

Expectations

The foundation of providing customer satisfaction is living up to your customers' expectations.

High noon at the fast-food drive-through window. With three cars in front of you, you order a Number 3 Combo. What are your expectations?

The order will be filled in, perhaps, 183 seconds? A little more or less. But not 10 minutes, and not 10 seconds. What about cost--$4.95? Maybe the super size for $5.75?

High noon at the New York Plaza's Garden Room. Order the luncheon special. What are your expectations?

Walk through the lobby. Wait to be seated. Wait for the menu. Wait for your drink. Wait to have your order taken. Have your drink refilled. Lunch is served. Check is delivered. Credit card is presented. Receipt is given.

Forty-five minutes? An hour? Two hours? What about cost--$25 plus a tip?

It is human nature to have pre-conceived notions as to time, cost, and worth.

The fast-food franchise and the Garden Room are both providing noontime nourishment. However, in each case, the noontime diner has entirely different expectations of the product he or she will receive.

If either establishment provided the product of the other, the purchaser would be disappointed.

This same principle can be extended to the expectations your customers have for the products your company delivers.

A service department in a small rural area can be very effective in providing next-day service, whereas a business located in the Aleutian Island Straits is pleased with 5-day fly-in response time, and the downtown law office in a metropolitan area is known for demanding a field technician within one hour.

My personal all-time most impatient customer called at 8:10 a.m. one day requesting service. Upon trying to enter a new service call, I realized someone else from their office had placed a call at 4:10 p.m. on the previous day. In fact, the tech was scheduled to start with this customer's machine at 8:30 that morning. I did not tell the customer of the previous day's service request. Instead, I politely gave the service call confirmation number and said a tech would be out by 8:30 that morning.

The customer's curt response was, "That's not acceptable. We need someone NOW."

"Our techs start work at 8:30," I responded. "You will be the first call of the day. The tech will be there in about twenty minutes."

In a gruff, disconcerting tone, the customer retorted, "See what you can do to speed it up. This is an emergency."

When a service department deals with customer satisfaction, expectations are more important than execution. Customers who are accustomed to two-day response time rarely complain if your tech arrives within eight hours. On the other hand, customers who were told (in writing) they have guaranteed four-hour response time are outraged if the tech arrives in 4.5 hours.

I am always amazed at how often "paper jam" and "emergency" are linked in the same sentence. Heart attack, World Trade Center, and Black Hawk Down are words more logically connected with emergencies. An inline stapler jam is an inconvenience. Human blood pressure and machine jam counts should not be related.

Since our service department has taken on network administration, the frequency of the use of "emergency" has diminished. We make a conscious effort to schedule network administration and installations first thing in the morning. Our customers have become accustomed to placing the network service call today and happily receiving service tomorrow morning.

Customers are more willing to switch off a printer than to attempt to clear a copier paper jam. Customers understand that they can unhook, move, and reinstall a back-up 30-50 pound HP printer. Yet they are unwilling to walk to the copier, lift the purple handle, and gently pull the paper out. Their expectations include fast copier repair service and slow printer repair response.

As your company takes on new products and services, make sure your sales, service, and accounts receivable departments agree on appropriate expectations.

Expectations Are a Two-Way Street

Take a look at your company's billing system: Due upon receipt, net 10, or net 30 days. Your company has an expectation that all customers pay their bills. We all know those slow-paying customers who tend to use the square root of the time due for payment of an invoice. The sooner you require payment, the sooner you will have an expectation of receiving payment.

If your goal is to receive prompt payment, change the expectations. Change your company's policy to, "Invoices are due upon receipt." You can still allow net-30 days to your trustworthy customers. This change of phrasing can allow you a 30-day advantage on trying to collect on the perennial slow payers.

If you want your sales people to close the majority of their sales before the 30th of the month, change their expectations. Pay a bonus for all sales closed and turned in before the 20th of the month. Try changing to a four-week month. This will instantly create a 13 "month" year. You will have one additional rotation of sales being finalized each year. Those who are using the 13-month year system have realistic expectations of increasing their yearly sales.

Do you have a problem with tardiness and absenteeism at the office? Do you have and require employees to use a time clock? If management has no expectations of a recording system of time worked, why should employees care what hours are spent at the office?

Do you have problems with accurate car stock parts inventory for your techs? How often do your require accurate inventories to be taken? What types of checks and balances are used to maintain an accurate ongoing car inventory? Do your techs have realistic expectations of what is required?

Changing and reinforcing expectations can make an enormous difference in your business. Don't disappoint your customers or employees by saying one thing and doing another. Have a plan and work it. You can be innovative in a very consistent way. Under-promise and over-achieve. Fulfilling expectations is the key to customer and employee satisfaction.

$100,000,000-Worth of Opinions From the Buyers

At an industry gathering, I attended a panel discussion made up of six high-level purchasing agents who were in charge of acquiring office reproduction equipment. As a group, they had the responsibility of personally overseeing more than $100,000,000 in annual purchasing budget money.

For two hours, members of the audience had the opportunity to question these buyers. The panelists spoke with candor and knowledge, and they even took a few well-deserved potshots at the traditional selling methods of today's "solution" speaking sales reps.

As a life-long service professional, I listened intently to these purchasing agents. I was impressed with the articulately asked questions from the audience. Most questioners had an air of "sales professional" firmly injected into their insightful questions. I would like to share with you the key points I took away from this interchange of perspectives.

Key Points

Sales people need more training; buyers expect the sales people to know more than they do; team selling is not customer friendly. As a group, all agents dislike multiple sales representatives showing up, with or without forewarning. Buyers find it distasteful to have one rep do all the talking, while the other rep(s) just "stand around looking at the ceiling." The reason is, "if the non-speaking guy does not know enough to talk, he definitely does not know enough to be awarded my business."

There are several dichotomies in America's work culture. One has to do with paper usage. Everyone is trying to cut down on the number of paper copies/prints being made, but they still want a physical copy. From the panel: "As ecologically sensitive buyers, we all profess that we want to go paperless. Unfortunately, most corporate cultures still judge a person's productivity by the amount of paper on their desk."

The more we talk about paperless, the more we print. Now we are scanning and printing; people still trust paper. Most businesses are too busy taking care of the day-to-day needs of their work to learn how (and pay for the necessary training) to optimize the worth of "the solution." The next generation may be paperless, but this generation needs the security of paper.

Where is the end user going to get the necessary education? Sales representatives must know and understand their customer's business. All sales reps promise to save the customer money; that line does not work. Sales reps must have passion for and knowledge of their product. Repeated contacts (by the representative) before and after a sale are necessary. For instance, a customer buys hardware; he or she demands ongoing communication from the sales rep to earn repeat business.

Do not ask a customer to sign off on something that is not right. Do not ask for a premature sign-off so the rep can win a trip or meet their quarterly bonus. The sales rep must deliver the promised goods and provide world-class service every day.

As a nation, we are lazy and possessive. Who is going to tell the boss that he/she cannot have an HP printer at the desk? Cost is always an issue. Believe it or not, cost can often be buried in someone else's budget, a scan here and a print there.

When dealing with government agencies, do your research and follow the money. Many departments have separate funds to buy special equipment. Color, plotters, and high- and low-end printers can easily be purchased outside of the published bid specifications.

You must work your way slowly into government. Usually there is a big pay-off when they finally sign, such as a referral to their friends and business associates. Representatives must understand the customer's business; customers must have better technology than they have now. Reps must be able to meet all government rules for the deaf, sightless, wireless, color, postscript preloaded, etc.

What Customers Want

Buyers remember that if your company has the ability to consistently do more than the customer was promised, it should. "We want to do business with someone who has proven they were there in a moment of need," they pointed out. "We are looking for a poised, professional, and knowledge-based worker who has more technical expertise than we have."

Tag-teams of multiple reps showing up to sell a product were unanimously disliked. Customers do not like to be overpowered with young trainees. Buyers want to deal with someone who knows more about the product than they do. Tell the customer ahead of time why there will be additional people attending a sales presentation. They, in turn, might bring their own buying team, and it will be more difficult to sell to many personalities. The best approach is using one knowledgeable sales rep to sell to one approachable purchasing agent.

It is okay to tell a customer "I don't know" or "We can't do this."

Copying has gone from decentralized to centralized and back to decentralized. Sales reps always seem to be trying to get you to do something else.

As a group, all of the panel members admitted to not having a real strategy in dealing with their in-house printing needs. "We are all making a lot of copies and no one knows why or how these copies are being used. The true total cost and ultimate value to the end user is unknown." Universally, there is little managing of what is actually being printed. Electronic information is always being blamed for the loss of vital information. A hard copy is safe. If it is not printed here, at least we want it printed somewhere. People still want paper. Input here, printed there. Scan many, print many somewhere else.

Dealing With IT's and End Users

If the Information Technology person says no, go to Purchasing.

No one ever got fired by buying HP. Sales people must change the customer's HP comfort level. IT professionals want a proven winner with no complications.

Purchasing agents need to be more knowledgeable to be able to work with ITs. Purchasing can talk the IT guys into trying something. A sales rep only has one chance to impress the IT staff. Bring everything the first day or forget it. ITs won't give you a second chance: "One strike and you're out."

End users really do not know what hard copies actually cost. They may know the hard cost of the original program, but not the people cost involved.

When leaving a voice mail, identify a specific need that will catch the buyer's attention.

Do not believe what customers say—listen for what the customers mean. Learn to read between the lines. They may call and request information on a new printer. When the rep arrives with printer brochures and price quotes, the customer points to the copier they plan to replace. Reps need to always draw the customer out with appropriate questions to qualify that "what they say is what they really mean."

Do not send a rookie with someone else who does the talking. Everyone who shows up must take part in the sales process. If you are not going to say anything, do not come.

Manufacturers must become familiar with the end user's favorite software systems. If your printer will not work with the software the customer currently uses, forget the sale.

Buyers still believe it is more cost effective to have separate equipment for making black and color prints.

Less than three percent of the US government's defense department copiers are connected to a network. The government foresees a security risk in networked equipment.

Conclusions

At the end of the two-hour session, the panel was asked to share some of the most important elements of the selling process:

-- "Get to the point fast, be honest, and admit what you don't know."
-- "Partnership. We are in this together. Be responsive. Answer any e-mail or voice mail immediately."
-- "Learn my business."
-- "Under-promise, over-deliver."

-- "Keep focused on the customer's needs."
-- "Make your customer successful and you will be successful."

Over 500 people attended the general session, where they listened to sales promotions, advertising campaigns, and details about this year's dealer incentive trip. However, when the time came to listen to the customer, less than 100 people showed up. Over 80 percent of the attending dealers did not choose to listen to purchasing agents who control over one hundred million dollars of purchasing power.

Panelists commented: Why were so few people here to listen to our message? Most sales people do not really care about the customer. All they care about is what is in it for them. The customer is only a necessary evil of the selling process.

Selling is hard work. Over the past five years, most service department personnel have worked very hard to recreate their knowledge base. The old way of servicing and selling will not provide your dealership with business. Even if you just want to sell "the box," effective sales representatives must understand what is in "the box" and what that "box" can provide to the customer.

The 100 attending dealers who chose to invest their time in listening to the customer are already ahead of the curve.

Switching Gears: Service Makes a Sales Call

Yes, I am the service manager. Service is my primary point of interest and expertise. Run on a separate profit and loss statement, the service department with its manager is responsible for generating a specific amount of revenue each month. When a sales representative or customer requests that I go out into the field to make an in-person visit, I must make a revenue-based decision. I must determine the best use of my time for the good of the department and the company.

An in-person sales call can help to make a sale. However, too many out-of-office calls can break your service department's revenue goals. When done properly, a customer visit requires about 30-90 minutes of preparation and follow-up time. Two-way travel, wait time, and the actual meeting require another two to three hours. Each time a customer or sales rep requests a field meeting, I need to figure about four hours.

On occasion, customers will call to request a personal visit to discuss the renewal of their service agreement. In a highly congested urban area, even the shortest of visits takes three hours of out-of-office time. Invariably, it is a low-end user who thinks a personal visit will enable him or her to intimidate or impress me. Ultimately, most expect that a personal visit will enable them to reduce the cost of their service agreement.

I have determined that, in most cases, making these types of visits is not utilizing my time for the good of the service department. My typical response to these requests is, "All of your records are here at your corporate headquarters. I will be glad to send you any pertinent information that you may need to make a decision. I can answer any questions or concerns you may have over the telephone or through e-mail. I know how valuable your time is. What information can I get for you to help you make an educated decision?" This tactic has always worked for me.

I will also guiltlessly say "no" when a sales representative requests my presence at a demonstration on a 20-print-per-minute machine, ten miles from the office. I simply cannot justify the loss of income to the service department.

There will be instances, however, when time away from the service department is important and a necessary part of creating service department revenues.

For instance, when a sales rep asks me to attend a sales presentation within our office, I always oblige. A few minutes in the showroom can be easily worked into my schedule. Also, when a potential customer calls requesting an in-person visit to review the possibility of taking over a 100-machine service contract, I ask, "when and where." It is worth the necessary time for the potential business opportunity.

Effective Use of Time

When a customer or sales representative requests an appropriate field meeting, use the process outlined below to maximize the effectiveness of your visit.

1. Find out a little about the customer ahead of time. If it is a current customer, review their equipment history, buying

patterns, payment history, and usage, and make a note of the names of a few contacts. If there have been any concerns in the past, make sure you know how the situations were rectified. If the meeting is with a potential new customer, ask the sales rep for a bit of history on the account. A quick Internet search may give you a little more background information on the company.

2. Put together a customized folder or small notebook of information for the customer. This includes a personalized letter of introduction with a list of sample pricing for service agreements, parts, and supplies. Try to bring examples of similar type customers, including copies of similar purchase orders or service agreements. I try to match similar types of businesses (even more than similar equipment). Churches, city government, schools, car dealers, etc., normally are more impressed with your company doing business with people in similar work environments.

Always include copies of your workman's compensation and liability insurance, a one-page history of service department and company achievements, and a list of references. Include a business card within the handout material. I always make an extra copy of the presentation to keep on file. This can be used for a quick reference when the customer calls back. It also can be reused with minor changes for another customer meeting.

3. Once you have set a time for the meeting, telephone or e-mail a confirmation which restates the time, location, and purpose of the meeting. Remember to include the names or positions of the people who will be attending. Leave a telephone number, just in case there is a last minute cancellation or time change. This can be done the day before or morning of the meeting.

4. Always be on time for the meeting. By this, I mean be early. Use those extra few minutes to review your presentation material, go to the bathroom, or brush up on the industry with the most current news (I always keep something in my car or briefcase to fill up a few extra minutes). Arriving ten minutes late, parking in a red zone, or forgetting what is in your presentation package will not make a memorable first impression.

5. Dress like a professional. Dress similar to or one level better than those you expect to meet. A pressed shirt and polished shoes make a statement. Professionalism is a state of mind.

6. Repeat each person's name as you are introduced. Give each person attending the meeting your business card. If a business card is given to you in return, treat it with respect.

7. When the time is appropriate, give each attendee a copy of your handout folder. As part of your pre-meeting preparation, always inquire how many people will be attending. Always bring one more than you think is needed. You can use this as your file copy if it is not used. If it is needed, you appear very prepared.

8. Listen to what others have to say. Service personnel are considered experts. If you talk too much, your knowledge level may be challenged. Periodically nod in agreement and take notes. Never disagree with what anyone else says. Follow the conversation. At any time, you may be asked a question or your opinion requested. When answering a question, always use the questioner's name in your reply. If possible, refer back to a previous comment or reaffirm an earlier comment made by the customer.

9. Speak with an appropriate level of sophistication. When you are talking to IT people, use every acronym and computer jargon you know. When talking to the controller or CFO, talk dollars, percentages, and profits. When you are talking to the office manger, talk about ease of operation and user-friendly options. Try to mirror the person to whom you are speaking. Using a similar tone of voice, speed of speech, and body position will subconsciously allow the listener to feel more comfortable with you.

10. Take notes. Jot down each person's concerns and needs. When appropriate, use the person's name. Always recap any concerns that were discussed. Give a specific time when you will follow up on their specific requests. Ask how each person would like to receive the needed information, whether it is via telephone, fax, or e-mail. When the (potential) customer responds, refer to their business card to confirm that the appropriate information is on the card you have. Always attach an appropriate time frame when you will "get back" to the customer. Eye contact and a smile are never out of place.

11. Follow up in a timely manner. A "Thank You" card with an enclosed business card is always appropriate. At the very least, include a "thank you for your time and interest" or "thank you for the opportunity to earn your business" as part of the follow-up e-mail message. If you do not hear from the customer, do a general follow-up in a week or two. E-mail or voice mail works great for this. Leave your name and phone number again. Restate a thank you for allowing the meeting. Reconfirm that you are available for any further consultation.

If it is worth your time to do a customer visit, do it right and make a winning impression. The service manager is an extension of the service department. Being on time, displaying professionalism, being knowledgeable, promptly following up on all requested information, being personable and respectful constitute a large part of the winning equation. When a customer is contemplating a 60-month, all-inclusive equipment lease and service commitment, providing peace of mind can make the winning difference.

Keeping Customers: Is It the "Impossible Dream?"

Service professionals are sometimes overwhelmed with the amount of work that is expected of them. The demands of setting up new equipment, refurbishing used machines, attending to in-house demands, and caring for demos, do not begin to address our main role of attending to billable and maintenance-agreement customers.

The additional challenges of digital installations, changing software, and customers who know just enough about their network to be dangerous, provide a new twist to today's service professional. Instead of being excited about customers calling us for needed work, we sometimes tend to resent the customers we already have.

The ABC's of successful business management speak to this concept: Always Be Closing. The service department must stay acutely aware of the need to retain current customers as well as to actively recruit new ones. As a child, I remember singing, "Make new friends, but keep the old, one is silver and the other's gold." As a working adult, no truer words were ever spoken in terms of sustaining and growing a business.

In today's tough business world, customers seem to go in and out of business faster than DSL transmission speed. Here, "The Man of La Mancha" and I share an impossible dream. It is my goal to sustain 100 percent of our current customer base. Additionally, we must continue to lure as many new customers as possible.

Retaining your entire customer base is virtually impossible. A well-run customer-conscious business will lose approximately 15-25 percent of its current customer base per year through no fault of its own. Customers die, retire, go out of business, consolidate, merge, change management, move out of your area, file bankruptcy, or just decide to change their vendors.

Loss of part of your sales and service base is something that is going to happen, whether you plan for it or not. Based on these statistics, after three non-growth years, you will have lost almost half of your current customer base.

A proactive service department can be your number one line of offense to help your business grow. To maintain a very moderate 5-percent yearly growth, you must succeed in gaining at least 30 percent more new business annually. The most common way to generate new business is to capture dissatisfied or complacent customers from other businesses. Alternatively, you can gamble on newly organized companies that might last long enough to pay you for the services you have provided.

Word of mouth (referrals) is the best and most economical form of advertising. Satisfied service customers are the best endorsement any company can have. Teach your technicians to ask your satisfied customers if they know someone who desires or is in need of the products and services your company provides.

Make sure your techs have a speaking knowledge of all the products and service your company currently handles. Teach them to be highly aware of their surroundings. Have them actively be on the lookout for other service and sales opportunities for your company. Reward them for regularly providing leads to other members of your staff. By simply looking into the windows of businesses they pass, techs may identify potential new customers.

Teach your employees to be aware of any competitor's delivery trucks. If one of your present customers has a demonstration machine from a competitor, make sure the tech informs someone at your company. New business usually comes from people who are already familiar with the type of goods and service that your company currently sells.

Maintaining customers requires that you keep in touch. Have a responsive understanding of each customer's individual wants and needs. It is inherent in human nature to deal with people we like, respect, and trust. Technicians have the unique ability to gain the trust, confidence, and friendship of the customers they service. Use your field service infantry to attract new customers when they are out working on the front lines.

At least 50 percent of your friends and business associates use some of the products your company sells. Your doctor, dentist, veterinarian, insurance person, gardener, auto mechanic, banker, travel agent, and relatives should all be made aware of your business expertise. Any tech that cannot give out at least 200 business cards each year is not networking with enough people.

Make sure there is a formal structure within your company to process and disseminate leads. At the management level, there should be a regular secondary review to process all leads and to make sure there is prompt follow-up.

Encourage your field service staff to Always Be Closing. Teach your technicians to be ever vigilant in retaining the current customer. Be aware of the ever-constant need to grow your base. By being proactive on a daily basis, your business can withstand the natural attrition of customers.

Bargaining Can Be a Win-Win

Bargaining. Does that describe your purchasing habits? It is a virtual given that the customer will bargain on equipment price, lease rates, or service and supply cost. (Potential) customers try to get the price adjusted on each aspect of the sale. In the office equipment business, bargaining is an acceptable part of the purchasing process.

The listed "retail" price is often considered to be nothing more than a line item in advertising material, not really a marketable selling price. Many sales representatives cannot remember the last time they sold hardware at the full listed retail price. Now may be the time to re-examine your company's purchasing habits.

In the day-to-day running of our own businesses, we sometimes forget to continue this bargaining trend. Someone in your company--service manager, parts manager, purchasing agent, or owner--is responsible for acquiring needed parts, supplies, and equipment. Too often, the person who actually makes the buying decision is not inclined to regularly check your vendor's prices or ask for a better value.

In some organizations, the computer system determines the buying decisions. A receiving clerk acknowledges the arrival of the order. A purchase order is then cross-referenced to the received order. An accounts payable clerk adjusts the purchase order if there is a difference between the cost of the product and the referenced price on the invoice. The vendor's invoice is then processed and a check is produced to pay for the order.

At some point, clerks and computers are merely tracking prices. Somewhere along the line, the buying process has become automated. Cost accountability has slipped through the cracks.

The wholesale cost your employees use to price a product may be regularly updated by your computer system, using a software program that automatically averages prices to account for changing wholesale costs. What happens to the printed sales list that has not been updated this century? How are cost increases passed on to your maintenance agreement customers? Who is aware of price increases on regularly purchased products?

Sometimes it pays to look again at the pricing on products you resell and use in your business.

The time and energy required to do educated bargaining will vary from product to product. There is a broad line between spending hours of research and bargaining to attain a 5 percent savings on a $3 bearing, and receiving a 25 percent discount on a $10,000 drum order.

All You Need to Do is Ask

I make a habit of approaching each of my major vendors twice a year. We regularly examine our purchasing relationship. For those who do not feel comfortable with the person-to-person "bargaining" process, there is a painless alternative. Ask your vendor to re-examine your buying patterns. Asking, "Is there any way I can alter my buying patterns to increase my discount levels with your company?" could reveal amazing discounts from your vendor.

Before you place a large order, ask if there are any specials or free freight programs currently available. Ask for multi-item discount price quotes. You may only want to buy one item, but it costs nothing to ask. Once the representative quotes a discounted price, you know there is room for negotiation. You can agree to pay the regular price today. and request the multi-unit discount when you purchase this product again.

I also try to help my vendor reps be able to fulfill their own needs. Most have monthly, quarterly, or yearly quotas. You can become their working partner. Ask if you can receive any additional discounts if you order "today." Some vendors will even allow you to place an order for items you won't need for a while. I receive special price consideration for giving a purchase order number for items I want shipped 90 days from now. I will be given 120 days to pay for the product. It's a win/win situation. All you need to do is ask.

Use the Internet as a resource to find a product's base cost. Then call your regular vendor. Mine talks with me, provides me with personalized service, extends product information, passes on industry gossip, sponsors my local BTA meetings, and has become a professional friend. I share the Internet price with my rep, and then ask for his best price.

I am willing to pay a little more than the raw price I have located on the Web. By throwing out the low-ball price, I make my vendor aware that I am an educated buyer. It is my vendor's responsibility to keep me as a loyal customer.

I am acutely aware of the need for all businesses to make a profit. My wholesale vendors need to make a profit on me, as I need to be able to make a profit when I resell this product to my customers. All three parts of this triangle of success (distributor, wholesaler, and end-user) must be in place to make the business cycle successful.

Having an open, respectful, mutually profitable working relationship with your vendors is a win-win partnership. Be an educated buyer who is willing to pay a fair price when receiving added value. Always ask your vendor, "is that your final answer?" You may not become a millionaire, but you will save your company money.

Two Guys Named Mike

Decades-old Video Still Holds Valuable Customer Service Lessons

Customer relations complaints seem to increase periodically. For instance, you might hear from three customers in a row who take the time to call about a slight technician indiscretion, whereas you usually only hear one complaint every few months. While listening to some feedback, my first thought is, "Boy, are these customers getting picky."

The more I think about it, the more I realize the error of my thinking. Creating an atmosphere of regularly fulfilling every customer's extreme expectations is a service department's ultimate goal. Creating an atmosphere of exceptional customer service raises the bar of your customer's expectations. More importantly, it will insure you of their remaining as your customer.

One of the best ways of keeping your customer base loyal is to provide an atmosphere of exceptional expectations. The ability for a customer to feel comfortable enough to call and make a comment adds value to the overall vendor-buyer relationship.

You could dismiss the calls, blaming the hectic nature of the season, back to school, or the full moon. As I recently was jotting down some points of customer service I needed to discuss during the next service meeting, my mind wandered back to a customer service video I had viewed when I was a working field service tech in the late 1970's.

The half-hour video was commonly referred to as the "Mike and Mike" film. I remember its being shown every couple of years. It was a painless way to spotlight the good, bad, and ugly of customer relations skills.

Customer Service vs. Customer Relations

During the past few years, much of our effort has been focused on enabling the technical staff to become "digitized" and network savvy. Our service department lending library is full of A+, MCSE (Microsoft Certified Systems Engineer), CNE (Certified Novell Engineer), and other self-help computer-focused material. I took a look into the cabinet, where I last remember seeing the Mike and Mike video. Way in the back, I spied the 30+-year-old video, covered by a heavy layer of dust.

My initial fear that was this dinosaur of a customer service video might be too outdated to still be effective. Many of our service techs were not even born when this video was made. I took it home that night and braced myself for a bit of nostalgia.

"Two Guys Named Mike" brought back memories of Happy Days and the Andy Griffith show. No tattoos, no body piecing, no purple spiked hair. Clothing and office equipment were a bit dated, but good manners remain unchanged by the passing of time.

The premise of the video is to show two different technicians, from two different companies, arriving at an office at the same time to fix different equipment. The first Mike graphically breaks all the rules of acceptable customer relations. The second Mike is professional in everything he does. I was pleasantly surprised to discover good customer relations have not changed much.

As the next service meeting started, the announcement of an R-rated video was going to be shown today piqued everyone's curiosity. I quickly added it has a CR rating, for customer relations. The mere mention of "Two Guys Named Mike" brought groans from the older techs and blank faces from the younger set.

As in past viewings, the customer relations blunders committed by Mike # 1 bring random laughter from around the room. This video never fails to identify the current customer relations problems different techs recognize in themselves. The more they laugh at a viewed situation, the greater the chances they are guilty of regularly committing that social error.

"Two Guys Named Mike" displays the wrong way and the appropriate way to deal with everyday situations such as field techs encounter. Self-introduction, signing in, talking with the key operator, diagnosing a problem, work habits, the actual repair, acquiring needed parts, leaving the equipment in a down condition, the cost of the repair, buying a maintenance agreement, promising a return date, getting the service bill signed, cleaning up the work area, signing out, and leaving the office—they're all there.

If a picture is worth a 1,000 words, viewing this video will save the service manager 10,000 words of pleading for the need for improved customer relation skills.

When "Two Guys Named Mike" was created, wet electrostatic copiers, teletypes, and dictating machines were the state of the art.

Despite all the technological changes over the years, good manners, clean and neat work habits, the ability to listen, and (un)common courtesy are still valued by our customers. Better yet, teaching and encouraging these traits will insure they remain our customers. Help your techs help themselves, by providing regular customer service training.

Strategies for Savvy Sales Leads

I am always confounded and a little perplexed when a long-time service customer questions me: "Does FKM sell copiers?"

Do we sell copiers? Of course, we sell copiers. Selling copiers is our main business. Yet, many of the service customers I deal with on a day-to-day basis fail to view our company as a seller of equipment.

What are we doing wrong? We spend thousands of dollars on advertising. We employ over 50 sales people. "Sales, service and supplies" is on all of our printed literature. Still, more often than I care to admit, some of our core service customers inquire, "Do you sell copiers?"

The best customer is an educated buyer. The more your current customers know and understand about your business, the better chance you have of keeping their business.

As a manager of a highly-motivated service staff, my first responsibility to my employer is to provide top-notch, consistent, and profitable service.

On a larger scale, I have a responsibility to do everything possible to ensure the prosperity and longevity of our company as a whole. The office machine industry is sales driven. Without a customer base, no service would be required.

Anything service employees can do to aid the overall day-to-day selling of copiers, fax machines, and printers will directly insure the success of the service department and the continued employment for all our techs.

We have an ongoing service tech lead program which compensates any service employee who turns in a lead that culminates in a sale within 90 days. Technicians do not do the selling. They merely turn in a contact name from any current customer who expresses a desire for new equipment.

The tech earns $25 or 10 percent of the sales representative's commission (whichever is greater). About 25 percent of technician-provided sales leads turn into actual sales.

An Economical Way to Reach Customers

I had the privilege to speak at the Business Technology Association in Atlanta, Ga. Gathered together at 8:30 a.m. on a Saturday morning was a group of industry leaders talking about the challenges of transitioning into the selling and servicing of digital equipment. Following my presentation, a question-and-answer period provided me with a great new advertising idea.

Jeff Jehn of Cincinnati, Ohio, shared an information-gathering technique that is used at Waltz Business Machines. "When we fax our monthly meter reading questionnaires, we include a couple of questions inquiring if there is any need for new equipment."

Jeff's shared idea is what I call an "instant truth." Immediately everyone in the room recognized Jeff's idea was so simple a concept that we had all been overlooking an easy, economical way to reach our customers by sharing new products we sell and unobtrusively asking for a little help in better assessing the customers' own needs.

Upon returning from the conference, I immediately started using Jeff's suggestion on our own meter reading forms. We are asking questions, mentioning new products we are selling, and sending a one-page "infomercial" along with each correspondence we fax.

After a couple of weeks, the response rate was better than 80 percent. Compare this to a normal mailing campaign response rate. The use of the fax questionnaire knowledge-gathering campaign is new to us. We are perfecting it on a day-to-day basis.

I've put together a three-month plan. We will change the information sheet and questions asked every 30 days. This way the monthly correspondence will stay fresh and interesting to our customers.

I plan to tie in a Thanksgiving, Christmas, and New Year's theme to the future fax-questionnaires. We may even offer a monthly prize to be awarded, by random drawing, to a customer who responds to our questions.

The fax has to be returned anyway. Checking off a simple box or two is much easier than tracking down numbers on the copier. Questions should be limited to no more than three. Answers should be a simple yes or no. Always ask if they would like any additional information. Keep it simple.

The asking of questions on the "Meter Reading Request Sheet" has a psychological advantage. We have a specific end-user contact. The meter reader usually is not the decision maker, but he or she usually has an inside knowledge of any immediate or future equipment needs or anticipated purchases.

This infomercial page briefly shares with our readers a little information about our company, our latest community activities or industry awards, new products offered, and any specials we are running.

Rethinking Mailings

Putting together the fax questionnaire allowed us to rethink our other mailing programs. It has been a few years since we used "envelope stuffer advertisements" when mailing company correspondence and invoices. So, we made a full color (made on one of the color copiers we sell) advertisement sheet to insert in each envelope that is sent out.

Neither of these ideas is earth-shattering or even original. But, they allow us to take advantage of simple, low-cost methods of educating our customers.

We were so busy spending money on advertising, we had forgotten how to utilize those free opportunities that are available to us. We must take advantage of reminding our current customers of all the products and services we offer in every way possible.

Colorless Profits

"Business is slow. How can we make more money in the service department?" I receive this common question via my e-mail or voice mail on a regular basis. There is no easy answer to such a broad question. Each of us must be continually aware of the need to optimize the opportunities for profits within our own company.

Many of us receive daily offerings via the fax and through e-mail from sellers of surplus supplies. The one constant feature being offered by these various surplus suppliers' hot sheets is COLOR: color toner, color developer, color duplicator ink, color drums.

Dealers always seem to purchase more magenta, cyan, yellow, and black items than is needed by our retail customers. I do believe unsuspecting dealers have enough unused color supplies on their shelves to create a paper rainbow that could cover the earth's circumference a thousands times over.

There is a fine line between always being out of a needed supply, and buying and warehousing products that will never be sold. The cost of employing purchasing clerks, the wholesale cost of the product, the shipping cost, the warehousing expenses, the cost of inventory control, and the potential cost of lost business, must all be balanced against having to wholesale unused products for pennies on the dollar or throwing away unsellable supplies.

Whenever you sell products that use color supplies, encourage your customers to keep at least one extra bottle of each color (toner, I.U. developer) product on hand. Diplomatically explain, "We always want you to have fresh product on hand. We place orders for color products once a week."

After years of being stuck with thousands of dollars of unsellable color supplies, I have made the business decision to minimize my inventory on all color related products.

If the color equipment is on the showroom floor, I will keep one or two containers of each needed color product in stock. For every 20 color machines I have under a full supply contract, I will keep one bottle minimum of each color supply item on my reorder list. This number may vary depending on the monthly usage of some high-volume machines.

Review Your Customers' Supplies

As a rule, every six months, you should make a complete review of leases that are due to expire. When picking up off-lease equipment that was covered under CPC (cost per copy) or total-care agreements, check for leftover supplies in the customer's office. Those unused containers of toner, developer, oil, drum units, etc. you find in the customer's supply room belong to you, the dealer. Even if you are not the re-selling dealer, those supplies are yours. The customer's CPC rate only pays for copier/prints that are used.

Toward the end of any lease or service agreement, monitor the amount of supplies that are sent to the customer. Train your staff politely to instruct your customers that you have a limit on the amount of supplies that can be shipped. Theoretically, under a cost per copy program, the toner should run out the same day the 36-month lease ends.

Have your technicians diplomatically review the number of supplies any CPC customers have on their shelf. Toward the last few weeks of an existing service and supply agreement, pick up any extra supplies. Have the tech or sales rep give the customer a receipt for the items taken. If questioned, explain that appropriate credit will be applied. Appropriate credit is zero. Only toner that is used on copies/prints that are made is paid for by the customer.

Adding the phrase "supplies and preventive maintenance service will be provided at rates consistent with the manufacturer's recommended intervals" allows you to charge for excessive need of toner. The customer who calls for a not-yet-due complete preventive maintenance and a new drum one week before their service agreement is due, can be denied. Simply explain it is not consistent with the manufacturer's recommended serving intervals.

The Cost of Extras

In today's digital world of low CPC pricing, servicing dealers must be prudent. There is little room for error. If every customer has one extra bottle of a product that is rated at 50,000 copiers / prints, hundreds of thousands of dollars of your potential profit can be thrown away (or picked up by another dealer) at the end of the lease or full service agreement.

In the late 1980's, the average wholesale cost of a container of toner was in the $15 range. Today, the wholesale cost of some containers of toner exceeds the $100 mark. Figure in also that color products require four (different colors) of everything.

When you walk through your warehouse, consider each one of those supply containers represents a $100 bill. During the lazy days of summer, take a closer look at your supply inventory. Reduce the number of color supplies you stock. Monitor the amount of supplies that are freely sent to CPC customers coming to the end of their leases.

Make sure supplies help provide your company with positive cash flow, real profit, and no need ever to have obsolete products.

Service Records Rewards

Service professionals have long debated the use of leaving an accurately completed service history card inside the equipment at the customer's location for each service technician to briefly write down the date, problem, parts used (or needed), meter reading, etc.

Some fear a competitor will be able to access too easily the equipment's service history. Others do not want the customer to be able to easily find the frequency or infrequency of the actual servicing. Other non-history-card users cite their inability to get their technical staff to consistently record every service call. Or it just takes too much time and discipline for the field techs to write everything down.

The old cliche, "No job is finished until the paperwork is done," will become ever so much more meaningful as more and more former copier, typewriter, and calculator dealers cross over into selling and servicing connected digital equipment. For years, successful VARs (value-added resellers) and computer service companies have realized the importance of having a customer pay for sharing knowledge, organizational skills, and retrieval of lost information.

Keep Records

It is vitally important to have on paper (or a floppy disc) a written history of everything which is done to a customer's computer system. This includes work done over a remote modem. The time the technician spends documenting all work accomplished or changes made is also part of our billable service hours (or use of prepaid time block).

The history card concept (documenting all the work that is performed) is expanded to a sellable, value-added living history. Do not fear that your customers or competitors have access to the work you have done. Use this accurate record keeping as a sellable commodity. Marketing and knowledge makes all the difference in the world.

Every time your staff touches a customer's keyboard, a written history should be documented and left with your customer. Additionally, a separate copy of this work should be kept by the servicing dealer. Technicians using laptop computers can download all new information into the customer's history file.

The power of having documented, correct information is an insurance policy against being blamed for a customer's computer problems. It also enables any trained servicing professional to be able to continue a job someone else has started. Too many companies are held virtually hostage to the one person who knows their system.

I recently read of a major hospital that spent over $300,000 updating their computer licensing and documentation of records. No new software or hardware was added. The new hospital administrator was merely making the hospital's current computer network legal. No one at this hospital had kept accurate records of when and how new stations, software, printers, programs, etc., had been added. When the hospital tried to face the awesome task of preparing for the updated programming, the new administrator discovered an even greater problem: No one had kept accurate records of software licensing. Nowhere could anyone find any documentation of thousands of computer changes.

Documentation Pays Off

Start gathering newspaper and magazine articles, as well as information available on the Internet, dealing with companies that have spent large amounts of money to update (make legal) undocumented business computer systems. Use these as part of your site seller or service sales literature.

Educating your customers to their potential for future problems is a new, profitable part of the selling and servicing cycle. This documentation can increase your presence in the customer's office. The documentation book that is kept at the customer's office should be professional looking and customized to each company. It must be updated each time your field or sales rep makes any changes. The customer's documentation record book that is kept in your office is an excellent source of referrals. It can be used to show potential customers how carefully and completely you care for your current customers.

Consumer studies have shown potential network purchasing customers depend more heavily on references than do businesses just buying stand-alone hardware. The checking of company-provided references has become part of the buying cycle. Having satisfied customers who will articulately express their satisfaction with the technical work your company has provided is an absolute necessity when dealing with the selling and servicing of connected products.

The extended version of the accurate, consistent use of the servicing history card can become a new source of revenue. Documenting every programming change, software purchase, movement of equipment, etc., will provide you and your customer with an added sense of security, professionalism, and profit.

Sell Telephone Technical Help:

Put Their Money Where Your Mouth Is

There are times in business that you cannot afford to deal with people or businesses that drain your time and patience.

One of my shop employees asked me to talk to a bothersome "customer" who was continually calling to request technical help. The caller did not have his user's manual or the general technical knowledge that was needed to repair the equipment.

My technicians wanted to be polite and help the caller. On the other hand, they understood the cost of our labor hour ($75+) and knew this was not appropriate use of their time.

The caller felt he had the right to ask questions and receive answers because he was our customer (having purchased one $27 item fourteen months ago). It was now time for me to politely tell this non-customer we could not afford to do business with him.

After a short introduction, I explained that any future technical information would be billable in advance, with a credit card number being necessary. During our conversation Mr. Ask-Everything informed me that, "I deal with 138 other vendors. You are the only vendor that has threatened to refuse me technical help."

"One hundred and thirty eight vendors," I repeated in my mind. "I bet they all have 800 numbers. And they all must dread the sound of this would-be buyer's voice."

I tried to keep my tone of voice pleasant and professional. "With 138 vendors to choose from, I am sure you will be able to get the needed technical information from someone else. Budget requirements will not allow our technical personnel to provide free telephone assistance in the future."

"Don't count on any more business from me," the caller threatened.

"I understand, thank you, good-bye." I hung up our 800 number. I was no longer losing money to this non-customer.

Good managers train their employees to practice restraint. You must know when the investment of your time and knowledge has a statistically viable chance of making a profit.

Think of it as a bet at a racetrack. As a department head with a conservative management style, I will not gamble my company's resources on a 100-to-1 long shot. The odds are very low that this type of customer will purchase enough of our products to cover the cost of a technician's time. Endorsing unlimited telephone help for free is tantamount to setting up guidelines that encourage stealing.

You must understand your cost. Every time you give something away for free, you must charge the next customer twice as much to recover the necessary profits to stay in business. If you don't have the structure and self-discipline to say "NO" in the first place, you create a downward spiral. You are always trying to catch-up on recovering lost profits.

There is a fine line between helping customers and being taken advantage of by thieves. Any request for technical assistance is always filtered through a "gate keeper" at my dealership. As the customer begins to explain their question or need, the gatekeeper can quickly look at the customer's history of doing business with us over the past year. Ongoing purchasers with prompt payment histories have earned the right to speak with someone that can provide "free" technical help.

I have learned through years of disappointment that people with very old, small copiers or faxes will never buy from a dealer of our size. The superstores with $99 copiers, faxes, and printers will get their business. My job is to politely end our conversation in less than 90 seconds, explaining that we may be able to sell them supplies in the future. Thank you. Good-bye.

Technical Telephone Time

Callers with chronic past-due accounts or no history of an ongoing business relationship are screened. "I see you have an outstanding invoice over 90 days past due. Who should I have our accounts receivable department talk to before I have a technical specialist call you back?" This is a fair and just approach. Anyone who does not live up to your purchasing terms (net 30 days) is stealing from you. Why would you do business with a known criminal?

I am always amazed at dealers who are afraid of getting a non-paying (non)customer upset. People who pay slowly are a COST to your company. Every time you "sell" to them, it costs you additional money to receive payment.

Those customers who have not engaged in a profitable business relationship with you can purchase Technical Telephone Time. Be prepared to fax or e-mail your Technical Telephone Time price sheet. We offer an unlimited usage yearly Telephone Service Agreement, as well as "buy as you talk" plan. Always ask for a credit card number or a purchase order number in advance.

No customer has ever purchased our unlimited yearly plan. But it gets them off the phone and officially puts them on notice that technical knowledge is not free. Our good customers are always provided friendly, free, and knowledgeable telephone help. Their ongoing business relationship has already paid for this service.

As more of your incoming telephone calls request technical help, set up an in-house system that maximizes your potential for profit. Be prepared to provide written payment options to provide those who take advantage of "free" telephone help. Treat your company's technical knowledge with the same respect and cost basis as you do any other piece of sellable inventory. Value, advertise, and sell the knowledge your customers need.

Form Simplifies Need to Track Equipment

Your in-house service department (shop) can be a source of convenient revenue or a persistent irritant. Random drop-in service customers must be treated with respect as well as restrictions.

I used to be plagued by the random charge-call customer who showed up at the loading dock with an old piece of equipment. Many of these walk-in customers seem to be retired engineers who expect you to stop doing all your scheduled work to look at their antiquated equipment. In fact, they would like to watch you repair it. That way they can fix it themselves next time. And, yes, they take cream and two sugars in their coffee, thanks.

Those days of constant irritations, interruptions, and deadbeat customers who never return to pick up abandoned equipment, are gone. Customers who call ahead or drop by unannounced are politely given the guidelines of our repair shop.

"A $35 inspection charge is required to receive your equipment. Within eight business hours you will be contacted by telephone with an estimate of the must-do and should-do work. (A written estimate can also be faxed.) This non-refundable $35 inspection fee will be credited toward any work that you authorize. Our shop rate is $75 per hour, with a one hour minimum plus the cost of parts.

"We are able to offer this discounted in-shop servicing rate by being able to schedule your needed work into our time allotments. If you want to watch or pick a specific time, we offer our standard field service rate.

"Our receiving hours are 8 am to 4 pm." (We actually close at 5 pm, but I learned my lesson the hard way).

Customers used to regularly show up at 5:15. "Traffic was worse than I anticipated," they would apologize. I was often forced to pay someone overtime or disrupt my own after-hour's schedule. Stating a 4 p.m. closing time allows for the smooth handling of the late arrivals.

Orderly Authorization

Part one of the receiving process is having the potential shop customer fill out this "shop inspection/authorization form" (see example).

Any customer or delivery person who shows up without the ability to pay the $35 Estimate Charge is still required to sign the form. The equipment is received, but no one looks at the machine until payment is made. Usually a credit card number is telephoned in.

The $35 up-front payment encourages the marginal service customer to commit to having some work being authorized after the estimate is given. They have already paid for almost half ($35 inspection fee) of the $75 minimum charge. If they do pick up the machine without authorizing any work, your cost of receiving, storing, and estimating have been (partially) covered.

After the estimate is explained on the telephone, the customer may be required to submit prepayment for the cost of special-order parts. The customer is also offered overnight air delivery of parts for an additional fee. Service managers are usually able to sense a customer who is too willing to authorize expensive work. When in doubt, require a customer to prepay retail cost and shipping of any special-order parts.

SHOP INSPECTION AUTHORIZATION FORM

Name ____

Address____

City/State ___________________________Zip _________

Contact ____

Phone (_____) _______________________Ext. _________

Serial # ____________________________Model _______

Service Requested __________________________________

____

____

$35 Non-Refundable Estimate Charge

$75 Minimum Shop Servicing Charge

(Estimate charge is waived if $75 shop work is authorized)

If equipment is not picked up within 30 days, (________),
Insert Date

equipment will be unconditionally forfeited to

(____________________________________)
Company's Name

to offset the cost of repair and/or storage.

I have read, understand and agree to the above stated terms.

Signed _______________________________Date _________

Initial form of $35 payment _________________________

Many a customer has left a machine, a telephone number that connects to an anonymous voice mail system and a non-readable address. I used to send registered letters, leave messages, fax destruction authorization forms, and store abandoned equipment for years. With this signed form, I have full legal possession after 30 days.

Upon being told it will cost $800 to fix their equipment, the customer sheepishly admits they only paid $25 at a local auction. When they tell me to just throw the machine away, I quickly accept, knowing that I have their signed destruction authorization, plus their $35 is already in our bank account.

These tactics are not cold-hearted. They are simply good business practices extended to a portion of our service revenue that has been "given away" in the past. My shop techs do not work for free. Information is one of the many products my service department sells.

The use of the shop inspection form, including a prepaid fee, will simplify your need to keep and track abandoned equipment. It will generate revenue. Your shop can provide professional services to the walk-in customer while proving a constant trickle of revenue to your department's bottom line.

Paper Ponderings

Governmental legislation requiring the use of recycled paper continues to play havoc with our high-speed printers and copiers. Adding to this are businesses trying to reduce their day-to-day operational expenses by cutting costs in every sector of their business. Buying cheaper paper always seems to be at the top of the list. One of our largest customers buys the cheapest recycled paper they can find. Then they call our service department and complain that their copier jams in the duplex and is producing wrinkled and faded copies.

Paper can have an enormous effect on the short- and long-term serviceability of printing equipment. In today's business world, customers are often penny wise and pound foolish when it comes to purchasing paper. Many large companies, school districts, and municipalities are required to use recycled paper. Add to these the large office superstores that sell cases (5,000 sheets, 10 reams) of paper for under $12 per box, and you can see the problem.

As color printers and copiers become more commonly used at home and in business, the quality and suitability of the paper is having enormous effects on the overall serviceability and perceived copy quality of printing and copying equipment. Paper quality, finish, brightness, opacity, cut, dust, packaging, storage, handling, and end-user installation all have an impact on the end user's perception of how their printing equipment is performing. Part of your responsibility as the seller and supporter of printing products is to diplomatically educate the end user on the nuances of the paper they use.

At a recent visit to an office superstore, paper was being sold for $9.95 per 5,000 sheets (10-ream case) to $49.95 for 50 sheets of high gloss photographic paper. That is more than a 400 percent per sheet difference in price. I counted over 40 different offerings of paper in this one store alone. No wonder our customers, sales people, and technicians are confused.

To What End Use?

When trying to simplify your paper discussions with customers, here are some basic items to discuss. Figure out how the paper is going to be used. High speed copiers and printers with duplex and stapling ability require much higher quality paper than a 15-print-per-minute personal copier, fax, or printer. The quality of color prints and copies will vary from marginally acceptable to knock-your-socks-off gorgeous, depending on the paper stock used. Laser, inkjet, and color all need different types of paper to maximize print quality.

Paper Properties

Brightness:
The whiter the paper, the blacker the print appears. The contrast between paper and image makes the entire print appear to be of a higher quality. Copy quality problems can instantly disappear as the whiteness/brightness is intensified.

Opacity:
Poor opacity allows backlighting to wash out or overshadow the printed image. Opacity is the ability for the paper's surface to reflect light.

Cut:

Better quality wrapped reams of paper will have an arrow on the ream end paper label. This arrow represents the direction the paper should be placed in the paper cassette. This directional arrow reflects the importance of direction of grain and cut into the paper's usage. Cheaper paper rarely takes into consideration these areas of importance. Paper feed, transport, and duplex ability are affected by the direction of wood grain and smoothness of ream cut.

Dust:

Poorly cut or processed paper can bring bits of debris that can build up within the interior of the printing equipment. Soon, the printer interior will be covered with a layer of paper dust, affecting print quality and jamming.

Ream Wrapping Paper:

The strength, composition, and sealing process (glue) of the paper used to wrap the ream affects the amount of protection the paper receives during transport and storage. Torn ream wrapping can cause moisture invasion and bent, creased, or bruised sheets of paper.

Finish:

Paper must be slick enough to allow the toner to penetrate the surface. If it is too porous, the toner will blast, causing a fuzzy looking image. If it is too slick, the paper feed mechanism will have trouble picking up individual sheets. Very slick paper designed for color printers creates a clear, sharp, and colorful image. This same high quality (expensive) slick paper can leave excessive colored toner on the fuser rollers. The need to replace or frequently clean fuser rollers will increase as the slickness or the paper finish increases. When cheaper, more porous paper is used for color printing, copy quality diminishes as fuser roller cleanliness increases. This is one of the few times that poor quality paper actually increases the cleanliness of the equipment.

Other Issues

Types of Paper:
Multi-use is "good enough" for everyday copier use. Laser paper is usually 24-28 lb. with a smooth finish that helps minimizes curl and improves whiteness contrast. Inkjet paper is more porous, allowing the wet ink to penetrate the paper fiber. Higher quality laser and inkjet paper will specify a DPI range. Matching the DPI paper range with the printer equipment range will maximize print quality.

End-User Paper Care:
Even the best paper, when treated poorly, will play havoc with a printer's effectiveness. Paper should be stored flat, in unopened reams, in the vicinity of use. Paper that is stored in hot or cold environments and then brought into an office setting needs 24 hours to adapt to the new environment. Paper that is too cold is stiff; limpness is caused by high temperatures. Both paper feed and the ability to absorb toner are negatively affected by extreme temperatures or poor storage environment.

Paper Weight:
Twenty-pound xerographic quality paper is the standard. It is now common to have printing equipment rated for use from 14 to 120 pound paper. The use of different paper weights may require the use of the sheet bypass or universal paper tray. Duplexing may not be possible on some weights of paper. Customers must be made aware of the limitations of their equipment.

Recycled Paper:
This is a subject of confusion. The composition of recycled paper is as varied as the waste in your trash can. Each sheet has a history all its own. Without getting technical, some recycled paper works and some doesn't. As a former field tech, my favorite paper comes from the

"hard woods" of the American Southeast. Anything that says "recycled" is an unknown. Not only is it a potential for problems, but recycled paper can vary from sheet to sheet.

That simple piece of paper that is carelessly placed into a sheet bypass unit or paper cassette can increase or decrease the end user's perception of their printer equipment's reliability and your company's technical expertise. Technicians must be trained to identify, explain, and prove what the best paper is for the end-user's needs. Field techs can instantly prove the worth (or worthlessness) of the end-user's current choice of paper by always having protected (we use self-sealing plastic storage bags) sample paper (for color and black) as part of their car stock. A picture (sample print on the appropriate paper) can be worth a thousand words of explanation. Customer complaints of inferior print quality or jamming in the duplex or sheet bypass can be instantly explained and corrected. Indisputable creditability can be achieved when the tech can produce a non-jamming, high quality print by merely changing the paper that is being used.

If your company does not sell paper, make sure you provide a current list of high quality paper you recommend and a convenient place of purchase. Your customer may not choose to pay the price for premium quality paper, but the burden of providing trouble free, high-quality printing will no longer be yours.

Creating Budgets in Your Service Department

Budget time. Whatever time of year your company's fiscal year begins, every manager, director or vice president has to struggle to create next year's "guesstimate" of what they want to happen, how much it will cost, and how the money will be generated to meet the stated expectations.

Many things go into the budgeting process, including hopes, dreams, corporate mandates, personal bonus quests, labor hours, training costs, auto expenses, parts, cell phones, laptop computers, and employee bonuses, to name a few. The most difficult part of the service department's budgeting process is the huge support responsibility, with very little control of the revenue line.

More than 80 percent of my service department's revenue is price controlled by a non-service employee. Additionally, these non-service employees tend to personally lose money every time they increase the service department's revenue line. This is a classic win/lose predicament.

With the increasing overall percentage of equipment being acquired through all-inclusive lease agreements (equipment, service, and supplies), the customer only sees a total monthly cost. Every cent of the monthly payment that is assigned to pay for the service and supply portion of the cost-per-copy (CPC) lease lowers the overall amount that is assigned to the cost of the equipment.

Under traditional CPC leasing agreements, there is little to no incentive for the sales representative to charge a higher price for the service and supply portion of the CPC than what is already mandated. Very often, reps will plead with the service manager for a reduced rate on the service and supply portion of the monthly cost. This allows a higher price to be assigned to the hardware portion of sales.

Let me be more specific. Periodically, a company's owner sits down with the departmental heads of sales, service, and supply to set maintenance agreement (MA) and CPC pricing. At the end of these meetings (heated discussions) prices are set, but rarely to anyone's satisfaction. Service never receives enough money. Sales feel the service and supply pricing is not market competitive. Supplies know they are receiving the short end of the stick, especially when dealing with color and multifunctional machines.

Frustrations with Discounts

There is just never enough money to go around. Once the MA and CPC prices are set, the discounting begins. If the service or supply manager refuses to lower the listed price for this "very competitive deal," the sales reps feels their hard fought sale has been sabotaged. The sales manager quickly makes a call and talks about the need for you to be a team player, the competitive market place, bonus attainment, how "you can raise the prices next year," yadda yadda yadda.

The squeeze is on. Say "no" and you instantly become the villain. Say "yes" and you have just lowered the threshold of pricing on all future deals. Even worse, by agreeing to lower the price on service and supplies, you have reduced 60 future opportunities to generate profit. The equipment portion of the lease is paid up front in one lump sum. The service and supply portion normally has an escalation and overage clause. By lowering the initial service and supply portion of the monthly payment in favor of a one-time higher equipment cost, the dealership reduces the next 60 months of earnings.

Each time a rep asks me to lower a listed service pricing, I ask, "What part of our service program can I eliminate? Can I send an untrained tech? Is it all right if it takes two or three days to get to the customer? Can I eliminate overnight freight on needed parts? Can all incoming service calls go directly into voice mail? Will the sales department take over the technical telephone help desk? Can I reduce car stock inventory by 50%? Can we forego salary increases to all the technicians? Better yet, we can simply not offer vacation, sick time, or training for anyone who works in the service or supply departments."

Needless to say, the sales rep has no idea what I am talking about. "Of course you can't do that. You don't understand, just lower the service and supply rate this time. It is a very competitive deal," the salesperson usually responds.

"Is there any money in the deal on the sales side?" I ask.

After a long pause, "A little," the rep relies in a much softened tone.

"Let me make sure I have this straight." I say. "You have enough money in the deal to meet the base transfer price. Plus, there's enough money to allow you to make 'a little' on the deal. You will receive the lease bonus. You will receive your quarterly bonus, but service must lower their rate for the next 60 months. You want me to override the listed pricing so you can make a little more money today, all the while realizing the company will lose money for the next five years. If you need a lower service rate, you can buy it down with the 'little' money that is left in the deal. My responsibility is to make sure there is enough money in the deal to pay for five years worth of responsibility."

Setting a Balanced Ratio

Service managers have enormous budgetary responsibilities with little opportunity to control the source of their revenue. Service is a support department with an income responsibility. Service departments have multi-million dollar budgets that generate the largest portion of business profits, and yet the service department's management rarely has the final say on their pricing structure.

Adding to the service department's revenue-generating paradox is the desired ratio between prepaid (MAs, CPCs, rentals, warranties) and billable (time and material) service calls. Ideally, at least 80 percent of all service revenue should be prepaid. The better we do our job of selling prepaid service, the less opportunity service has to generate time and material billables. It never fails that when a service tech charges a CPC customer for a toner spill or network administration, the sales rep is on the phone to us, relaying the customer's complaints about the extra charges.

The new digital equipment needs fewer parts and service. The pricing curve has already lowered itself to a point of little return. The .015 to .02 cents per analog copy has already been replaced with .005 to .009 full service and supply pricing for digital equipment. My service budget is being destroyed by .02 per copy analog service agreements being "upgraded" to .0075 CPC pricing. With each new replacement, my service revenue is reduced by 50% or more.

Is there an easy answer? Not that I have figured out yet. But, at least I understand the question and the need for vigilance. The need to control 36 to 60 months of aftermarket revenue is the key to a profitable company. The long-term viability of any traditional copier dealership is ultimately determined by the month-to-month revenue generated from disciplined pricing established at the time of original equipment placement. Knowing the right questions to ask, replies to make, and attitude to project can be a big help in the world of negotiations.

The Service Survival Kit

Marketing is one of those two-bit words meaning "go sell something with a bit of flair." As a service manager, I have always tried to instill "marketing" concepts among the employees in our service department.

A few months ago, I challenged the service staff to come up with a new "marketing" idea for something we sell through the service department. I wanted my techs to expand their thinking to include a creative idea for packaging something we are already selling in a new and different way that would create a bit of excitement.

The concept of having service create a marketing campaign may seem to be a stretch. Techs are comfortable doing the work other create. In fact, most of the time the service department seems to have an overload of work. Why a quest for a marketing campaign?

Most traditional "copier" dealers work on a business model that requires the service department to generate the largest margin of profit within the company. As the servicing cost of digital equipment decreases, so does the amount we can charge for these services. In order to maintain the same level of revenue generated by the service department in the past, new areas for sales are required.

The Challenge

I created a marketing challenge for my techs: submit an idea or product that we can sell within the service department. There was a two-week deadline. Techs could work in groups or submit their ideas individually. The winner would receive eight hours off with pay. If it was a group win, a total of eight hours would be divided up among the group.

Immediately, the techs asked for guidelines and examples. "I want you to come up with your own ideas," I said. "If I give you an example, it will limit your creative process. You know our customers; you know the technical ability we have; and you know the products we currently sell. Our goal is to make a 40% margin. But 20% of something is better than 100% of nothing."

The looks I saw around the room expressed the techs' concern that this was going to be more difficult than tracing down an electrical short in a ten foot long wiring harness. "What if we can't come up with an idea?" one tech asked. I answered, "You increase your chances of losing your job."

"You mean I will be fired for not turning in a sales idea? That isn't fair. I'm a tech in the service department," retorted a frustrated technician.

My reply was this: "What I mean is, without sales there is no money to pay any of us. Without new ideas, the company cannot grow. Without growth, there will not be enough money to keep all of us employed at our current rate." I continued, "The service revenue on each newly-sold piece of digital equipment is less than the money we were receiving on the analog copier it replaced. The service department must find new ways to create revenue if we are to continue to be employed."

There was silence in the room. You could almost hear the thought processes going on in the technicians' brains. I could imagine them thinking, "We have all worked hard to become network savvy, digital techs. Now she wants us to become sales people, too."

During the two weeks, I received e-mails requesting guidelines or "what do you think of this idea" from my service techs. Parking lot conversations shifted from sports to marketing teams. Part of my goal was already accomplished. Techs were thinking in terms of marketing. It was no longer enough to just fix something; techs were being asked to be a part of the creative selling process.

Before you can understand the winning entry, you need a little background on my belief in "co-opetition." Co-opetition is the concept of cooperating with the competition. Working in a large metropolitan area, I firmly believe there is enough business for everyone to share. I have always helped out fellow technicians from other companies. I try to work closely with other dealers. I try to be friends with other service managers. We are all in this together. I would rather be friends with the competition than enemies.

Technicians, service managers, and owners of other companies regularly come to our office to buy (or borrow) a needed part, tool, or piece of equipment. We have an open door policy. We have even been known to allow sales reps from other companies to use our showroom for their demonstrations.

The Winning Idea

At the next service meeting, the techs brought in their new ideas. The goal was to have each tech or group present their marketing idea to the entire service department. The winning idea would be chosen by the other techs, which enabled everyone to take part. The techs were encouraged to present a demo or sales pitch of their idea in hopes of gaining a vote. The individual pitches also enables other techs to see how they could present ideas to customers in the future.

Through the years, our techs have become quite competitive with one another in a friendly way. There is a great deal of camaraderie and good-hearted teasing and joking. The presentations of ideas brought out laughter, applause, disbelief, and a few high-fives of approval.

The winning entry was the Tech Survival Kit. The idea stemmed from requests by dealers who dropped by to pick up parts and would ask to buy a spring hook or can of spray air or some other item they saw our techs using. The kit would show that co-opetition with outside companies could also be beneficial financially.

The Tech Survival Kit was made up of a pre-packed group of commonly requested items. The demo model was attractively shrink-wrapped, with each item in plain sight:

- 3M Vacuum filter
- 1 can of spray air
- 1 spring hook
- 6 poly gloves
- 5 shop towels
- 5 stretch towels
- 1 flashlight
- 1 Scotch Brite pad
- 1 original test pattern
- 4 alcohol pads
- A Tootsie Roll Pop (something sweet for the drive)

As a group, we priced out each item, establishing an acceptable profit margin. We then priced the Tech Survival Kit. After checking to see how much money each tech had with them that day, we determined our acceptable selling price was too high for an impulse point of sale purchase.

After much discussion, we decided that $15 would be our price point. In order to achieve this goal, we went back over the pricing to figure out what we could remove to keep the cost in an acceptable range.

Taking away the vacuum filter was the most obvious choice to lower the cost. But, once the filter was removed, the size of the kit was dramatically reduced. The techs didn't think it looked like a bargain at $15. The vacuum filter had to stay. The techs then considered the size, tech appeal, and cost of each object. There was even talk of considering this to be a "loss leader" type of promotion. Eventually the price was raised to $19.50 and the flashlight was removed. We compromised on a 26% profit margin. The labor time required to gather and package the individual pieces of the Tech Survival Kit and shrink wrap them would be carried in our general overhead costs.

Although we all agreed that selling Tech Survival Kits at $19.50 to walk-in wholesale customers was not going to save anyone's job, we sold about 20 kits over the next eight months. That amounted to about $100 in profit.

The entire service department learned, through a fun exercise in marketing, the importance of presentation and bundling of products. We created a market for a value-added product that never before existed. Creatively packaging needed items together, in an attractive value group, is a positive step to growing your business.

Chapter 3

Our Bread and Butter

Maintenance/Service Agreements

Sign of Success: The Importance of Having an Initial Sign-off Sheet

As part of a company's basic maintenance agreement, the importance of the initial (at time of completing the successful installation) sign-off sheet cannot be overlooked.

Documentation is the essential ingredient in being able to charge for additionally requested network administration, lost hardware, misplaced drivers or other software, upgraded operating systems, or anything else your customers think is your responsibility. The completeness of your installation sign-off paperwork is critical to your ability to charge for future network administration.

My service department has been installing digitally connected equipment for many years. I receive daily requests from customers for free network administration. Our dispatcher professionally explains, "Your requested network administration is not covered under your current maintenance agreement. We can provide the needed network administration at our standard hourly IT (Information Technology) support labor rate."

The customer's call is often followed up by the original sales representative calling me, stating, "The service department didn't do something on the initial installation (one, two or three years ago). Consequently, the customer should receive the additional network administration at no charge."

Verify By Documentation

I regularly receive requests for missing software, reinstallation of printing systems or drivers, installation of scanning or e-mail functions, additional workstations, added capability to run different size paper, or attention to whatever problem the customer has at the moment.

Most requests are framed within the context of a claim that the technician was negligent in the install. Something was done incorrectly or incompletely. Arguing with the customer is never productive. My initial response to these requests is, "Let me pull the original installation paper work. I will give you a call back within one hour."

We learned the hard way. Everything must be documented, signed off or initialed, and saved for future reference (proof). All conversations with the end user's offsite IT administrator are documented with their first and last name, telephone number, and/or e-mail address. IP addresses are listed and the specific workstations that were connected (we offer five as part of the install) are documented.

Originally, our sign-off sheet merely stated that all original software had been delivered. We quickly realized this type of passive sign-off caused problems. Many months or years after the installation, the customers were adamant that no software was left.

We now have a separate line item for acknowledging the delivery and acceptance of all pertinent items. The end user is required to give first and last name and initial the acceptance of each item. The sign-off sheet even has a space to write down where the receiving person plans to store the software. On many occasions, I have been able to tell the customer (who accuses us of not leaving the software) exactly where the missing software is stored in their company.

The sign-off sheet also proves that the original software license was purchased and received. If the software really is lost, we can legally make a copy and send it to the customer. For this, we do not charge the full price of new software. We do charge for making and sending a CD or floppy to the customer. We invoice the equivalent of half our hourly IT support rate plus shipping. We are not selling the software, but we are charging for the necessary labor to process the requests.

When an end user requests drivers, we always first refer them to an appropriate Web site. We also offer to provide anything they need at our standard networking support price.

When dealing with after-installation support, customers will take as much as you allow. The more you give in the beginning, the more they will demand as the relationship continues. The nicer (free IT support) I am in the beginning, the madder the customer becomes when I say "No" later on.

Any items that the installing tech feels may cause a problem in the future are clearly documented. Very often, the end user's IT person does not want to deal with a specific installation issue. They tell our installing tech, "Don't worry about it. I'll take care of it myself", or some other official proclamation of "Don't do this."

These are the items that inevitability come back to haunt us two years later. The customer wants us to come back (at no charge) and complete the installation. The ability to locate and fax a detailed sign-off sheet is a very powerful tool in saying "No" in a professional manner.

I also use a pre-authorization and agreement-to-pay form for those customers I do not trust. I learned the hard way. Several customers agreed to pay for the requested IT work, then refused to pay once the invoice was sent. By requiring a signed pre-authorization sheet, I am putting the customer on notice that there will be no room for feigning alleged misunderstandings of what is covered by their maintenance agreement.

Complete installation documentation is the foundation for next year's profit.

Connected Copier Agreement

Is your dealership still "giving away" those random labor hours that are required to install new drivers, update a print system, reset a frozen job, reinstall the scan function, update an Internet connection, change Internet providers, or train an end user? All those relatively simple tasks are quietly stealing away thousands of dollars of potential billable hours from service department revenues.

Making sure there is a clear understanding between the dealership and the end user about what is and is not included in any warranty, service agreement, cost-per-copy, rental, or hourly service rate is vital to earnings. When confusion arises about what is and is not "covered," the service manager must often give in to the demands of the customer.

The customer's perception is that a cost-per-copy (CPC) agreement or other type of maintenance agreement (MA) is all-inclusive. In the customer's mind, the copy and the print function are the same thing. If a piece of paper, with the appropriate images, does not come out of the copier when the print icon is clicked, the copier is broken. If the copier is broken, in the customer's mind, their prepaid MA or CPC takes care of everything.

You can rarely convince a customer to pay for something that is not specifically excluded (in writing) from the service agreement. How can you change the customer's preconceived notion that they are entitled to free service on the network administration of their connected equipment? After years of frustration, I have come to this conclusion: if you can't beat them, join them.

If the customer thinks that his or her copier network administration is (or should be) included in the prepaid service agreement, then let's offer to sell the customer what he or she wants.

Consolidation of Features

Our "connected care agreement" or CCA fulfills the customer's need. This is a hybrid between the standard cost-per-copy agreement and a prepaid network administration blocks-of-time agreement.

My service department is now offering three options of prepaid maintenance:

1) The standard maintenance agreement (MA)—includes labor, travel, parts, drums, preventive maintenance (PM) kits;

2) The traditional cost-per-copy agreement (CPC)—includes labor, travel, parts, drums, PM kits and toner, developer, oil, etc., billed through a lease agreement or directly by the dealer;

3) The innovative connected care agreement (CCA)—includes all of the above, PLUS copier / printer network administration.

It makes sense finally to charge a little bit more to pay for that which I repeatedly seem to give away. In the past, even when I initially got a CPC or MA customer to agree to pay for network administration, they somehow never seemed to pay that networking labor invoice.

"How can we put a customer on credit hold for one network administration invoice when they are promptly paying hundreds of dollars each month for their CPC?" our company's controller would ask, as he credited off the network administration service fee. Everybody is happy; except the service manager whose profit-and-loss statement just shifted a little more to the red.

Level of Connection

When establishing a pricing level for the CCA, I reviewed the list of our customers who most often call for network administration. Higher volume customers have more problems. However, they usually have in-house IT personnel who could be instructed over the telephone or e-mailed the appropriate "fix." If the IT person was on vacation or out sick, the network was usually in relatively good condition and could be quickly repaired by one of our digital specialists in the field.

The low-end user, with one or two workstations, usually causes a disproportionate amount of grief per print made. Smaller networks or peer-to-peer connections are often administered by the most computer-savvy employee, friend, or high school-aged child of the small-company's owner. Even when this person is knowledgeable, he or she is often unavailable. The network is a mishmash of patches, McGyver type connections, mixed platforms, no backup software, and multiple operating systems.

During a year of standard MA or CPC coverage, the high-end user is less likely to need an in-office network administration service call than is the low-end user. When setting up CCA pricing criteria, I factored in two service calls for the low-end user, one service call and three help-desk phone calls for the high-end user.

My goal was to generate an additional $200 to $300 per yearly CCA agreement. The customer who is only paying for 30,000 to 60,000 prints per year must pay an additional .005 to .009 cents per click to generate enough revenue. The customer who makes 500,000 clicks per year only needs to be charged an additional .0005 cents per click to generate that same $200 to $300.

In either case, the additional money that is generated from the CCA agreement is credited directly to the service department's bottom line. More importantly, the customer has a clear understanding of the limitations and inclusions of the services that are being offered at the time the equipment is purchased.

When I first approached our sales department management with the CCA concept, I was braced for a fight. I came with statistics, cost analysis, long-term customer satisfaction theories, and a prayer. Much to my surprise, the sales manager thought the CCA was a great idea. We were offering a needed product (low cost, all-inclusive copier network administration) that was unique within our market place.

The sales department is able to bring added value to the customer. We are offering our client an additional level of peace of mind. For a fraction of a penny, the customer can rest assured that their thousands of dollars worth of investment (their new connected copier) won't go down for want of a new driver or locked-out print queue. No need to haggle over who has the ultimate responsibility for making the copier work. Copier, print system, network card, memory, or a misguided end user; the remedy is a no-charge (prepaid) service call away. The CCA truly takes all the hassle out of connected copying.

CCA Works

Many of today's businesses are on their second or third generation of digital connected copier. The buying public has experienced the frustration of dealing with a printer/copier that won't print. The idea of being able to purchase a maintenance agreement or cost-per-copy that takes into consideration the real needs of the connected copier is value added.

The connected care agreement is working for our customers, our sales department, the service department, and administrative services. Our accounts receivable clerks no longer have to deal with customers who refuse to pay for the network administration service calls. The service dispatchers no longer have to ask for a purchase order number from customers who "normally get everything for free." The service managers no longer have to explain what is and is not covered under the customer's maintenance or CPC agreement. Our sales reps are happy because they have a new product (true peace of mind) to offer.

Is the connected copier agreement the next logical step for the industry or just a special niche we have managed to provide our customers? The CCA is already providing our company and customers a new level of security and easily administered profits. The next step is up to you. Be a leader, be a follower, or be left behind.

Determining the Actual Cost-Per-Copy

Currently, I am in the midst of trying to measure—FAIRLY—and predict the cost of service and supplies on digital equipment for long term cost-per-copy (CPC) maintenance agreements. Sounds simple enough—all I need to do is accurately estimate cost, over the next five years, for all of the products we are selling (or have ever sold).

To come up with an accurate CPC number, I must take into consideration the cost of parts, inflation, tax rates, office rent, shipping fees, world terrorism, wars in the Middle East, earthquakes, flood, hurricanes, lighting strikes, famine, gasoline prices, health insurance rates, auto expenses, profit sharing, a new DSL or T-1 line, cell phone expenses . . . you get the idea. Those are only the outside factors; I forgot to mention equipment reliability, upgrades (modifications when the equipment does not work as originally designed), PM (preventive maintenance) cycles, labor rates, and travel time. And, yes, this estimate must be extended out to four decimals (one thousandth of one cent) plus or minus .0001.

A Battle of Departments

Manufacturers will often present spreadsheets with a few raw costs, designed to convince the customer and the sales department that a fair and equitable cost of a single copy is .0034. I have always considered these pricing aids to be advertising material-interesting to look at, but not usable in the real world. As you can see, the appropriate, profitable pricing of service agreements is much more complex than manufacturers suggest.

By suggesting a .0034 CPC price, any internally published pricing over .0035, guaranteed for the length of the five-year lease, appears unjustified. "Service is waging a war against the sales department, insisting upon a service and supply rate of .0125 cent per copy," say our sales representatives who are constantly challenging service pricing. "Sales will never be able to beat the competition if the service department insists on making over 400 percent profit."

I hear it every day. "The sales department is being broadsided by the service department's unrealistic expectations of receiving more than a half-cent per copy for the service portion of the CPC revenue," the sales reps say. "The new digital equipment requires less service. We shouldn't lose any money at .007. That will cover our service and supply costs. We can't be competitive at .009 per copy."

The battle lines have been drawn: sales wants .0034 while service is asking for .0125. How can two groups of people, looking at the same facts, see such different results?

Follow the Rules

Rule ONE:

Never trust anyone else's numbers. You can use Internet sites, customized software, and manufacturers' pricing sheets; you can listen to your trusted sales manager, your controller, or even your company's president; but, remember, you are the one who is ultimately responsible. Personal agendas, mathematical errors, rounding numbers down, or stupidity always seem to come into play, so that numbers usually differ. Be sure of your numbers and how you went about getting them.

Rule TWO:
Six months after a product is launched, re-calculate the cost of service and supplies. Adjust your service pricing according.

Rule THREE:
Revisit your service pricing on a yearly basis. Be fair to your company and to the customer.

Rule FOUR:
Raise service agreement pricing each year. A slow, gradual increase allows you to recoup the necessary increase in costs over the course of the life of the equipment. When pricing is raised properly, somewhere between year three and year ten, it becomes economically necessary for the end user to upgrade to new equipment.

Rule FIVE:
When establishing your cost, calculate a specific amount of cost to cover the overhead of providing the parts, supplies, labor, and freight necessary to provide an acceptable level of service and supplies. I normally add a 17 percent markup to the raw cost of any needed part or supply to establish the weighted cost. This percentage is established by dividing the manufacturer's wholesale price by 83 percent (the reciprocal of 17 percent).

Rule SIX:
By adding in the 17 percent markup, the true cost of the part is established. Next, calculate your labor cost. This is also referred to as an hourly burden rate or cost of the service hour. A justifiable cost of the labor hour is between $42 and $95 per hour. While this is an enormous range, I seriously doubt if any dealership in America has an hourly digital tech burden rate under $42.

Profit is a Cost

Once you have your weighted the cost of parts, labor, and travel, calculate the cost of a reasonable profit. All too often, PROFIT is never calculated into the cost of a product or service. PROFIT is a COST of all products or services that we sell. Profit deserves a line item on your costing sheet. Profit must be a part of your pricing formula and is a necessary part of doing business.

Figure in your acceptable rate of profit as an actual cost of the product. If you are selling your products and labor without consciously adding the needed profit to your calculations, you are doing a disservice to your employer, vendors, and customers.

In order to stay in business, a consistent profit must be made. Consequently, pricing a product at a level that "covers your cost" is lunacy. Covering your cost is a one-way ticket to bankruptcy. Under-pricing your products will ultimately cause your company to go out of business.

I think back fondly to the days when 007 made me think about the adventures of James Bond. Now, .007 is my first point of negotiation for service and supply pricing on those competitive deals. It is the responsibility of the sales, service, and supply departments to "DO THE NUMBERS." Use the manufacturer's pricing sheet as a guideline for your own product pricing. Do NOT fall into the trap of allowing the customer or another company's sales rep to dictate the prices that will allow your company to make a profit.

Profit must be a part of your pricing formula. Profit is a legitimate cost of every business transaction—the cost of being in business.

Don't Let Sales Outweigh Service: Managing Service Pricing

Where do you draw the line? Your voice mail message starts out, "It's a very competitive situation right now. Two other dealers are offering similar equipment below my transfer cost. The delivery requires two flights of stairs, and we would need to return their current piece of leased equipment back to the Midwest. Can you work with me on the service agreement pricing?"

We have heard it all before. The representative tells me, "There is no money in the deal on the equipment side." After looking at the service and supply rates being quoted, I instantly realize there will be no money for service and supplies over the next 60 months either. My original thought about this kind of voice mail pleading is, "If everybody is losing money, this is not a viable deal. Why should I agree to lose money in service because the sales rep is choosing to be the lowest bidder rather than the best sales (solution) rep?"

I hope that I have matured a bit since thinking that way. It IS tough out there. Selling copiers, printers, scanners, multi-functionals, or solutions is not an easy task. As a service manager, one of my responsibilities is to make sure the company generates enough business to keep all of my technicians employed. Digital equipment is working so well at the moment that it is putting the longevity of some technical positions in jeopardy. My focus for the year is to create more work opportunities for service to receive payment at a lower overall cost. Otherwise, my job will soon be firing techs (their only fault is doing the job well), because there is not enough work to go around.

When I focus on the care-taking of my technicians, I realize I must help the sales representative. When there is money to go around, I want service to receive their fair share. However, when the deal is truly skinny, I must do what I can to help my people.

Discrepancy Forms

I came up with a compromise; it is called the Discrepancy Form. If the sales reps need to sell a MA (maintenance agreement) or CPC (cost-per-copy agreement), including all service and supplies, below the company's listed rate, they must receive pre-approval. This approval can initially be verbal. When the final paper work (lease or sales documentation) is turned in, the written terms of the servicing compromise must have a manager's signature of approval.

The service Discrepancy Form is a structured document that requires the rep to do a little extra work. The form must be filled out with the customer's name and address, as well as the equipment that is being sold or leased. Then, the sales rep must write down the total gross profit on the sales side of the deal, the specific type of service agreement requested, the listed transfer price of the requested service agreement, the number of copies being purchased, and the billing terms (monthly, quarterly, yearly). Next, the requested service pricing needs to be filled in with the amount of the total first year monetary loss (price difference) and a justification for the difference in the pricing.

It takes some getting used to. When I started using this form, sales reps feigned a need to lower the service rate, while thousands of dollars of commission and lease bonus points were being made on the sale; this repulsed me. Commissioned sales people were hard pressed to explain the need for compromising the service rate on a CPC, while the bottom line was thousands of dollars in the green. I had a few enterprising sales reps explain to me, "The company is making so much money on the hardware, that service and supplies can be given for free."

The concept of the service department's profit and loss never entered into the sales reps' equation. On the other hand, I could rationalize part of what the sales reps were trying to say as being true. The only problem is that the industry benchmarking of cost and profit allocations reflects how the service department generates the lion's share of the company's profits. The going rate of the profit margin required by the service department is 20 to 40%. Additionally, most company's controllers and owner(s) expect the service department to provide a higher margin of profit than is required by other departments.

Achieving Parity

No matter what the size of your company or the number of products you sell, your dealership requires a steady cash flow to grease the wheels of commerce. Even bad deals are sometimes necessary to keep the business flowing. Your goal should be to understand your cost and make sure there is parity. *Webster's Dictionary* defines parity as: "equality; equal status or pay." This word is more often used in the political word: tit for tat, quid pro quo, give and take. Parity is a principle of equality and fairness.

The Discrepancy Form is a diplomatic way to establish parity—i.e., a situational, "I know that you know that I know." If the deal truly is skinny, we will tighten our belts together. If there is money in the deal, it will be shared according to the pre-established rules of the sale (equipment price list, standard service rates). If there is still money in the deal, the sales representative has earned additional commission.

The days when sales made plenty of money and service did not make anything are gone. We share the good deals and the bad. Parity is being accomplished.

My secondary goal with the Discrepancy Form is to limit the reduced service pricing to the first year only. A well-managed service department can survive by providing the first year's service at a reduced price, because that still allows additional increases of the service (and supply) cost. Many think "additional" is tantamount to yearly. Why must increases be only allotted once a year?

Reviewing Reviews

In the "olden" days, service agreements were paid on a yearly basis, up front. A yearly increase made good business sense: pay once a year, have your price reviewed once a year. Now that most customers insist on monthly or quarterly billing, why do dealers stay with the once-a-year review?

Reasons:

Many of our vendors, including the manufacturer we represent, have no objection to (seemingly) random price increases. The cost of parts, supplies, and equipment often is increased more than once a year. Sometimes we must broaden our mindset. When a customer forces us to lower a price below our actual cost of business, something must be taken away or business will go away.

When agreeing to sell service and supplies below our lowest listed transfer price, I require a maximum of first-year only pricing. If a customer insists on a multiple-year guarantee of a set price, the sales rep is charged back for the average yearly increase that will be lost.

Use of the Discrepancy Form for service agreements helps to keep sales and service at parity. In turn, the company gains flexibility without animosity. The sales rep will think twice before low-balling the cost of the service agreement. Service management can help the sales reps achieve additional sales by lending a helping hand. Together, the sales and service departments can work toward additional revenue for both departments. Parity has been achieved.

Warranty Expiration Form

I received a telephone call from Tom Skerl, Vice President of Sales at North Coast Business System. After a little small talk, Tom paused. "I want to thank you. We finally took your advice and tried your *Warranty Expiration Form* idea. With the help of Jon Lewis, our Director of Service, we used a modified version of the form that you handed out in your seminar. Within a few weeks, it actually started to rain money. We received over $14,000 from customers who responded to your *Warranty Expiration Form.* My biggest regret is it took us over a year to try out your idea."

A big grin came upon my face. It is always very reassuring for me as a speaker and writer to learn that attendees and readers successfully make money with my suggestions.

But let me go back. Tom had attended one of my seminars. I talked about how I was able to deal with some of my past mistakes. When we first got into the digital era, I, like many other service managers, was unfamiliar with some of the problems we would encounter. I slowly learned that hard drives self-destruct, Fiery color interfaces and main boards malfunction, controllers stop working, and several other network/computer related items need to be replaced. In each case, the maintenance agreement (MA) or cost-per-copy (CPC) pricing (usually under a penny per copy) wasn't nearly enough to cover the cost of these needed parts.

My biggest surprise came when I needed to buy a replacement Fiery printed circuit board. The wholesale price was over $10,000. This is more than we would receive for the color copier's maintenance agreement over the entire five years of the lease. I felt like a babe in the woods and the big bad wolf was eating me alive.

In desperation, I tried to figure out what I could do to recoup some of the money it was costing the service department to replace the network specific or color specific items that were failing. How could we go back to a customer who had already had their equipment and maintenance agreement in effect for two or three years and asked them to start paying for something that was never mentioned in the past? How could I charge back to the customer additional money that was required to cover the entire network or color-specific items that were attached to their connected equipment?

A Lightbulb Moment

Then fate took its course. I was at work when a representative from Sony called me. It seems the two-year manufacturer's warranty on my Sony Vaio laptop computer was about to expire. The telemarketer wanted to know if I was interested in continuing coverage by buying a maintenance agreement. I'm not quite sure what the telemarketer said after that. The light bulb of discovering a great idea blinded my thoughts.

This was the answer to my problems. I could contact each one of our customers and explain that the manufacturer's warranty on their equipment has expired. If they wanted extended coverage, they could purchase a new maintenance agreement. In fairness to our customers,

I was merely providing additional coverage on items that were not included under a traditional CPC or MA. In good faith, our company had covered items that were never intended to be covered for under a penny a copy.

During the past couple of years I had realized that most companies offered separate maintenance agreements on the Fiery controller. External controllers and hard drives were often excluded from other company's maintenance agreements. I was merely getting caught up to the industry norms.

I started the process by going through our installed machine base, oldest to newest. I sent out letters (see example) explaining the manufacturer's warranty had expired on ___________________(listed a specific piece of equipment). I enclosed a service agreement proposal with each letter. I used company letterhead, individually addressed to each customer.

Immediately, the customer is diplomatically informed that they no longer have any coverage on the specifically named equipment. Additionally, the customer is offered the opportunity to buy additional coverage on the equipment whose manufacturer's warranty has expired.

When I first started this project, I chose the customers I felt most needed the extended warranty. Next, I sent letters to our customers with the oldest installation date. Each week I sent out a few more letters targeting the appropriate customers. It took over six months to research and send out all of the end-of-warranty letters.

Yes, I did receive telephone calls asking for more information. I made sure I sent only a few warranty expiration letters at a time. This allowed time to research each customer's situation, as well as protecting myself from a deluge of telephone calls.

Warranty Expiration Form

Our records show that the manufacturer's warranty has expired on your computer and networking equipment that is installed with your

____

(equipment make model and serial number).

(ABC Company) will continue to service your Fiery interface on a per call billable basis. Excluded from your current coverage are

____

(Fiery controller and external control unit).
Any labor, travel, parts, or other service will be billable at ABC Company standard service rate.

(ABC Company) is offering continuing coverage on the Fiery controller for your color printing equipment. You may purchase an extended warranty. Enclosed is a maintenance agreement that will provide coverage on your color Fiery controller. All parts and labor related to any originally installed Fiery controller hardware can be covered for $________ per month for unlimited copies prints.

Your current coverage includes maintaining the walk-up functionality of your copier. (ABC Company) will provide all maintenance that is required to enable you to be able to make a copy when the print button on the color copier operation board is pressed.

Please review the attached proposal. In order to continue uninterrupted coverage, please sign the agreement and return with appropriate payment. If you have any questions please call

____

(provide name and telephone number).

My initial hope was that customers would at least be notified that they no longer had coverage on the specifically named equipment. Much to my surprise, customers signed the enclosed maintenance agreement and sent payment for the extended coverage.

The End Creates a Beginning

This situation, which had originally been a costly oversight, had turn into a new service we could offer our customers. Over one-third of our customers chose to buy the new coverage and sent their signed agreements and money. The remaining two-thirds, who chose not to buy the extended coverage, were diplomatically informed in writing that any future service calls would be billable. Using our newly-acquired knowledge, we sold new equipment with separate maintenance agreement offerings on Fiery interfaces, densitometer calibrations, and other network related items.

A little hindsight had paid off. We were able to recoup some of the potential losses in servicing the Fiery interfaces and other networking computer hardware. Our customers were able to purchase additional peace of mind. And the company earned some much-needed money to pay for the added expense of covering Fiery interfaces and other network related items.

After sending out the initial set of letters with the Warranty Expiration Form, I was as surprised as Tom Skerl and Jon Lewis were when the money started coming in. The payment and signed agreements were a concrete reminder that new forms of revenue are possible. It also provided our customers with a realistic explanation of the coverage they currently have on their equipment.

Whose Default Is It?

Webster's Dictionary defines default as "a failure to react or to perform an action."

This service manager defines default as "our first line of profit."

The maintenance agreement administrator says, "The default is inconsistent and confusing."

The sales representatives are often confused, unaware, or won't discuss defaults.

The print-for-pay end user (commercial copy shops such as Kinko's or PIP) understands the liabilities of default settings.

Customer rarely ask about default settings until they receive their first overage click billing.

The importance of a properly set default setting on all equipment makes this worth your ongoing inspection. Most pieces of equipment with an internal or external click-counting ability have a default counter. The programming that determines the default is usually made through the diagnostic codes in the operation panel. There are different options for counting paper feed or paper exit. Imagine the difference a click can mean when a customer is running two-sided 11 X 17 full-color versus one-sided 8 X 11 black.

Some machines come with preset multiple clicks for each of the four drum passes required to make a color image. On these machines, a black copy only passes by the drum once. Four clicks for color, one click for black. When pricing cost-per-copy (CPC) or maintenance agreements, determine the desired price for color copies and divide by four. At three cents per click, a color copy will cost 12 cents; a black copy costs three cents.

Some equipment comes with dual meters. One meter records color copies, another meter registers black copies. Dealers usually charge a set amount for color and a lower cost for black.

Make sure your sales, service, and supply agreement billing representatives understand the variation in click counts on each new piece of equipment. Most digital equipment has the ability to do a printout of the usage report. However, these reports can create additional confusion.

It Takes Figuring

Upon introduction of each new piece of equipment, our set-up techs always try to figure out how the default is set and how to read the click printout page. The service agreement pricing is adjusted to each machine's print-count configuration.

Recently, several of us could not make any sense out of the print count printout page on a new model of color printer we were setting up. In desperation, we called the manufacturer's technical hotline. After waiting the traditional 28 minutes on hold, we asked for an explanation of the click readout page. We were told, "You are the first dealer to call for an explanation."

The machine was manufactured by another company. It had been engineered in Japan, manufactured in China, and the click explanation had been translated into Japlish. Jokingly, there was some further explanation involving an abacus theory. To make a very long story short, it took five days, seven phone calls, eight e-mails, and translation from Chinese to Japanese to English to figure out the most convoluted print explanation page I have ever seen.

The scariest part of the story is that we were the only dealer who had requested an explanation of how to read the printout report. This is the report that determines what constitutes a click, which in turn determines how much a customer will be charged. I firmly believe without the lengthy explanation (over half a page of single-typed directions) no clerk, customer, sales representative or technician could have dissected the utterly baffling set of numbers and letters on the printout page. Nor could anyone figure out and test how the defaults were set.

Count the Difference in Clicks

This brings us back to the importance of the defaults. The installing dealer has the right to have the final decision on how different sizes of paper are counted. The dealer has the right to charge more for an 11 X 17 inch full-color two-sided copy than a single-sided 8.5 X 11 black.

When the market is forcing dealers to charge under a penny-per-copy for full service and supplies, there is no room for mistakes. Your dealership has the absolute need to make sure you are being paid additional money for larger (than 8.5 X 11) and two-sided copies.

Equally as necessary as understanding the importance of the default setting is replacing the use of the word "copy" or "print" with the term "click" on all your service agreement documents.

Make sure your service agreements (CPC) sell CLICKS. Never sell copies or prints. When making a full-color 11 X 17 double-sided copy, many color machines will register 16 clicks. That is one click for each of the four-color passes on four 8.5 X 11 space units. At 10 cents per click versus 10 cents per copy, there is a $1.50 difference in each 11 X 17 image that exits the color copier (printer).

A customer who makes 2,000 two-sided 11X 17 copies each month could pay $200 at 10 cents per copy or $3,200 if they are paying by the click. Over the course of a 60-month lease, the 10-cents-per-copy customer pays $12,000 for service and supplies. The 10-cents-per-click customer will pay $192,000. That is an additional $180,000 when the default is set properly and you are selling clicks.

The click default on copiers/printers/MFPs is still a mystery to most. I have seen the same make and model of equipment come in with different default settings. Too many dealers trust their service and supply profit margins to be determined by a nameless worker on an assembly line 6,000 miles from the business, randomly deciding how the click defaults are set.

An internal company policy regarding the checking of the click default settings is imperative to maximizing service agreement revenue. Ongoing vigilance and constant monitoring of proper default settings is prudent. Each new piece of equipment must be tested to determine when and how clicks are registered.

When setting up pricing criteria on new color equipment, make sure you understand how many clicks correspond to each type of copying. By being proactive and knowledgeable about each machine's default click settings, you can be sure you are not at fault of lowering your service revenues.

CLICK Your Way to Profitability

Use the Click as Measurement for Payment in Service Agreement

Copies, prints, linear feet, square feet, originals, and solutions: we all have learned to change our vocabulary through the years. The name of the end product continues to evolve. That piece of paper that comes out of the equipment we sell is identified by many names. The newest innovation appears to be the "CLICK."

I share with you an experience that I first learned about through an e-mail. An owner of a dealership in Florida e-mailed me asking for guidance with an upcoming court case he was facing. After reading his e-mail, I contacted him by telephone.

The Florida dealer had leased a color connected printer/copier to a customer. The initial sale had been "very competitive." After much negotiation and several cost reducing proposals, the end user had leased an $8,000 color copier/printer. The full maintenance agreement coverage (including all color supplies) had been purchased directly through the dealer (not a CPC through the leasing company).

The customer had gone over all the lease and maintenance paper work with a "fine tooth comb." A few adjustments were required on both the lease and the maintenance agreement. The end user insisted on having a firm cost on the all-inclusive maintenance agreement for five years, even through it was only a three-year lease. The end user even agreed to accept a half-cent base increase over the normal .09 cents per copy, to adjust for the five-year no-price-increase clause.

"In order for all of us to be on the same page," the end user wrote up a separate "letter of agreement." This confirmed unlimited color supplies and service would be provided under the terms of the maintenance agreement for five years. In this "letter of agreement," it was further restated, "the customer will pay .095 per copy/print, with a base rate of 2,000 copies/prints monthly in advance, with overages billed monthly in arrears."

All of these terms were stated in their standard maintenance agreement, so no red flags were raised. The customer required a three-day contingency trial. All worked well. On the fourth day, the customer signed the lease, the lease acceptance, maintenance agreement, and letter of agreement.

The Florida dealer billed the first month's full service agreement for $190.00 (2,000 times .095). At the end of the first month, the meter reading was 7,420. The second month's billing was for $704.90 which included the base and 6,422 of overage changes.

The Trick to Clicks

That's when the trouble began. The customer adjusted (and paid) the invoice to the base amount of $190.00 for 2,000 copies. A note was attached stating: "The maintenance agreement was for a base of 2,000 copies/prints per month. We have only made 1,825 copies/

prints this month. Your calculations are incorrect."

The sales representative went out to double-check the meter reading and re-explain the terms of the maintenance agreement, if necessary. By the time the sales rep arrived for the in-person meter confirmation, the meter count was well over 10,000.

The customer smugly explained to the sales rep that all the images made were 11 X 17 two-sided prints. The printer was "clicking" four times for each print that came out of their newly leased equipment. The customer showed the sales rep a copy of the maintenance agreement and additional "letter of agreement." Nowhere was there any mention of a "click" charge. All written references and verbal promises had always referred to .095 cents per copy or print.

The sales representative tried to explain meter readings and clicks, the way it is in our industry. At .095 per two-sided 11 X 17 full-color prints, the dealership would lose thousands of dollars during a five-year contract.

The customer merely smiled. "I have a signed contract for 2,000 prints per month. Whether you make or lose money is no concern of mine. Please have all future maintenance agreement invoices reflect the number of prints we make."

Even if this dealer wanted to live by the letter of the agreement, there was no way to accurately register how many individual pieces of paper were coming out of the color copier. This particular color copier had a software default for the 11 X 17 to be metered as one or two clicks. However, a two-sided print was always counted as two metered clicks.

Is There A Moral?

There would never be any credibility to their meter reading. The customer had cleverly set the stage for paying for a minimum of 2,000 prints with any monthly meter reading under 8,000 clicks. The customer had shrewdly dropped their cost per 8.5 X 11 color copy to .025 per click.

To make a long, costly story short: The customer continued paying their base rate each month. The dealer stopped servicing and providing supplies for the customer because they were past due on paying each month's overage. The customer countered by taking the dealer to small claims court. The court quickly ruled in favor of the end user.

The customer politely told the dealer, "Hold up your end of the written maintenance agreement or it will cost you tens of thousands in real legal bills. In civil court, you have no supporting arguments. Small claims court was merely a warning. We are going to be business partners for the next five years. You need to start living up to your end of the agreement immediately."

The dealer smartly decided to lose a little money each month rather than go through a prolonged court case he felt certain he would lose.

Now is the time to take a new look at your maintenance and lease (CPC) agreements. Traditionally we bill by the click. Our maintenance and sales agreements enumerate service and supplies by the copy or print.

We can all learn from the mishaps of this Florida dealer. He paid dearly for using the verbiage that has served us all so well for 30 years. Use the "replace" option in your word processing application to simplify the task. Update the wording in all your documentation.

Good-bye copies, so long prints, hello CLICKS.

"Scan Many, Print Few"

Scanning is increasingly becoming an issue to be examined and manipulated by both the buying customer and selling dealership. Heavy users of the scanning function can create havoc with the profit margins anticipated under traditional maintenance agreements.

As end users continue to use traditional copiers as scanners, new servicing issues are emerging. Most copiers that scan have two separate meters: one meter counts the scans and another meter keeps track of copies (prints).

The traditional sales pitch of "scan once, print many" is turning into "scan many, print few." Many technologically advanced companies are using the scan feature more than the copier's printing function.

I have learned to categorize the three most common types of buyers (eventual users) of the scan function.

1.) The casual user who knows enough about scanning to have the subject included on their overall checklist. He or she does not currently have any particular need for high-end scanner usage.

2.) The knowledgeable, IT-type buyer who asks about scanning capabilities--speed, memory, ease of use, hard drive capacity, and job memory, to name a few. He or she brings up scanning early in the needs list, as a vital part of the buying process.

The buyer who openly asks about scanning in the proposal procedure will again address the scanning issue while negotiating CPC (cost-per-copy) or service agreement pricing.

3.) The shrewd buyer who is a potential heavy user of the scanning process and relies upon entirely different tactics. He or she will casually ask to see a multi-page document scanned. Questions on storage capabilities, memory maximization, job storage, network and e-mail abilities, come up in casually directed conversation during the demo. Normally the sales representative positively agrees to each enquiry or sidesteps the questions, deferring to the technical staff, who can show them how everything is done.
Late into the negotiations, when lease and service pricing have been established, the customer slips in, "The scans are not counted as meter clicks toward the service agreement." In most cases, the comment is spoken in the form of a statement rather than a question. This third type of purchaser is the one who concerns me.

Other Scanners

Another sign that a high-speed digital copy system is predominately used for scanning is the savvy IT purchaser who requests low per-copy-pricing on the maintenance agreement (no supplies). The issue of monthly or yearly minimums will be purposely ignored. CPC pricing or other all-inclusive service agreements will be rejected.

Often, it is during the site survey (usually conducted by the technical staff over the telephone or by e-mail) that the scanning function enters into the equation. Once the technician starts communicating with the IT personnel, the scanning issue quickly moves to the forefront. The copying function is being reduced to a secondary position of need.

When negotiating the service portion of the agreement, the customer commonly asks for high-volume copy pricing with no monthly minimums. In the past, dealerships could slide on the insistence of requiring a minimum monthly usage with little fear of low-volume usage on higher priced models.

As more and more companies understand the practical usages of fast scanning equipment, dealers must become aware of new usage patterns. High-end copiers may no longer generate hundreds or thousands of dollars in monthly click-charge revenue.

Service Needs Will Change

During the past few years, I have always kept my ears open for service managers who have encountered negative scanning experiences. I talked with several service managers who are losing money on customers who scan more than they print.

An upstate New York dealer was required to do a complete automatic document feeder rebuild. Also needed were a scan motor, eight scanner cables, and all the associated hardware. All this at 563,000 scans and 10, 485 copies. "We got caught on this one. We sold the service agreement at .005, no supplies, no minimum. So far, we have received less than $60 for service," said the dealer. "The scanner rebuild alone cost over $500. We learned a lot from this customer. We now charge for both meter clicks and scan clicks."

Another dealer, in Minnesota, related a similar situation: "630,000 scans, 110,000 copies. Not enough revenue to cover the cost of the scanner rebuilds. I wrote-off the cost of repairing the scanning system to training. Fool me once, your fault. Fool me twice, my fault. Fool me three times, and we are out of business."

Admittedly, the digitally connected equipment requires much less service than traditional analog copiers. Some savvy, price-conscious customers are ahead of many dealers' learning curves. Smart buyers know they can require more aggressively priced service agreements.

Many dealers have reduced the price of their traditional servicing agreements. It is now imperative that pricing accommodations are made to recoup the cost of servicing equipment that make more scans than prints. Also, we must be aware of the cost associated with embedded CPU's, memory, network cards, lost software, and accompanying labor costs.

A simple way to protect your profits from the potential of copiers that scan more than print is to add one line to your traditional service agreement. "The customer will pay an additional .0025 cents per scan, when the scans exceed service agreement minimums or actual print usage."

Scanning is becoming an increasing portion of our business. Now is the time to effectively prepare for the future. Have a written plan to recoup the long-term cost of servicing the scanner portion of digital copiers. Better yet, structure your service agreements to generate revenue on each scan your customer makes.

Profits Hinge on Preventive Maintenance

Preventive maintenance servicing can make or break the profitability of your service department. Creating formulas, functions, and checklists for each service call will maximize your profitability potential.

Your service department is no stronger than your weakest technician. For some, this can be a very scary thought. I try to inspire all my technicians to achieve the "McDonald's Theory of Reliability" into their daily work habits.

Let me explain. A McDonald's™ hamburger purchased in Hong Kong looks, tastes, smells, and is wrapped just like a hamburger served in Kansas City. Like McDonald's, a successful service department establishes and monitors consistent rules for success.

If I want every tech to approach and complete each service call in a similar manner, I must make sure there are written, reasonable guidelines. Printed on the back of each of our customer service orders is a checklist enumerating the various duties that may be done during this servicing.

This form is a cross between a working "cheat sheet" and a "Get Out of Jail Free" card. The check sheet is a handy reference to verify the completeness of servicing for each machine. Any item not checked means the tech consciously did not work on that function. This is especially important on billable servicing. Chargeable customers have a habit of expecting everything to be warranted forever while only paying for one hour of service.

Check It Off

Using a checklist clearly explains to the customer (or a supervisor who follows up on a previously completed call) what work has been done. If a technician only works on the sorter, as marked off on the checklist, there is no implied warranty on the automatic document feeder.

When my technicians are performing preventive maintenance (PM), they use the manufacturer's PM checklist and our own customized service call checklists. Additionally, when dealing with high volume, console copiers' PM cycles, there are several different levels of required service. In order to assure that the correct PM servicing cycle is completed, my supervisors have made individualized PM checklist charts for each machine we service.

These charts graphically show which PM kit (group of parts) should be replaced at each successive copy count. Sometimes multiple PM kits are required at a single servicing. The PM cycle for the RADF (document feeder) is also listed. All PM kits, drum, and developer part numbers are noted for easy access.

At each PM, all the simulations, jam counts, and self-diagnostic codes are checked, recorded, and cleared. A simulation checklist has been made for each model. This sheet is kept with the service history card in the copier.

We use the manufacturer's suggested PM cycle as a starting point. Actual field experience will dictate real life serving requirements. The life cycles of developer, fuser rollers, drums, and automatic document feeder parts, etc., often vary greatly from the manufacturers' written life spans. Do not be misled by written manufacturers' expectations.

Find a Proper Procedure

Make sure your company has a way to recycle PM kit parts that are not used. Allow your techs to make educated decisions when not to replace parts that are included in a PM kit. Encourage your techs to return the unused parts. Have procedures to recycle these parts into your active inventory and have them credited back into service's parts and labor.

Establish a procedure to rebuild a PM kit if a single part is taken from the kit to do a needed repair. I have seen dealerships throw away unused parts and scrap entire PM kits for want of a computer (bookkeeping) system that allows returns for these variations.

For those companies who do not use manufacturer's pre-packaged PM kits, establish your own in-house packaging of regularly needed PM parts. It is management's responsibility to help the field tech be productive.

Completeness and correctness of work is simplified once all the techs get in the habit of accurately following written procedures. My customer service order requires a listing of the next meter reading that will require a PM servicing and which level of PM will be required. This previously obtained information is used as a quick reference before dispatching a tech to future calls. If there is not enough time to complete an anticipated PM, or if the needed PM kit is unavailable, the PM is rescheduled (before the technician is dispatched).

Technical and customer relations procedures are important to standardize in written form. Technicians must be accountable for specific actions. If management is unable or unwilling to do their job of establishing written standards and expectations, your field technical staff will probably emulate this laissez-faire attitude.

Most employees want to do a good job. The use of service call and PM checklist will provide your service department with McDonald's-style reliability.

The Cost of Nothing: There is Always a Cost to Maintenance Service Call

"It was nothing, just a dirty toner sensor. It will work like new now."

I have heard these words, uttered by service technicians, quoted back to me by customers on many occasions. The customer is unhappy for being billed more than $100 for service that the calling tech said was "nothing."

At the time of the initial service call, the unsuspecting tech was told this customer was on a maintenance agreement. The tech had worked on this copier many times over the past several years, often not even bothering to get anyone to sign the service order. It was just a simple no-charge service call.

Little did the tech know that the customer had not renewed their maintenance agreement.

After several attempts to get the customer to pay for the renewal of the service agreement, the customer admitted, "We are cutting back on expenses. The tech had told us that our copier was 'just like new' and the service call was 'nothing.' We have no intention for paying for 'nothing' on a copier that is just like 'new.'"

"Nothing," this service manager thought, "has a very high price."

As the customer continued to complain about being charged for a service call that the tech had said was for "nothing," I silently started adding up what fixing "nothing" cost the dealership.

What "Nothing" Costs

There is the cost of the technician's cell phone to connect with his lap top computer, which dials into an Internet service provider to obtain the information the dispatcher has entered into the master computer system. The City Map book (Map Quest takes a long time to provide misleading information) allowed him to drive 20 miles across the toll bridge. The tech's labor hour, hiring, training, 401K, health insurance, vacation and sick time, training, parts, technical manuals, car stock, and a percentage of overhead are a few of the costs that crossed my mind.

The basic tech mentality is to be worker-bees. They traditionally downplay the value of their technical knowledge and troubleshooting talents. Techs have learned that when a customer asks, "What did you do to fix it?" what they really want to know is, "Does it work now." Techs tend to simplify and leave on a positive note.

It is important that technicians are trained (and receive on-going reinforcement) to value the importance of what they say and how they say it to the customer.

The tech who earns $15 per hour has an hourly cost (burden rate) to your dealership of $50 to $90 per hour. The technicians' cost to the dealership is the same each hour, whether they are driving, troubleshooting, instructing a customer, doing a preventive maintenance call, attending a company meeting, or fixing the equipment.

Every time a tech asks me if it is "OK if I don't charge the customer; all I had to do is to re-attach the sorter?"

I respond with, "Do you want to receive mileage reimbursement for driving to the customer? Do you want to be paid for the one hour (you logged on your service report) it took you to hook the sorter up? Do you want to accrue sick and vacation time for this hour? Should we deduct a portion of your health insurance and 401K payment the company pays for you?"

Very quickly, the tech understands there is a high cost of his doing "nothing" for an hour.

Techs, dispatchers, service managers, sales reps, and company owners must understand that doing something for FREE has a cost. Every time labor is given away, or you have unworked paid labor hours, you are digging a hole that will require twice as much work to refill.

Full-time service techs in the United States are paid for eight hours per day, 40 hours per week, 52 weeks per year. It costs the dealership the same amount of money for the technician's hour whether or not any customer is paying for their time and knowledge.

The Price of Value

Teach your techs to appreciate the cost and worth of their time and knowledge. There is a cost for the tech to walk through the customer's door. If a customer requests a field service call, the customer and the tech must understand there is a cost to the dealer and a price to the customer.

A tech who has adequate training and experience to be able to identify and correct a problem in 30 seconds should not be penalized by a customer. Would the customer feel that he or she had received a greater value if an incompetent tech had spent 60 minutes figuring our how to properly attach the sorter?

Never tell a customer “It was nothing.” A four-year-old piece of equipment will never be as “good as new.” Every field tech must be taught to maximize the worth of their ability. Never discount your knowledge. Common words and expressions, spoken in haste, can come back and haunt the dealer.

CPC:
Calculating Profits Carefully

No matter how connected and digitally advanced your copier dealership has become, the question remains: "How can you make money selling supplies when the majority of your customers have cost-per-copy (CPC) coverage?" The problems, resulting from all-inclusive (everything except paper and staples) full-service agreements, continue to plague the dealership's bottom-line.

There is more to CPC profitability than merely losing the opportunity to sell supplies through traditional retail channels. The bigger question is, "How can I be sure we are not losing money on the CPC supplies that are being provided to our customers?" The escalating costs and diminishing returns of selling all-inclusive service agreements is a two-decade-old problem. Tracking toner usages and accessing accurate meter readings continue to concern the dealer.

Common pitfalls of CPC agreements:

-- Connected equipment will naturally use a larger percentage of fill than standard walk-up copying;

-- Customers lose the toner sent to them or seem to be selling it on eBay;

-- Shipping costs continue to escalate;

-- Tracking payments received from lease companies that reimburse for the service and supply portion of the CPC is time-consuming, and reimbursement always seems to be a few months behind the customer's actual payment history;

-- Acquiring accurate meter readings takes time and ultimately becomes a cost factor;

-- A few bottles of supplies are never accounted for on lease returns.

CPC Considerations

Here are some tactics that other dealers are using to say ahead of the CPC game. Select the ones that are most appropriate for your local customer base.

1.) Limit the amount of toner provided under a CPC. If your marketplace allows you this limitation, it may be worth a try. You may, however, find that the cost of tracking the amount of toner provided to a CPC customer is actually greater than the cost of the product that may be lost, misused, or fraudulently obtained. The time and money spent, energy depleted, and negative feelings created when a customer is told they must pay for additional supplies are often self-defeating. Customers feel that they are being double billed or that an unrealistic usage was allotted.

2.) Provide all allotted products at the beginning of the contract. This controls the amount of product and eliminates several freight bills. However, the instant cost to the dealership of a year's worth of product is substantial. This method should only be considered for very low volume agreements that are paid up front in a single payment.

3.) Utilize different rules for different classifications of customers. Churches and real estate offices seem to use more toner than lawyers and CPAs. Some dealers merely add a clause to their service agreement that states, "Supplies will be provided based on the manufacturer's listed usage rate." This clause can be invoked if a customer repeatedly requests excessive amounts of toner. Many dealers train the clerk that inputs supply orders to quickly review the ordering history of each customer before shipping out more supplies. Attention should be focused on the renewal date and payment history of each CPC customer. A customer whose agreement expires next month or who pays slowly should not be shipped six months worth of supplies.

4.) Weigh the cost of product against the cost of shipping. A common practice is to ship three months' of product at a time. This works especially well if the majority of your customers pay quarterly in advance. Common sense must be used when providing supplies. The customer who has a low-end copier, whose toner wholesale cost is $4 per cartridge, can be sent a year's worth of supplies upfront. Quarterly shipping will cost more than the product.

5.) Whenever possible, do not ship developer. Have technicians carry it in stock and install it when necessary. Make sure technicians record accurate meter readings when they are servicing equipment. If a customer has multiple machines, the tech can quickly record current meter readings from several pieces of equipment.

6.) Special attention must be paid to high-end users. The customer running 500,000 copies per month, paying monthly, in arrears, can be sent two month's worth of the $268 per cartridge toner. These customers will become very demanding if they run out of toner. A delicate balance between their payment history and the amount of toner they can be sent in advance of payment must be established.

7.) Recover excess quantities. During the early years of a long-term lease, you do not need to worry about sending more toner than the CPC payments would cover. However, toward the end of the lease term, diligence is necessary. If another company sells your client new equipment and takes responsibility for returning the leased machine, you will never see the extra bottles of toner the customer has on their shelf. At the end of any agreement that provides supplies, you have every right to be proactive and pick up any unused products, as well as the surge suppressor that was originally placed with the equipment. This can be done with a UPS pick-up tag or by having the technician, sales representative, or delivery person pick up surplus supplies. Tens of thousands of dollar of returned supplies can be added back into to your profit column.
Customers on an all-inclusive service agreement are not entitled to a cash refund for the supplies that were not used. Issuing a receipt for returned supplies justifies the picking up of the supplies in the customer's mind. "Your account will be appropriately adjusted" is a true statement that can accompany the issuing of a receipt.

8.) Bill monthly CPC service agreement customers promptly, base upfront and overages in arrears. Encourage quarterly billing up front. When a customer's account reaches 31 days past due, immediately stop providing service and supplies.

Never ship toner to a customer with a past due account. Be polite, but firm. Dealers cause their own problems by setting themselves up to be put in an adversarial position. The more lenient you are, the more animosity is created when you put a customer on credit hold.

9.) Make sure your company is set up as a credit card vendor. You will be amazed at how many of your customers will be willing to pay their (past due) bills with plastic. Make it a company policy to always offer credit card billing. You can even set up for periodic (monthly or quarterly) automatic billing to a credit card account to pay the periodic service agreement charges. Some of you may be shaking your head and asking, "What about that one to four percent vendor fee charged by credit card companies?" Your ability to increase cash flow and shorten your receivables will more than make up for the few percentage points that are lost in credit card transactions. Think how much is written off on a regular basis from customers who always seem to short pay an invoice or refuse to pay shipping.

10.) Whenever possible, encourage quarterly, semi-annual, or yearly billing cycles. Change your terms to "due upon presentation" or "due net 10 or net 15 days" when you are billing the customer directly. The cost of carrying a delinquent customer can quickly become greater than the actual cost of the toner you are providing. Track payments due under lease agreements as aggressively as you would any other customer. Accurate monitoring and crediting payments are essential.

Smart Billing

No invoice should be processed for under $100. It is not profitable for either party to be sending invoices and processing checks for small amounts of money. The cost of processing a single invoice ranges from $27 to $72. The cost to receive, authorize, and pay this invoice is similarly expensive to the company that pays the bill. Neither your company, nor the vendor, nor the receiver of the payment can afford to process low-end monthly service agreement bills. Educate your customers, your salespeople, and yourself. The billing process is a genuine cost factor in your business. In many dealerships, the actual invoicing cost is greater than the price of the shipped supplies.

Toner is becoming an increasingly larger portion of the total cost of all-inclusive service agreements. The successful dealer must be conscientious in reducing costs in all aspects of the service and supply equation. Know your customer; track payment history, usage patterns, toner cost, freight costs, expected fill volumes, expiration dates, and profitability to ensure that both you and your customers come out ahead of the equation.

Chapter 4

Motivating Field Personnel, or "Out of Sight,..."

Technicians and Human Resources

Test Your Interview Skills

I am a service manager, not a human relations expert. However, I am responsible for recruiting, hiring, and training all of my employees. Over the years, I have developed a few no-cost techniques that can serve as pre-employment testing procedures.

The wrong hiring decision can be very costly. You (the potential employer) ultimately undergo the greatest test. You have the most time and money at stake during the interviewing and hiring process. It is your company or department that can be most affected by the results of how you test an applicant.

Although there is not one perfect pre-employment test, many professional testing firms can provide you with specific testing products. These tests can range from $25 to over $500 per test.

Testing can begin before there is actually any contact between you and the potential employee. If you are looking for a person that is computer literate (able to actually hook up a printer), request that a resume or personal statement of qualifications be e-mailed. As a first test, request applicants to include one or two specific pieces of information in their e-mail. This can be as simple as asking that all e-mailed responses be addressed to Mister CADE Tialevia, c/o dept 42238.

This may seem a little contrived. However, this simple response instantly tests the applicant's ability to follow directions, use numbers, spell foreign words, pay attention to detail, and make independent decisions.

Will the e-mail be addressed exactly as requested? Will Mister become MR.? Will dept be corrected to dept.? Will CADE be changed to Cade or Tialevia capitalized to TELAVIA?

A good technical representative must be able to read and interpret details. The importance of lower or upper case cannot be overstated in using some computer software. If you are not sure what the "appropriate" answer should be for an aspiring technical rep, pose the same "test" to one of your best technicians or to someone in the business you respect. See how they respond.

The next test you can pose to a potential employee is the first telephone experience. When you call the number listed on the resume, are you greeted with a recording that gives you comfort as that person's future employer? Is there wild rock music in the background with a message of "Dude, I'm lightin' up right now" or a crying baby, or a homemade family-sung jingle, or a "god bless you" at the end of a formal recording? Each gives you a little insight into the lifestyle of the applicant.

If you are looking for someone to answer your incoming calls or anchor the phone support to customers or technicians, the telephone interview is of enormous value. This type of job requires a telephone personality. Ask the applicant when would be a convenient time to speak uninterrupted for a while. Set up a formal telephone interview.

The Eye of the Beholder

If you need a field technician, the eyeball test is essential. Your company's receptionist is the best judge of the way the interviewee appears as he or she enters your office for the interview. The receptionist best represents the sort of person in your customer's office who will first see your tech any time he enters for a service call. If your receptionist gives the applicant a thumbs-up, continue the interviewing process.

When I make an appointment with an applicant, I always explain during the first telephone interview, "We normally follow a four-step interview process. The process starts with this telephone interview and a visit to our office to fill out an application and take a couple of tests. Upon the appraisal of the test results, you may be contacted for a return interview with the departmental manager. References are then normally checked and an employment offer may be made."

This allows me the luxury of not having to waste any time with an applicant that does not pass the "eyeball" test. An applicant who arrives with a pierced eyebrow, wearing a T-shirt with obscene words, stained, ripped Levis, and sockless sandals, is not worth my time for a one-on-one interview.

If the applicant looks acceptable and passes the eyeball test, you can easily appear and say you would like to break with tradition and do a brief first interview. Again, you have allowed yourself the option to be able to abbreviate the interview at any time if the applicant fails any portion of the one on one interview.

Moving On to the Next Test

The applicant's being on time and dressing appropriately are tests number one and two. Test number three is, did the applicant bring a pen or pencil? Was a clean print of their resume presented? I am always amazed by third-generation copies or streaked prints being presented by the hopeful printer or copier technician.

I always give at least two written tests with each interview. My real knockout test is a simple 20-question, 6th-grade level, word problem math test. I provide a pocket calculator. Preventive maintenance cycles, part numbers, sales tax, and billing of invoices require an applicant to be comfortable with numbers.

I am amazed at the number of people who are out looking for work and are unable to do 6th-grade level math.

Whatever tests you use, double-check their worthiness by having the best person in your office (who has a similar position) take the test. Better yet, have that person write up a customized test dealing with job specific issues.

Whatever test you use, be consistent with all applicants. United States government and state hiring laws require you to keep all applications for at least one year. Check with local labor relations board for specific rules in your area.

People are usually at their best during an interview. If their very best is not up to your standards, do not lower your standards. Keep interviewing.

"Boss Do You Have A Minute?"

"Boss, do you have a minute?" Those words can be more disturbing to a manager or company owner than any upset customer demanding their money back. Management, who seemingly has all the power, sometimes is at the mercy of the workers. Employees always seem to ask for that "minute" at the most inconvenient times.

By the time you actually manage to set aside a few quiet minutes for the requested conversation, your stomach is in knots, and you can feel a migraine headache starting to form. "What is going on now? I have enough problems with customers, vendors, manufacturers, and the IRS. I am already looking for a new receptionist, and now my best technician 'needs a minute'!"

At the appointed time, your technician joins you in the conference room. *He* closes the door. "Oh great," you think. "He's quitting, demanding a raise, or going to tell me some horrible news." The knot in your stomach continues to tighten. You smile tentatively and wait for disaster to strike.

Get Ahead of the Question

One way to prevent this scenario from ever happening in your company is to regularly perform human resource PM's. Preventive maintenance servicing is standard operating procedure in the office machine industry. We try to service the equipment in a timely manner before it breaks. We update our software, install the latest versions of anti-virus software, and try to keep up with current technology. An ounce of prevention is worth a pound of cure.

We, as owners and managers, must take the same proactive approach with our company's most valuable resource--our employees--as we do with our computer systems. By doing regularly scheduled human resource PM's, we, too, can keep our employees focused on doing their jobs. Employees need to focus on taking care of our customer's needs. A disgruntled or confused employee will spend too much energy worrying about his or her overdue review.

One reason we neglect "reviewing our employees" on a timely basis is our tendency to make the performance review a "big deal." It is time consuming. There is stress on both parties. Few managers or company owners feel comfortable playing psychoanalyst, mentor, interrogator, or personnel professional. Some tend to put off that which makes them uncomfortable or will cost the company additional money.

A Form of Prevention

I offer here two simple evaluation forms that you and your employee can fill out on a monthly or quarterly basis. By having the employee independently fill out the same review form you are using, you (or their supervisor) can become aware of any differences in opinion or performance expectations. Often, an employee will have an entirely different concept of their job performance rating than you perceive.

By doing routine monthly evaluations, the review process will become less stressful. Small concerns can be addressed before they turn into large problems. Ongoing re-enforcement of proper behavior can be painlessly monitored. When the time comes for a (yearly) compensation adjustment review, there are no surprises.

These monthly evaluation forms can help you through your next employee review session.

The first evaluation is designed specifically to rate Field Service Techs. It addresses specific requirements and details that techs encounter. This form can also be used during the pre-employment interview process to specifically explain the requirements and your expectations of the daily behavior of the field service tech.

The next form is more generic. It can be used for almost any position within the company. You can use both forms when reviewing a field tech. You can use them simultaneously, or alternate them on a monthly or quarterly basis. In either case, give the employee a copy of the evaluation form(s) you want them to self-complete. You can set up an appointment to for the review after their self-review is turned in.

As a manager, you can decide how to handle employees who never return their evaluation form. You can ignore the need to do their evaluation. Lower their score on incentive and following instructions. Realize if they don't care enough about themselves to turn in the self-evaluation, they probably don't care much about your company either.

Either of these forms can be modified to accommodate your specific needs. Different positions have special needs. Use these forms as a catalyst to create a check list of desired actions within your company.

The easiest way to relieve the tension, fear, and general uneasiness of random periodic reviews is to get in the habit of doing regularly scheduled evaluations. The key is to have both you and the employee fill out these evaluation forms separately. Then sit down together.

Monthly Evaluation Report
Field Service Technician

Date________________Evaluated By ________________

Employee __________________________ Total Points Earned ________

Rate yourself on the following criteria on a scale of 1 through 5 points, with 5 representing the best.

1.	Attendance	________
1A.	A Punctuality	________
2.	Ability to find customers office and work on the assigned equipment	________
3.	Productive and profitable work habits	________
4.	Car stock (having the appropriate parts in an organized way)	________
5.	Tools (clean, neat, orderly, meters and flashlights that work)	________
6.	Initiative (doing all the work that is needed in a timely cost effective manner)	________
7.	Customer relations (always treating customers in a professional manner)	________
8.	Ability to identify and diagnose problems	________
9.	Transportation availability (car working properly, full of fuel, money for parking)	________
10.	Ability to use service and parts manuals, Internet and Web sites effectively	________
11.	Seeking technical help in a timely manner... using manufacture's hotline	________
12.	Productivity, creating value for the company for the work you do	________
13.	Adhering to the companies policies and procedures	________
14.	Paperwork: complete, appropriate billing, legible, signed by customer, turned in promptly	________
15.	Using your individual talents to help the entire company	________
16.	Turning in leads that generate new profitable business for the company	________
17.	Contributing a special project or idea that benefited the company	________
18.	Optimizing the full use of the work day	________
19.	Positive attitude toward work and your fellow employees	________
20.	Meaningful participation in service meetings	________
	Total points	________

Additional comments ____

____

____

EMPLOYEE PERFORMANCE PRE-EVALUATION

NAME:______________________________ DATE:______________

DEPARTMENT: ______________________________ JOB TITLE: ______________

CHECK ONE OF THE FOLLOWING:

U – Unsatisfactory F - Fair
S – Satisfactory
G - Good E - Excellent

	U	F	S	G	E	COMMENTS
1. Job Understanding: Employee possesses a clear knowledge of the responsibilities and the task he or she performs.						
2. Job Performance: Neatness, thoroughness and accuracy of employee's work.						
3. Job Productivity: The quality of the employee's work in terms of being on time and completion of tasks.						
4. Dependability: Can you rely upon this individual in terms of completing tasks in a timely manner?						
5. Attendance: Employee is on time for work daily: at work regularly.						
6. Cooperation: Ability to work willingly with associates, managers, subordinates and others.						
7. OVERALL RATING:						

General comments as to your strengths, weaknesses and action taken to improve job performance: ______________________________

____

Review the two forms and discuss the similarities and /or differences. By openly discussing each other's viewpoints, you will both become more cognizant of your mutual and diverging needs and abilities.

Model Performance

You will probably find that, the better the overall quality of the employee, the more critical their self-review will be. Perfectionists tend to always be striving to be better and accomplish more. Your average "C" type employee will tend to evaluative him or herself on the high side. The reason they are mediocre workers is that they have no great self-expectations or lack an appropriate mentor or role model.

Sometimes you will find an employee who will make giant strides of improvement with the help of a conscientious manager. By specifically charting a course of desired actions, a motivated employee will improve.

Evaluations and reviews are part of the American work culture. If you want your employees to excel in their jobs, make sure that management does its job. Make the time to consciously evaluate your employees' job performance. Help them, help your company, be the best employees possible.

With the regular use of the self-evaluation forms, you can avoid ever having to face your employee's request of "Boss, do you have a minute?" In the future, *you* can make an appointment to go over your evaluation forms, shake hands, open the door, and you can both leave the room smiling.

How Can I Improve The Quality Of Our Staff?

Dealing with Personnel Problems

"How can I improve the quality of our staff?"

"Some of our techs have not taken an interest in the digital world."

"Car stock inventories are out of control."

"How do we deal with attendance and tardiness problems with field personnel?"

These are typical of the questions I receive from other service managers and company owners. I'm not quite sure how the authors of these queries expect me to respond to their concerns. These are not questions that can be easily answered with a one-paragraph fax or return e-mail.

Instead, I share with you a few "instant truths" that can help create the type of employees we all seek. I consider an "instant truth" to be something that can be universally acknowledged as factual or a good idea.

Rather than focusing on an employee's behavior during the workday, around your office or department, look at the bigger picture. A successful employer or manager should strive to help improve the entire lifestyle of their employees. Help your staff be better parents, spouses, siblings, and community members. Teach them how to have a better life outside of work and their job performance will improve.

I share these simple ten philosophies to create a better life. You can help instill these simple daily "rituals of success." Every person's life can be improved if you teach and encourage these simple activities.

Rituals of Success

1. Give thanks to someone for something each day. Some cultures call it prayer. Others believe it is just politeness. Conscientiously acknowledge something worthwhile that is happening in your life. Openly give thanks.

2. Read (anything) for ten minutes each day. Keep your mind stimulated. Learn something new. Reading allows you to have an educated conversation with someone else. Knowledge will impress your friends and co-workers. More importantly, knowledge will increase your self-respect.

3. Laugh out loud. Children and animals are enormous sources of humor. When you discover you have done something foolish, laughter continues to be the best medicine.

4. Listen to music. Melody helps to connect the brain with the heart. Loud or soft, fast or slow, music helps filter the day's happenings into useful experiences. Singing out loud or playing an instrument gives you bonus points.

5. Give something away. Sharing your time, wisdom, money, or material possessions will increase your self-respect. Something you have will probably be enjoyed and cherished by someone else. The person who gives, ultimately receives the most in return.

6. Live on a budget. Structure is good for the human soul. Being monetarily disciplined gives you more freedom in the

long run. Having money to spend, rather than spending money, makes life much easier. The difference between an emergency and an inconvenience is money. You must save money in order to have it to spend. Financial freedom is created one dollar at a time.

7. Throw something away. If your car doesn't fit in the garage, take a long look at your priorities. What do you have stored in your garage that is more valuable than your car? Less is more. Purify your life by freeing yourself of clutter. If you haven't used something in one year, get rid of it.

8. Write something each day. Keep a journal. Write a story. Writing sharpens your mind and clarifies your thoughts. Putting a wish into written words is the first step to success. Writing can create your own history of thought and purpose. Re-reading your words, written in the past, creates your own history.

9. Write a thank you note. E-mail and phone calls are appreciated, but a thank you note is cherished, saved, and remembered. A note that is mailed, slipped under a pillow, packed into a lunch pail, or left on a car's windshield becomes a gift of caring. Thank you notes are saved in scrap books or taped onto the refrigerator door for all to see.

10. Exercise. A healthy body will enable your mind to function at its highest level. Good health is the foundation for a strong heart, even temper, and high spirits.

There is nothing magic to these ten steps, but each of these actions will help you live a happier, more enjoyable life. They are all free, relatively painless, and will reap enormous benefits.

Many of our employees are so busy living life, they forget how to enjoy life. In your next departmental meeting, set aside a few minutes to share a positive thought. Ask your employees to share something good that happened to them yesterday.

Take a vote on who is their favorite customer. Ask them to share something that another tech did to help them. Praise a positive action. Thank your employees for being on time.

The first step to having better employees is to have better people work with you. Read, laugh, give, listen, budget, exercise, write, simplify, and be thankful. Good people make great employees.

Managing Change: Improving Your Service Techs' Behavior

One of the most common questions I receive by e-mail from my readers is, "How do you get your techs to do the required paperwork?"

Managing non-commissioned employees who work in the field (away from direct supervision) requires an entirely different management style than working with commissioned or in-house employees. Field technicians need to "buy into" any requested change. You must make it easier for the techs to do things your (newly desired) way than to do things their (old familiar) way.

Change takes time and ongoing reinforcement. In fact, consistent reinforcement may be the key to changing an established behavior. Many "Type-A" entrepreneurial personality types honestly believe that asking their employees one time for a desired radical change of behavior is sufficient. Disappointment and frustration set in when the newly requested behavior does not take place instantly.

An essential tool of management is repetition and tenacity. It takes an average of 30 repetitions of a new behavior to break the cycle of a previously established behavior. Most managers will not verbally request and reinforce the need for change two and a-half dozen times before expecting compliance.

Change Establishing

Before you can expect your employees to change a habit, you or the person requesting the change must be committed to following through until the successful change of behavior has been firmly established.

Here is a sample step-by-step guide to establishing a change in a field technician's behavior. I will use, as an example, the simple request of requiring a signature on each written service order form.

1. Establish in writing what change needs to take place. This written declaration is as much to solidify the commitment to the service manager (owner) as it is to define the specific change to the tech. There is no room for excuses when the new procedure is put into writing.

2. Once you have established the need for a new procedure, figure out why this procedure is necessary. Think of your field techs as a jury. What reasons for change can you enumerate that will make the techs buy into the new procedure. "Last month over $2,000 of billable service calls had to be credited. Many customers refused to pay because no one signed the service order. Over the past twelve months, over $25,000 of service revenue has been lost."

3. You must have a compelling answer to the ultimate question, "What's in it for me?" You must provide the tech with a solid self-interest to encourage the change. "This money could have been used for salary increases for service technicians. Taking an extra 60 seconds to get a signature on each service call may provide enough additional profit to enable you to receive a salary increase next year."

4. Have a contingency plan for problems. If you are unable to get a signature, it is your responsibility to make a note in the customer signature area. "No one there, left for lunch, refused to sign, no one authorized, or even, I forgot." Establish a way to allow your tech to follow the procedure, even if they fail. Have an option to provide a metaphoric "get out of jail free card."

5. Establish a consequence that you can and will actually enforce if the signature line is left blank. Depending on your company's policies and labor laws in your area, create a reward that will be withdrawn for non-compliance. Notice that I did NOT use the word punishment. I stated "withdrawal of reward." This is the key to creating winners rather than teaching technicians they are losers. Those who do it right receive extra benefits and approval. Those that do not comply are left out and ignored. Techs have a desire to belong and to be appreciated.

6. Have each tech signify understanding and personal agreement to conform to the new procedure by signing and dating an agreement form. I _______(tech's name)______ accept the responsibility to have each service order be signed by someone in the customer's office before the service call is complete. Signed ______________________________ Date _____________

7. Have a dispatcher (receptionist or you) check over each service order. Separate any service reports that do not have a signature. You must follow through on the pre-established reward withdrawal. Give a copy of the non-signed report to the errant technician. Do not chastise or publicly humiliate. Just remove the reward.

If a tech takes the time to complain about the injustice of the loss of a reward, listen politely. Offer to allow him or her the opportunity to go back to the customer's office to get a signature on his or her own time, without being paid for mileage (or use of the company car). Or use any another mutually agreed-upon consequence to reinforce the need to follow the procedure.

The goal is not to punish, but to make it easier to get the signature the first time, rather than to deal with the repercussions.

The Follow-up

Your job is to be firm and consistent. If you do not follow up on your part of the job, the employees won't do their part. This is not a one-time process. If you expect your techs to always get a signature, you must be willing to always check their work, follow up, and follow through on the predetermined negative consequences for less than acceptable work habits.

Some readers may think this is a rather childish way to treat adults. Some employees will always respond to a single word said or suggestion made. But human nature will compel many workers to take the path of least resistance. Your job is to make sure it is easier to do a job the correct way than the shoddy way.

If you want to improve the quality of your staff, then improve the quantity of your management. Establish written goals, have your staff "buy into" the procedure, and follow up, follow up, follow up.

Service Call Report: Paperwork—A Service Manager's Nightmare

N/C, no charge, no service report, no history cards, no business records. I see it all too often—the incomplete or faulty paperwork from the field technician.

While teaching a recent service seminar, I posed a series of questions to the attending service managers:

1. How many of you require written service orders for each service call?
2. How many do not allow "N/C" to be written on non-billable (M.A., CPC, rental, national account) service orders?
3. How many require a complete written documentation of all charges (service, travel, parts, supplies, and sales tax) that would have been billed, if the customer were not on a prepaid service program?
4. How many have someone in your office inspect every completed service order for completeness, including a customer signature and all appropriate non-billable charges?
5. How many use history cards?
6. How many require a copy of the history card to be turned in with the signed service order?

7. How many require a first and last copy to be included with the signed service order and copy of the history card?
8. When dealing with digitally connected equipment, how many require the appropriate summary print-out be attached to the service order?

With each question, fewer hands were raised, signifying yes. Some service managers became defensive. Others looked at me with amazement. The company owners that were attending did not have a clue what I was discussing.

There were a couple of very smug-looking service managers. They were able to say yes to all the questions. They had attended several of my service management seminars in the past and implemented the management skills they had been taught.

I will address each of the numbered issues separately:

1. Many service departments do not require a written service order on prepaid (no charge) customers. This is especially true with smaller service departments, or service departments headed by a former technician who has been promoted to service manager. Techs hate paperwork. The promoted service manager can finally become free of all the hassle of paperwork. When bookkeeping errors allow a billable customer to be treated as a no-charge prepaid service customer, there is no paper trail of customer acceptance to pay for any charges.

2. N/C, No Charge, means "worthless." Before long, both the customer and the technician believe the service and parts provided under a prepaid service program have no worth. Therefore, techs are free. Service has no value. When the time comes for the tech to actually charge a billable customer,

he is appalled by the outrageous prices he is supposed to charge. Many techs wonder why they are only paid $15 per hour, while charging $150 per hour. Techs who spend 80% to 90% of their time writing N/C, feel very uncomfortable when the random billable service call is required. Technicians have been known to apologize for the high prices they are forced to charge. Others continue in their "No Charge" habits and give away billable hours or discount part charges. Prepaid service customers tend to call more often because everything is "no charge." When the monthly, quarterly or yearly service agreement renewal shows up, they are upset at the high price of their no charge (worthless, free) service.

3. A safeguard to assure that the dealer has the right to charge for any service call is written documentation of a complete written and signed service order. This document will note all retail charges that must be paid if a prepaid service agreement is not in effect. Two separate columns can be included in the service order. Service Charges and Billable Charges can differentiate the retail value of the service delivered from the actual cost that is being charged. A line of explanation, above the customer's signature, might say, "I agree to pay all service charges if our account is not current or if this equipment is not covered under a fully-paid servicing agreement."

4. Have you ever tried to follow-up on an unpaid service call only to find there is no customer authorization for the work done? No one signed approval of the charges. The customer emphatically states that no one ever authorized the $1,000 billing. "We only wanted the equipment cleaned." No signature, no money. Even worse would be the absence of any written service order. How could you even prove a technician serviced the equipment?

5. The mere mention of service history cards can bring looks of horror from some sales representatives; they feel it is an open book that the competition will use. Date of install, modifications needed, easily assessable usage history, written documentation of constant service problems, the list is endless. Some companies feel an up-to-date history card is tantamount to opening up all your files to the competition.

6., 7., & 8.

From a tech's point of view, a well-documented history card allows a quick and convenient record of past and future needs. No need to call the office or struggle with a copy quality problem when the history card quickly confirms it is time for a developer change. A history of customer errors will signal that key operator training is more important than machine adjustment.

Effective management of field service representatives requires a special set of checks and balances. Too much control and the techs will revolt. Too little supervision and guidance, and you lose control of your field workers. Requiring prudent structure and practical actions helps techs know what is expected. Those who desire to follow the rules and optimize their personal achievement have guidelines for success. Those techs that tend to try to take short cuts and minimize their personal effort will have guidelines for minimally acceptable performance. In either case, the desired work is achieved.

Requiring first and last copies (prints) to be turned in with the completed service order means that the technician must take the time to test the equipment before work is started. The last copy is a formal documentation that the equipment was left in proper working condition. I require the "last copy" to be a combination: half a page copy or the test pattern and half a copy of our 5.5" X 8" history card. This gives proof the copy actually came from the customer's machine and the history card was filled out properly.

Faxes, printers, and digital equipment need to have a print of the test page, jam counts, or appropriate printout. In each case, the tech must turn in paperwork proving the service call was completed appropriately. Management receives documentation that can prove the fieldwork was successfully completed. This type of paperwork is invaluable when dealing with accounts-payable clerks, office managers, and small-claims court judges. A complete, professional history of work accomplished is a testimony to the professional approach your company represents. Great paperwork is an extension of competent work.

Overcoming Questions

1. Will this type of complete, accurate paperwork take more time? Yes
2. Will it create a more professional work ethic among your field techs? Yes
3. Will some complain and refuse to change their ways? Yes
4. Can creative managers overcome their lazy tech refusal to change? Yes
5. Will change happen overnight? No
6. Are the results worth the effort? That's up to you.

Failure is always immediately easier to accomplish than success. Working hard to accomplish a worthwhile goal is always easier and more rewarding in the long run.

Imagine if every time you spent $200 with your American Express card, no paperwork was generated. No records, no signature, no charge, no legal rights. Would you pay your monthly statement?

Written service orders, complete documentation of all retail worth, signatures, checks and balances, and a filing system that allows you to quickly find the information, are all indications of good business, quickly paid invoices, a structured field staff, and responsible management.

The Scouting Report: Sales Leads From Service Techs

"How can a get our techs to turn in leads?" This is a typical question I am asked by sales mangers who attend my service seminars. "We offer to pay them for any sales leads, but money doesn't seem to matter to techs."

As usual, sales and service seem to be speaking different languages. Although money is important to technicians, offering money as an incentive to sell is not effective. The "technical type" employee does not feel comfortable in a selling environment.

The mere thought of having to ask customers a sales-related question strikes fear into the heart of most techs. Turn the situation around: Offering your best sales person $100 to track down switch 7's open position on a schematic will not improve their chance of success. The same principle holds true for the technician who is a virtual fish out of water when requested to employ sales skills.

Sales managers sometimes ask their techs to just keep their eyes and ears open. "Listen for branch expansions, talk of need for new equipment, or a newly-awarded contract. Just let us know what is happening. Take advantage of the luxury of being welcomed into the customer's office."

But, technicians are focused on the equipment in need of service. They have learned to tune out the customer's office environment as they concentrate on the task at hand. A tech's goal is to get the entire job completed as quickly as possible, without disturbing the customer. The goal is speedy completion of the repair.

When they do turn in leads, technicians complain that they never hear what happens. Sometimes a "hot" lead may take months to actually result in a sale. A technical mentality deals with instant gratification.

Feedback Sharpens Ability

If you want to keep technicians interested in turning in leads, the sales department must supply ongoing feedback to the techs. Techs live in a four-hour response time mentality. Giving weekly updates on all tech-generated leads will also provide the feedback to sharpen the tech's ability to identify a buyer from a talker.

Rather than just asking for a sales lead, I sat down with our sales manager and asked, "What type of information do you need? What will help the sales team identify a hot prospect?" Next, I wanted to make the process fun for the technicians. The majority of my techs are male, so I instantly thought of sports as a natural common interest. I decided to call our lead form a "Scouting Report."

The Scouting Report appears less threatening to the technical staff than the traditional lead form. It provides them with a selling schematic to follow when noting the information our sales manager had requested. It is written proof of who actually turned in the lead and on what date. Finally, it makes tracking payment of the lead fee easier and facilitates the follow-up on the sales staff's time management.

Techs Become Scouts

You can modify the Scouting Report to fit your business. You should make it mandatory to attach a scouting report to every service order that is turned in. Establish a specific length of time that a lead fee will be paid after a report is turned in. Assign someone at your office to review every report and record pertinent information in your contact management system. Predetermine how multiple reports turned in on the same lead will be handled if a sale is made.

Some companies may want all completed Scouting Reports to be given directly to the appropriate territory sales representative. If a sales secretary or dispatcher gets involved in the processing of the Scouting Report, then he or she, too, should be considered for a share of any lead fee ($10 to $25) earned when a product is sold.

When asking the technicians to fill out the Scouting Report, do not require that every space be filled in. By allowing the techs to fill in only relevant information that they know is true, you have a much greater potential of receiving accurate, meaningful reports.

Let's say a good lead must include at least three items in the office. Ask your techs to fill in at least three of the questions on the Scouting Report when they get back to their parked vehicle. Caution your staff not to ask direct questions or appear to be "casing" the customers office. Train your techs to be observant, while being professionally discreet.

Allow your technical staff to be aware of the direct help they can be to the overall success of your business. A properly-designed Scouting Report will allow your field staff to know what questions need to be answered before the sales staff can begin the selling cycle.

Scouting Report

Company Name____

City____

Number of employees at this location __________

This prospect is HOT ______WARM______COLD______

Call (person's name)-- ___________________________________

Interested in ____

Telephone number ________________________ ext. _______________

Best time to call a.m. p.m.

Decision Maker _________________________Keyoperator ____________

Current equipment ________________________Monthly volume __________

(Please circle answers that are listed in *italics* on the Scouting Report.)

Other locations *yes* *no* *unknown*

Locations ____

Other business equipment being used _________________________

Color Copiers *Color Printers* *Wide Format* *Connected High Speed*
Networked Printers *Individual Desk Top Printers* *High Speed Copiers* *Hole Punch*
Saddle Stitcher

\# of Faxes _____ *Plain Paper* *Thermal ribbon* *Thermal Paper*

\# of Computer monitors _____ *LAN* *WAN* *Mixed*

Operating System _________________________

Wide Format *Originals* *Copies* ________being used

Color Originals *Color Copies* ________being used *In-house Newsletter*

Other servicing companies tags on any equipment Yes_____ No_____

Name on service tags _____________________________________

Company appears: *High Tech* *Mom & Pop* *Prosperous* *Middle of road* *Just getting by*

Years in business: _________

Appears: start-up .com *Family owned* *Privately owned* *Publicly owned*
Branch office *Corporate headquarters*

What does this company do? ________________________________

Was there any mention of:

opening new offices *other acquisitions* *new contract*

Does the customer appear to be a prospect for any products we sell? Yes No

If so, what products? _____________________________________

Uses recharged cartridges *Buys from office warehouse type stores*
Appears to do own servicing? *Uses OEM supplies?* *MIS on staff?*

Other comments ____

Technician _______________________________Date _______________

You Make the Call

The moon was full on Wednesday night. Full moons always seem to affect the mood of call-in service customers. I should have known trouble would be waiting Thursday morning.

The day started as usual. Thirty technicians were taking care of business. With our single-call dispatch, live dispatchers take service calls and talk with our technicians. The techs receive their morning call on the previous evening, after they clear their final call.

When I hear from a tech before 9:00 am, it usually means a problem. This day, the tech's call was transferred to me at 8:50 am. The full moon had wreaked its havoc.

Dispatch had given "Sam" his first call for Thursday morning on Wednesday afternoon. He was to go to our storage facility (where parts are dropped off on a daily basis) and pick up parts that had been originally ordered by another tech, who was out sick for a few days. After "Sam" picked up his parts at the storage facility (15 miles from his home), he was to drive 33 miles to the customer's office in Westwood (home of the UCLA Bruins).

"Ronelle, I have a problem; I completely jelled." The tech quietly spoke the words. "I went directly to the customer's office this morning. I actually went to the copier and started to work on it. No one there even knew why I had come. They said no one had called for service.

I read the history card and saw the notation that Tom (tech that was out sick) had ordered parts. Then I remembered. I was supposed to go to the storage depot and pick up parts before going to my first call. I'm sorry, I just wasn't thinking this morning."

"OK," I said, feigning composure. "What did you tell the customer?"

"I told them I needed to call the office," Sam said in a half whisper.

"Apologize for the confusion," I instructed. "Tell the customer that after inspecting the copier, there are a couple more parts you need. Tell them you will be back later today to complete the call."

I then continued, trying to make the best of a frustrating situation: "Go back to the storage unit. Pick up the parts. Let's just start your day over. I appreciate your being honest with me. As long as we work together, we can work everything out."

I hung up the phone, smiling in acceptance of a field tech's life and shaking my head in management's despair. When I was a field tech, I remember the sick feeling I got in my stomach when, after arriving at my first call, I discovered I had left my tool case at home. The blown PC board, a scratched drum, a copier that no longer worked after the PM was completed: I know those feelings first-hand. If you work in the field for a few years, you know that all technicians run into problems caused by inattention.

The Cost of Failure

As a manager, I must calculate the *cost of failure.* If each technician made one mistake each month, similar to Sam's forgetfulness, the direct cost to our dealership would exceed $79,000 per year. This includes labor, travel expenses, and parking fees.

Sam was not the only tech that was involved in an "I jelled moment" that week. Maybe it was time for a wakeup call for our field technical department.

The next service meeting was started by a questionnaire (see below) being handed out. Each tech was required to decide on a fair way to handle this specific situation. No names were given. Several other specific examples of technicians "jelling out" were also discussed.

The completed questionnaires were collected. No names were required. Some techs were very forgiving; others made Saddam Hussein look like a nice guy.

The ranges of the direct costs to the company were from $100 to $120,000.

After the questionnaires were handed in, we discussed practical, real-life actions a technician must include into his nightly routine. Actions taken the night before can help take the strain out of getting to their first call on time, with the correct parts, and being mentally ready to work.

Memory Can Be Checked

At the end of the discussion, I handed out "Ronelle's Rules: A Night Before Checklist for a Successful Day." The tech's biggest morning enemy is all the little things that take time or distract attention. Each little item may only take three to five minutes to correct. However, on any given morning, three, four, or five separate little distractions can make a technician 20 to 30 minutes late. Furthermore, the little things can cause them to be in a distracted, frustrated mood before their day's work even begins.

Two weeks after the questionnaire was filled out and the Checklist for Success was distributed, everyone was back on their best behavior, on time, ready to work, tool case, parts, and a winning attitude close at hand.

There is no need for you to wait for the next full moon to discover that your service techs are unprepared. I hope you share this "A Night Before Checklist for a Successful Day" with your techs before the problems occur.

QUESTIONNAIRE:

You Make the Call

Situation: Tech calls in at 8:50 am. "Ronelle, I have a problem, I completely jelled. I'm in Westwood (33 miles from storage depot/120 minutes round trip in Los Angeles morning traffic). I forgot to go to the storage depot and pickup my parts for my first call." Arrives at storage depot 9:45 a.m. Drives back to the customer's. Arrives at 10:45 a.m.

What should the company do?

_______ Do nothing. He didn't do it on purpose.

_______ ____

Should mileage be paid?

_______To the customer's office for original trip

_______To the storage depot, from the customer's office

_______To the customer's office, from the storage unit

Should parking be paid for the original trip to the customer's office?_______

Should the tech be paid his regular wage starting at:

_______ 8:30 when he originally arrived at the customer's office without parts?

_______ 9:45 when he arrived at the storage unit to pick up parts?

_______ 10:45 when he actually started the service call with the parts?

_______ Let him use sick or vacation time starting at _____:______am

Estimate the approximate cost of the "jelling" of the tech:

to FKM $______________ to the tech personally $____________

Have you ever forgotten to pickup your parts, tool case, gone to the wrong call

If yes _____ How many times in 2__ __ __? _______ NO _______

I take the 5th _______.

Do you think this signals a bigger problem or simply a momentary memory loss that's part of the job?

What can every tech do to make sure this type of mistake does not happen in the future? ______________________________

If each service employee made one such mistake each month, approximately what would the total yearly cost be to the company? $ ____________________

Ronelle's Rules:
A Night Before Checklist
For A Successful Day

- ❒ IS THE CAR FILLED UP?
- ❒ KNOW WHERE YOU ARE GOING AND HOW YOU ARE GOING TO GET THERE
- ❒ WHAT'S THE WEATHER FORECAST?
- ❒ DO YOU KNOW WHAT YOU ARE WEARING?
- ❒ ARE YOUR CLOTHES CLEANED, IRONED AND SHOES SHINED?
- ❒ LUNCH IS PACKED / COOLER HAS ICE / OR LUNCH MONEY
- ❒ EXTRA $ FOR PARKING / CHANGE FOR TOLL ROADS AND STREET PARKING
- ❒ ALARM(S) SET TO PROPER TIME
- ❒ WHOSE TURN TO TAKE CARE AND FEED THE ANIMALS?
- ❒ WHOSE RESPONSIBILITY TO TAKE THE CHILDREN TO DAYCARE?
- ❒ ARE YOUR OLDER CHILDREN READY FOR SCHOOL?
- ❒ PAPERWORK FOR A.M. CALL READILY AVAILABLE
- ❒ CHECK FOR OP PARTS FOR A.M. CALL
- ❒ ENOUGH TIME FOR BREAKFAST
- ❒ DO YOU KNOW WHERE YOUR BEEPER, CELL PHONE, AND KEYS ARE?
- ❒ ALL PARTS AND TOOL CASE IN VEHICLE
- ❒ TALK TO SIGNIFICANT OTHER. CO-ORDINATE ANY SPECIAL NEEDS FOR THE NEXT MORNING

Taking Stock of Your Car Parts Inventory

Car Stock Inventory--these three words bring fear to the hearts and minds of field technicians, service managers, and owners. The annoying but persistent problem of the car inventory is always hovering in the background of all conscientious service professionals.

Periodically, the car inventory issue raises its ugly head. There is a fiscal need to find out exactly what dollar value of parts and supplies are being carried by field techs. Hours or days of seemingly non-productive labor hours must be spent counting and verifying each field tech's car stock inventory.

No matter what type of company you run, the inventory issue can make or break the profitability of your business. The inventory that rides around in the back of your technician's vehicle is truly a ticking time bomb.

The list of inventory-related questions goes on and on: How much is enough? What does each tech need to carry? How does heat and cold affect the inventory's condition? How is it organized? Who is responsible for lost or broken items? How is it restocked? How and when can the tech return unwanted items? Do the techs keep their inventory when they go on vacation or to out of state training? Are manuals, parts lists, and bulletins kept as part of the car stock?

Keep Records Up To Date

It is vitally important that each technician have a computer-generated (or written) parts and supply inventory list that is updated on a regular basis--each service meeting is a convenient time. Doing rotational inventory, or checking different sections of the inventory on an on-going basis, is relatively easy. By continuously updating a small part of the total, the need for an enormous amount of time all at once is eliminated.

Designate time during the regular workweek, whether at a service meeting or some other point, for taking inventory of car stock. The little bits of time left over time at the end of the workday can be assigned as inventory upkeep time. When the field technician calls in at 4:15 p.m. to clear his call, both of you realize there is not adequate time to travel to and complete another call. Rather than sending him home, assign the tech to update his car stock inventory until 5:00 p.m.

When I give this response, it is perfectly all right if the tech disregards my request. I expect the tech to try to get a jump on the evening commute and start the evening drive home. It is perfectly OK. The tech has just been allotted 45 minutes of company paid time to work on his inventory. It is my responsibility to keep an accurate record of the time that has been allotted for updating his car stock list.

I use a 3 X 5 index card for each technician. I note the time off (4:15) and the date. If you keep track of this thrown-away time, by the end of the month, you will have given the tech eight full hours of time allotted to organizing and tabulating his or her car stock. When the time comes for a complete inventory to be turned in, the company is not responsible for allotting any more time. The technician may have to work all day Saturday to get his car stock straightened out. You owe nothing more. You have already provided the needed time during regular working hours to finish the task.

Inventory = Money

A fiscal miracle usually happens after techs update their car stock inventory. When they count and record the parts they are carrying, they usually decide they don't need about 25% of what they are issued. Car stock inventory will decrease in direct ratio to the frequency it is monitored. The more often technicians are required to count their inventory, the fewer parts they will carry. I allow each tech to establish his or her own car stock inventory.

Many variables go into establishing an appropriate level of parts and supplies that should be carried by technicians. For instance: How far away is their working territory? How many models of equipment are being serviced? What level of technical expertise does each car stock have to support? What size vehicle does the tech drive? What temperatures can the technician expect to encounter? Is the technician neat and organized or messy and unorganized? Does your service depart have a location for parts drop? Is there a parts driver or an arrangement for UPS home delivery of needed parts? Is there a problem with excessive breakage or theft? These are but a few of the variables.

Some dealerships minimize the cost and hassle of maintaining car stock by having their techs come into the office each morning to pick up needed parts. I firmly believe that carrying NO inventory is extremely expensive--much more expensive than even a $10,000 car stock.

Wasted Time=Wasted Money

Calculate the cost of time wasted each morning for the technician to come into the office, have a cup of coffee, share a few friendly words with other office staff members, and have an additional conversation with other techs in the parking lot before leaving to drive to their first call.

Using a conservative number of half-an-hour wasted each time the tech comes into the office and an additional half-an-hour to drive to the first call of the morning—a realistic number of one-hour daily of non-productive time—these daily trips to the office cost over $14,500 per tech, per year. (Five hours time 45 weeks, allowing for training, vacations, and holidays, times $65.00, the cost of one labor hour per day for a technician making $15.00 per hour, equals more than $14,500 per tech.)

Wasted labor hours can never be recouped. On the other hand, unused parts in a car stock inventory continue to maintain their value.

A continually updated inventory is vital to effectively completing service calls. Most computerized dispatch software programs have a built-in inventory system. It is much more effective to look into your computer files to see which tech currently has a needed part than to randomly send the next available tech who may or may not have the part.

Accuracy Means Efficiency

As natural attrition occurs, the machine population will shift from older analog equipment to newer digital models. It is imperative to reevaluate the levels of parts purchases and the type of parts carried in the warehouse and car stock inventory. An accurate inventory allows the technician who has diagnosed a specific problem to quickly check their updated car stock inventory (which is conveniently stored in their tool case). This eliminates the time-consuming and frustrating search of their vehicle to try to find the needed part.

This type of efficiency enhances the level of service that can be delivered to your customers. It will greatly shorten the turn-around time required on calls waiting for parts installations. It will ultimately increase your customer's level of satisfaction.

One of the greatest ongoing costs to all dealerships is the inventory of parts that are necessary to deal with the daily servicing of equipment. Depending on the size of your operation, hundreds, thousands, or even millions of dollars are invested in an attempt to have the correct part in the right place in a timely manner. This simple concept has been the nemesis of thousands of service managers.

The delicate balancing of time, monetary resources, storage, and the availability of needed parts will be simplified by carefully monitoring car stock inventory.

Sharing the Power of Knowledge

It doesn't seem that long ago when I wasn't sure of the difference between analog and digital. I keep hearing about the changes taking place with the Internet, dot.com, e-commerce, CNE. I wasn't very concerned. After all, I had lived through carbon paper, wet-estate copiers, dry-estate, plain paper wet and dry copiers. This digital thing couldn't be much different.

Boy, was I wrong!

We have been witnessing a technical and sociological revolution. Two-hundred years from now the world's scholars will look back at this period—I call it the Dot Com Era-- with the same reverence as the Renaissance or Industrial Revolution.

Several years ago, I was asked to write an article about the process required to earn a See and E. I didn't want to show my ignorance, so I blindly agreed to write about the requested subject matter in my next column. I did not have a clue as to what this See and E was. I started my research without the aid of the Internet.

Before long, I realized I was really researching CNE certification. Even then, there was confusion over Certified Novell Engineer or Certified Network Engineer. Thus started my baptism into the digital world.

The more I learned, the more concern I had for the 40 traditional (analog) technicians I was managing. How was I going to create an environment to help my techs bridge the gap? I had learned the hard way; paying techs time-and-a-half on Saturdays to attend technical training didn't work. In fact, it cost the company a great deal of money and only bred resentment from the techs at having to work on Saturday. Little was learned.

Teaching to Learn

However, I found that a group becomes a team when all members are sure enough of themselves and their contributions to be able to praise the skills of others.

I started a VOLUNTARY, peer-to-peer (techs teaching techs) training--friends teaching friends, in a relaxed atmosphere, on Saturday mornings. The teaching techs began to gain in self-esteem. They found the truth of the adage, "The more you teach, the more you learn yourself." Those Saturday morning sessions have become a tradition. The learning techs increase their self worth. We all have a good time.

The company provides healthy food and the use of the shop as our training room. I unlock the door and make sure learning starts at the appointed hour.

In the beginning, I would periodically ask general questions to keep the conversation flowing. Now, I sit in the back of the room, oblivious to the meaning of most of the discussions. Over a dozen of our techs have achieved computer certifications.

How did we go from ground zero analog, to knowledgeable, network savvy, digitally proficient, certified technicians?

Peer-to-Peer Training Works

A couple of my techs appeared to be computer savvy, but I did not know enough to be able to make an accurate value judgment. I hired a CNE whom I knew to show up that first weekend morning. A dozen techs choose to spend Saturday morning at the office.

We built a computer, installed a new hard drive, loaded software, and explored the Internet. A couple of us had laptops. We shared tips on using PowerPoint and Excel. Five hours passed quickly. At the end of the learning session, the CNE gave me evaluations on the knowledge level of the attending copier techs. Now I had a better point of reference on the actual knowledge level possessed by my employees.

I approached a couple of these more computer literate techs and offered to swap comp time for them tutoring future sessions. This was a decade ago. Yet, the Saturday training session continue, once every other month.

Today, we sell only digital equipment. About 50% are connected at installation. Over one-third of our copier techs have computer certifications. No one is paid to attend these voluntary learning sessions. Sometimes we give away gifts. Technician Dads have even brought their children who seem to be more computer literate than some of the adults.

These Saturday training sessions have no dress code, and no timetable. The talk of computers, copiers, and faxes is intermixed with baseball, football, and basketball. Fishing trips entangle with software tales.

The idea of peer-to-peer training has become friend-to-friend sharing. These training sessions are a friendly meeting place for field service technicians that normally work in singular isolation. They willingly share their knowledge.

The relaxed (no one is being paid) atmosphere allows for the added element of camaraderie that most service departments lack. These feelings of friendship extend into the work that is accomplished in the field, Monday through Friday. Techs are more willing to help one another. Sharing a new idea or suggestion on how something can be better accomplished is seen as helpful rather than as unwelcome criticism. Techs feel comfortable asking questions of a friend that would never be queried of an unknown worker.

Baseball teams have been formed, fishing trips organized, god-parents and a wedding's best man chosen from friendships formed on these Saturdays.

The Extended Impact

Our company's owner has expressed his amazement and pride in a technical work force that repeatedly shows up on Saturdays to improve their working skills.

One of the luxuries of being a female service manager is my ability to make our working atmosphere a little softer and kinder while getting the job done. I congratulate births, graduations, sports victories, and accomplishments of all kinds. Praise is free, but it reaps a high dividend.

I have never brought beer to our Saturday learning sessions. My techs are offered low fat milk, orange juice, fruit, and granola. My goal is to set a healthful example. I always leave industry-related magazines in the men's bathroom. I strategically place junior (community) college class schedules where they can be seen.

Once we are back to our Monday through Friday work week, I try to schedule end-of-the-day service calls close to the attending techs' college classes whenever possible. I am a little lenient at finals time, allowing techs to start working at 7:00am (whenever possible) so they can get off early to get an extra hour of study time in before their final exam.

I make of point of asking them how class is going. What are you learning this week? Are there any books you can share with other techs? We have a video training and book lending library in the service department. We encourage shared learning.

As each tech achieves a new certification, he or she proudly donates the previously needed books to the service lending library. "I never want to open this book again!" is said with a grin of accomplishment.

When I was growing up, my mother, a first generation daughter of illiterate immigrant parents from Portugal, stressed the importance of education. It was the central point of my upbringing. Education once achieved can never be taken from you. Knowledge is the greatest renewable resource a human can possess. Learning transcends all boundaries of race, age, money, physical handicaps, social, and economic barriers. Education is the bridge to personal improvement, growth, and pride.

The business manager that can tap into his or her employee's learning abilities will earn enormous dividends. The level of your work force will improve in direct ratio to the ongoing schooling that is pursued.

A chain is only as strong as its weakest link.

Don't Water the Weeds

As managers, parents, and friends, we tend to spend much of our time focusing on those around us who are in need of help. We counsel, criticize, and console those who are in need of personal and professional improvement.

I have often been accused of not treating all of my employees equally. "You show favoritism to some techs. It's not fair."

I agree 100% with this assessment of my management style. I do have favorites. Each person is different. My employees are treated in direct ratio to their daily actions. The tech who manages to work eight full hours, have accurate parts inventories, turn in legible paper work, display superior customer relations, show great troubleshooting ability, attend networking school at night, and turn in leads, is paid more and treated better than those who never display any of these qualities.

It took me years struggling with my "C" workers, trying to make them superstars, before I realized the error of my ways. The harder I worked to help the average worker reach the next plateau of excellence, the more frustrated we both became. Meanwhile, my superstars were continuing to succeed at a moderate level of growth with little help or encouragement from management.

The individuals who were self-starters, high achievers, and highly competent were usually left to their own means of achieving success. They did not require my continual attention to get their job done.

The 80/20 rule seems to apply as much to employees as it does with profits from customers. Twenty percent of mediocre workers can easily take up 80% of your management time.

As a former horse trainer, I learned early in my career to never waste time on a mediocre equine. I focused my time, energy, and customer's money on enhancing a horse that possessed the innate natural ability to attain greatness. I fed and watered all the horses in the barn. I just didn't waste my time trying to enhance their lack of natural talent.

At some point in my service manager life, I recalled this lesson from my horse training days: Don't water the weeds. Focus your attention on those resources that have the greatest potential for attaining future success. Spend 80% of your time on the 20% of your employees who really are ready and willing to make a significant difference in your company's productivity.

Invest your energy in the employees who have a proven track record of showing up and being prepared to succeed. With additional guidance and encouragement from a supportive manager, imagine how much more can be achieved.

Train Your Successors

If you empower dummies, you will get bad decisions faster. Be confident enough in your own abilities to invest in individuals who may someday out-perform you. Achievers understand that before you can be promoted, there must be someone who is able to take over your current position. Training those around you allows everyone to succeed.

In service meetings, I try to specially acknowledge technicians who display superior work habits. "Thank you, Rick, for leading an evening network study group. Martin worked until 6:00 p.m. to complete the installation. John sent a creative modification to the manufacturer's technical hotline. Ken did a great job with our new e-mail list. Oscar has turned in three leads that resulted in equipment sales this month." I am not only praising the achievers, I am presenting a readable road map for success for those up-and-comers to emulate.

It has taken me years to accept that there are "C" employees. I ask about their family, I commiserate about their car trouble, lost expense checks, and faulty alarm clock that made them late. I accept the fact that their wages are being garnished and their credit cards are maxed out. I do not spend extra hours of mentoring on these people nor do I chastise them for allowing such things to happen in their life.

Some people can barely manage "C+" behavior. I softly guide and allow them to work at their own level and give them appropriate work assignments. Some employees have such turbulent lives that they really need a non-threatening, non-challenging work environment to rest their frazzled emotions.

Let Them Blossom

Superstars will respond to challenges, have a strong work ethic, show initiative, and creativity. These people will continually pay back dividends when you invest your time and the company's money on their future. Look for people who have the physical and mental traits that can handle the challenges that go along with winning.

No company can succeed with all leaders. In order to be a great leader, you need followers. Allow your leaders to make a smooth road for the "C" workers to travel. Give yourself permission to ignore the weeds. Invest your time in watering, fertilizing, and providing sunshine to those who have earned the right to share 80% of your time.

I Know That You Know That I Know

Service managers must always be on the lookout for field habits that waste time, decrease productivity, or cost an inappropriate amount of money. When counseling a field employee for doing something that is inappropriate, discretion is the better part of valor.

A field employee who thinks he or she has been unjustly reprimanded for an action can cause havoc in the field. After a confrontation with a manager a field worker can have the attitude of, "out of sight, out of control."

The technician who would never dream of stealing any tangible object from the company may think nothing of starting 15 minutes late, adjusting their mileage, or doing a free service call for a customer who has become a friend. Stealing can come in many forms.

I have learned to use the "I know that you know that I know" counseling method. This is an effective way to put an employee on notice that his or her actions are suspect without accusing of doing anything wrong. When counseled properly, the employee is encouraged to be a team player and praised for hard work and contributions to the overall effectiveness of the service department.

Let's say that you suspect a technician of exaggerating the mileage he turned in on his expense report. For some companies, cheating on one's expense report is very common. Rather than accusing the tech of lying and stealing and making the counseling session an interrogation, I depend on the "I know that you know that I know" method.

Counseling Effectiveness

If you want to have an effective counseling session, you must do your "homework" in advance. When counseling field personnel, make sure you have physical proof (examples) to back up your concerns. Have several expense reports with questionable entries. Highlight any questionable mileage entries. Run a computer history of the tech's service calls for the time in question. Have appropriate copies of local street maps with highlighted driving paths from each of the techs listed service calls. You can also use computer-generated directions and mileage from Map Quest or other Internet sites.

Depending on the severity of the problem, you can ask the tech to make a special trip to the office to talk with you. Or, you can wait for a seemingly causal meeting, asking the tech to come into your office when he is there to pick up parts, etc. Closing the door to your office or going into another room will emphasize the seriousness of the conversation.

Questioning, not accusing, is the key to letting the tech know that you know something isn't right. This will let them know that in the future you will not accept these actions.

Have some non-highlighted copies of the map ready for the tech to show you how he or she traveled from point A to point B. After the tech shows you on the map, ask for an estimate of how many miles this distance is. Maps all have a mileage scale, or use an educated guess as to the distance between service calls. Ask the tech, "Do you remember anything unusual that day that would have caused you to make a detour or use a longer driving distance?"

Ask the technician to compare the mileage he or she just gave you to the mileage on the expense report. When there is a significant difference, ask, "Can you remember how you arrived at such a different number of miles?"

Only Ask Questions

The key is to never accuse. Only ask questions. "What route did you use? Did you go anywhere else? Was there any reason you did not go in a direct route?" I have found the technicians that are just lazy and guess at their mileage, shrug their shoulders and readily admit they have not been doing an adequate job of tracking their miles.

One tech told me, "I disconnected the speedometer cable on my leased vehicle so I won't have to pay for overage on miles when I turn in this leased car. I just guess at the miles I put on my expense report."

"What criteria are you using when you guess at the mileage?" I asked. "Do you think your guesses are accurate?" In my mind, I was thinking, "What you are really saying is you are stealing both from the leasing company and from our company."

When asking questions, always wait for an answer. This silent time puts the burden of proof on the employee. It makes them realize the severity of the conversation and that they are ultimately responsible for their actions.

The techs who quickly provide a very specific answer as to why their mileage is excessive is usually guilty of premeditated cheating. In either case, your job is to let the tech know that from here on out you will not accept this method of calculating the mileage expense report.

The "I know that you know that I know" method puts everyone on notice that you will be watching and expecting a change.

The $15,000 Beers

Drinking alcoholic beverages before driving can have major consequences on you and your employment.

It was just another Saturday afternoon softball game. The service department's team had won. Traditionally, the winning team went out for pizza. They played a little pool, had a few beers, and everyone had left by 6:00 p.m.

The incident that ultimately affected the next seven years of one technician's life had started so innocently. Most of the softball team members worked as field service techs. Often, their spouses and children attended the games. They all had some good, healthy fun. Saturday afternoon softball had become a weekend tradition during the summer.

It was still light out when one of the technicians drove away from the pizza parlor. Suddenly, he realized there was a red light flashing in his rear view mirror. "My seatbelt," he thought. "My seatbelt is not on. That's good for a $179 fine." The technician cursed under his breath. The technician had a habit of not putting his seatbelt on until he was driving. Now he was going to pay for it in more ways than one.

The technician's first thought was to try to sneak the seatbelt on and click it before the officer appeared at the side of the door. But the highway patrolmen approached him very quickly.

"Good evening, Sir. May I see your driver's license and car registration?" The patrolmen said without a smile.

"Just my luck," the technician thought. "This guy is going to go by the book."

After he looked at the tech's driver's license and registration, he commanded, "Stay in the car." He went back to his patrol car and entered some information into this his laptop computer.

"Technology," thought the technician. "A cop with him and a laptop."

The technician sat in his car, watching the digital seconds flash by on his dashboard clock. Finally the highway patrolmen returned and asked the technician to step out of the car. "Have you been drinking?" the officer asked.

"No." The technician instantly responded. As the words left his lips he thought about the three beers he'd had along with the pizza. "Well, I did have a couple of beers, but that's not really drinking."

Before the tech realized what he was saying, he had just admitted to drinking and driving. He was handcuffed and unceremoniously assisted into the back seat of the officer's patrol car. He had just been arrested for driving under the influence of alcohol.

Before the night was over, he was required to leave his car (which was towed to an impound yard) at the side of the road; he was booked, photographed with a number across his chest, allowed to call his wife (who in turn called his parents, who then called a lawyer), and locked in the cell with a bunch of common criminals. As he sat on the floor of a cold, dirty, rancid-smelling jail cell (filled with some very dangerous looking people), the tech slowly began to comprehend how this one action would affect the next several years of his life.

A Look Back, With A Sigh

In hindsight, the tech felt fortunate he did not harm anyone else or lose his job. His family stood by him. He did not receive a ticket for not wearing the seatbelt. But drinking those three beers certainly changed the next few years of his life.

There was the cost of paying for his car being towed and the retrieval from the impound yard. The lawyer sent bills for the next six months. He missed several days of work going to trial, meeting with his probation officer, and having to attended rehabilitation classes. The judge sentenced him to weekends in jail for six months, 50 hours of community service, and then two years of probation. He was required to pay a fee for each one of the weekend stays in the county jail. Ultimately he had to go to court three separate times. His driver's license was suspended for six months. All of which meant he could no longer do his job as a field service technician.

Fortunately, he had an excellent past work history and his company was willing to work with him through this crisis. He became a shop tech. The structure of eight hours a day inside was a real culture shock. He was not used to working in one place, with the same people, all day long.

He did not receive a raise in his salary that year, but he was grateful that he didn't lose his job. He learned how difficult it was to take the bus, ride his bike, car pool with his wife, friends, and parents. The absolute inconvenience of being at the mercy of someone else or the public transportation system was not only humiliating, but extremely inconvenient.

At first, he blamed the cop, other members of the baseball team, his wife, the judge, his probation officer . . . everyone except himself.

Eventually, he realized that anyone who is a field technician or who earns their living while driving a car should think long and hard before an alcoholic beverage is ever put to their lips.

Finally, he took responsibility for his own actions. The tech was amazed as the costs of this incident continued to grow: towing fees, car storage and recovery, incarceration cost, lawyer fees, court costs, weekend incarceration charges, lost wages, loss of his company car, loss of his yearly salary increase, increases of his car insurance for the next seven years, visits to his probation officer and community service and the disruption of his life. The final tab was over $15,000. Those three beers cost about $5,000 apiece.

The moral of the story: if you're a field service technician, think very seriously about the possible repercussion before you drink and drive. If you are not responsible enough to understand the possible harm you can cause others by driving under the influence of alcohol or drugs, ask yourself, "Is this drink worth $15,000 and maybe even my job or my career as a field tech?" The answer is up to you.

Personal Business

There comes a time in each employee's life when focus and energy are distracted by personal matters. Be it a birth, death, accident, or just relatives visiting from out of town, personal responsibilities sometimes overshadow work responsibilities. Each person establishes his or her own code of ethics concerning priorities of family, business, and personal matters.

Managers can encourage open communication with employees by being sympathetic to their personal needs. By always offering encouragement and understanding, you can establish honesty and an open line of communication. Managers should be sensitive to other employees' needs for emotional joy or healing.

Each person deals with life-altering situations differently. The birth of the child can be a time of great joy. It can also create havoc for the first-time parent. A sleep-starved technician must be treated appropriately. A three-hour drive to a remote location could spell disaster for a technician who has had no sleep while tending to his fathering responsibilities.

A grown child grieving over the death of a parent can become equally distraught and distracted. Extra sensitivity from office support staff may well be needed. Depending on the personality and responsibilities of the adult child, a few hours or days off may be necessary for the health and well-being of both employee and employer.

In Time of Need

The appropriate time for an employer to deal with an employee's personal tragedy or joy is before the situation happens. Employees must be encouraged to value their paid vacation and sick time. It is important that employees are encouraged to save accrued time off. This will enable the employee to still receive a regular paycheck while dealing with unexpected events.

All too often, employees blame management for their personal lack of the available paid time off required to attend to personal needs. Management should periodically (monthly or at least quarterly) provide all employees with a current written accounting of their previously used and available paid time off.

If your tenured staff is young, you'll be dealing with marriages, births, car accidents, drunk driving arrests, and new home purchases. As your staff matures, you'll deal with chronic physical problems, employees having to deal with physical and mental problems of their own parents or adult children.

An employee who works in the office can arrange their time and space (filings of personal data, etc.) to deal with telephone calls to a hospital, funeral home, Social Security office, or insurance company. The in-office worker may be distracted and have constant interruptions, but part of the time can be safely focused on work.

Time Without Great Loss

The service manager must be especially sensitive to a field worker who is dealing with a personally disruptive situation. Rather than have the technician take the whole day off, you might schedule a half-day of shop time or in-house self-training. This will allow the technician time in the office to make and receive telephone calls. You might even provide a separate room that will provide privacy to deal with personal issues or grief.

By being sensitive to employees' needs, you ultimately can optimize their work time. Providing workable options, allows you to minimize missed work time. Management must try to evaluate what a preoccupied employee is capable of doing in a safe and effective manner. A distracted or distraught employee should not drive, work on machinery, or deal with upset customers. The computer programmer who loses focus can cause irreparable damage by a misguided keystroke.

Try to keep an open ear to the personal involvements of your employees. It may be helpful to ask a dispatcher or the 'Chatty Cathy' of the office to make sure that you are informed of any circumstances (revealed in lunchroom conversation) that may require a little extra attention.

When you do find that employee who is having a personal situation that may directly affect his or her work, take time to express your concern and your willingness to help. Open communication can be the difference between helping the employee and causing long-term negativity.

The more compassion and sensitivity you show your employees, the sooner they will be able to handle the external situation that can affect their internal work habits. A part-time worker is better than a full-time problem. When in doubt, it is better to err on the side of compassion and helpfulness. An employee who is responsible enough to take care of personal responsibilities is probably an effective member of your work place.

Be Equipped For A New Job

Acquiring a new job is listed as the third most stressful time in one's life. I continue to be amazed at how ill-equipped most interviewees are in understanding the process of *earning* a new job.

I use the word "earning" because many unsuccessful applicants do not grasp the fact that acquiring a new job is very hard work. Employment today is not guaranteed to last. Many long-time employees are losing their jobs, and companies have to deal with the reality of possible lay-offs at some time.

Whether you are in pursuit of a job, are doing the hiring, or are trying to find your technicians a position after a downsizing, there are certain factors to remember in the job search. To be successful, you must do your homework, act like a professional, and approach job hunting as a major work and research project.

Why Are You Looking?

For those on the outside looking in, here are a few tips to improve your changes of making the cut.

Applicants must first take some time to figure out why they are looking for a new position. Why are they out of work? Did something go wrong? Or why are they unsatisfied with present situation? They must also look inward, take a realistic view of their work history (if any), and assume responsibility for their present situation.

Many people think they are invaluable or that someone else will be laid off. The first to go is often the "experienced" employee making more money than he or she is directly generating. Six-week vacations, higher wages, extended smoking breaks, comfort level of the "good old days," little on-going self-education, and complacency are not the actions of a long-term employee. Job security is being worth more than a salary.

Job seekers must write or rewrite an up-to-date resume. Accuracy will be tested in the interview process. More than three-quarters of all interviews identify areas of discrepancy in an applicant's resume. The potential employer can easily conclude that such applicants are either ill-prepared or liars. In either case, their worth as future employees diminishes.

The Facts of the Matter

When the time comes to go looking for a new job, or to help a departing employee find work, keep these tips in mind:

Be aggressive. If an employment advertisement gives a fax number, e-mail address, or P.O. Box, send your resume to all the addresses. Don't be afraid to follow up.

Earning a new job has a great deal to do with timing. Sometimes new job openings happen with a moment's notice. Successful applicants who find a company that appeals to them must be persistent.

Applicants should be prepared to be contacted by telephone. There needs to be a pen or pencil along with paper at hand near every telephone. Any members of your household should be alerted and prepared, as well, to be polite and take accurate notes. Messages need to spell the caller's name correctly, include a return telephone number, and be timed and dated accurately

An answering-machine message should reflect the image that will earn the applicant the respect and return call for an interview. Loud rock music followed by "Do it at the beep" will not endear anyone to the personnel office of a potential employer. If the portable telephone has static, walk across the room and use an old-fashioned telephone that works clearly.

The Interview

For an interview, being on time is crucial. Arriving a few minutes early is even better. The applicant can then mentally review interview strategy, glance through his or her current accurate resume, and calm down.

Tools for the interview include two pencils, two pens, a card-sized calculator, an original up-to-date resume, portfolio of past accomplishments, certificates, school records, references, newspaper articles, and special accomplishments. Whenever possible, a set of these documents should be prepared to leave with the employer.

Clothes need to be clean, ironed, properly fitting, and job appropriate. Shoes should be polished or at least unscuffed. Get a haircut. Don't chew gum.

After a telephone or in-person interview, the applicant would be advised to send a follow-up letter restating a few personal strong points of how their qualifications will meet the needs of the applied-for position. The letter should open the door to another meeting and thank the interviewer for their time and information shared.

Not every job is right for every person. Not being offered a job should have nothing to do with a person's self-worth. As the world economy races toward a digitized Internet economy, the need for changing employment is inevitable. The best time to prepare to acquire a new job is before it is needed.

Chapter 5

Management Is A Verb

General Management Concerns

What's in a Name? The OEM Dilemma

Sometimes we forget that new people are always entering into our industry. All the knowledge we take for granted has to be acquired one fact at a time.

At a recent seminar, during a discussion on parts purchasing, one brave soul raised his hand and asked, "What is the significance of OEM? I know what the letters stand for--original equipment manufacturer--but I am not sure why I should care, or when and why I should buy an OEM product rather than the cheaper non-OEM product."

I could tell by the number of blank looks on several attendees' faces that a little explanation was in order. I will share with you some of our discussion.

Original Manufacturing?

The value of purchasing OEM parts and supplies confuses a lot of people. To OEM or not to OEM? Sometimes it seems to be a little like Hamlet's dilemma.

OEM, or original equipment manufacturer, is actually a misleading designation. Most manufacturers outsource (buy from someone else) many of the parts that are used in the "original" manufacturing of equipment. Many manufacturers sell the same exact product to several different companies. The product is then re-sold under the name of the company who has the reselling agreement with the original equipment manufacturer.

Many companies who make parts to resell to manufacturers have "exclusive distribution agreements." Legally, the fine print will vary in these contracts. The companies who manufacture the official OEM parts sometimes seem to only alter the look of the packaging before they sell them (legally--at a discounted price) to other non-OEM resellers.

The OEMs often claim that their official OEM parts are "guaranteed first quality" by means of costly quality control techniques. Their marketing departments sometimes imply that non-official-OEM products, when manufactured by the same company their OEM companies buy from, are selling off their "second" quality product. At some point, it all may become just a word game.

Creative purchasing of parts and supplies can make or break the profitability of the service department and ultimately your entire company. Someone at your company should take the responsibility to keep informed about the availability of alternate sources for parts and supply purchases. All too often, price has little to do with the ultimate value of where and how you acquire your parts and supplies.

Your primary responsibility is obtaining a "good enough part" at an "I can make some money on it" price. As equipment gets older, you may not need a first quality part for a customer's rarely used printer or copier that is located next to the warehouse's loading dock.

Confused Yet?

Admittedly, not all parts are equal. Some OEM part manufacturers will sell off their "second" quality merchandise to non-OEM resellers.

These parts are genuine OEM, but they are not top quality. Genuine OEM parts that have already been replaced by a newly modified (improved) item are often sold at a discount. The unsuspecting buyer pays a premium price for a discontinued or substandard, but genuine, OEM product.

Some non-OEM parts are equal to or superior in function and less expensive than the OEM equivalent. Some non-OEM products are superior in function and much more expensive than the OEM.

There are times when the OEM will run out of a product and actually buy a similar part from a previous non-OEM seller. This previous non-OEM seller has been instantly elevated to an OEM distributor.

Some high usage, expensive parts are worth shopping for in terms of price and quality. Buying from a non-OEM can often save hundreds of dollars. On the other hand, saving 85% on a one-dollar item that is rarely replaced is not worth your time or effort.

Many independent servicing dealers learn to mix and match a couple of "name brand" non-OEM suppliers with some independent distributors of various OEM products.

Some authorized dealers' contracts require them to use only OEM products. Different manufacturers enforce this clause with varying tenacity. The use of non-OEM drums, toner, developer, and fuser rollers can cause the manufacturer disdain. But the use of non-OEM bearings, lamps, and cleaning rollers often goes unnoticed.

Some OEMs prohibit authorized dealers from selling their product to unauthorized dealers. Other manufacturers encourage their dealers to sell the product to anyone. Make sure you know the rules in advance. If you plan to break a few, be aware of the repercussions if you are caught.

Getting the Best Deal on Parts

Most non-authorized dealers can acquire 80% of all needed parts and supplies from legitimate non-OEM wholesalers, at or below the legitimate wholesale cost that authorized dealers pay. The remaining 20% of small or specialty parts can be obtained through wholesalers who have a direct access to authorized distribution. These parts are usually priced between the wholesale and retail price.

Anyone who purchases parts must take into account the reliability, availability, and cost. It is good business to cultivate backup vendors and to alternate purchases between the vendors. This tends to keep you abreast of industry trends and gossip. If one vendor is out of a product, you have a backup product source without having to deal with credit applications or COD deliveries. You maintain familiarity with catalog usage and ordering procedures.

Non-OEM board repair depots are often superior to the OEM's in-house repair departments. Those companies who specialize in board repairs offer 24-hour turn-around and lower cost than the OEMs. Some OEMs actually outsource their board repairs to independent companies.

Non-OEM parts and supplies play a significant role in the dealer convenience and profitability. Their sales staff is usually friendlier, more knowledgeable, and has a longer tenure in the business. Their parts selling staff often works on commission. On the other hand, original manufacturers' parts staffs are often entry-level positions, non-commissioned, and work under the constant strain of having to explain to upset dealers why a part is on back order or not covered under warranty.

Buying Patterns

Non-OEM suppliers are needed to keep the manufacturers honest. When there is too great a price difference between OEM and non-OEM products, the dealer's buying patterns shift. OEMs are forced to reduce their price. A high OEM-priced product inspires non-OEM resellers to find an acceptable replacement product at a lower cost.

All dealerships should make sure that somewhere in the "fine print" of their service agreement they acknowledge the fact that replacement parts will be "dealer approved" or other such language that implies or states: replacement parts may or may not be new and/ or OEM.

There are many variables to consider when choosing vendors for needed products. Purchasing is a dynamic process. Complacency can become an expensive luxury. Stay knowledgeable, always ask for this month's specials, negotiate freight charges, keep abreast of industry trends, and keep track of life spans of the different OEM and non-OEM products.

Accountant, Teacher, Firefighter: All Part of Service Management

As I teach service seminars across the United States, I am repeatedly asked, "Who in your company keeps track of all these ideas you have just presented? Who keeps track of contest winners, late starters, technicians who contribute special projects and turn in sales leads? Who does all the work that creates the winning margin of excellence?"

I often wonder what other service managers do all day long. Historically, we talk about service managers spending most of their time putting out fires. It is the old excuse of "urgent" taking the place of "important."

The starting point of all successful service departments is with understanding the goal of optimizing the time available for work. Knowing the cost and use of the service hour is essential for establishing a profitable, effective service department.

If the service manager does not respect the value of the service department's main inventory item--the labor hour--the profitability of the service department will never be optimized.

I share general income and cost figures with my entire field service staff. I make sure that the technicians who work on prepaid servicing all day (MA/CPC/Rental/National Accounts/Warranty) understand their work is directly related to billable income.

I am proud to work for a profit-driven organization. All our techs know that their salary, security, benefits, pension plan, and the welfare of their family and retirement depends on how correctly we all do our jobs.

The manager who shrugs his or her shoulders and says, "There is nothing that can be done about wayward techs," is not a manager, but an acceptor.

It's Your Responsibility

The behavior of technicians is the direct responsibility of the service manager. Good intentions and long hours do not guarantee a profitable and customer-friendly service department.

Helping field techs achieve effective work habits requires a very special management style. Managing non-office, non-commissioned technical employees in the field requires constant monitoring, feedback, and creativity. A manager must set up expectations, establish procedures, monitor progress, and reward or chastise the resulting actions.

Each service department leader must blend his or her own management style with each technician's personality and the company's business philosophy. The key is not the particular way you manage, but what results are achieved from your managing.

Start Small, But Start

If you are not sure how to get a true management program going, start with some baby steps. List one action you would like to see immediately improved within your service department:

(It's your job to fill in the blank.)

Next, list three very specific actions (changes) that must take place within your service department to help bring about this new habit:

1.
2.
3.

Put in writing the specific consequence that will happen to the offending employee. Better yet, reward all the technicians who do achieve the listed behavior. Try to get peer pressure, pride, a new tool, money, time off, etc., to help you achieve the new goal.

Post the achiever's name and/or photo in the service department for all to see. Send home a letter of appreciation acknowledging this employee's specific contribution to the company's well-being.

Whenever I hire an additional technician, I make sure the new employee gets an old tool case, vacuum, and meter. I reward an existing tech who has proven himself as an achiever with new equipment.

I acknowledge the action that is being rewarded. "Jim has had perfect attendance for the past six months." I present the new tool case in the service meeting for all to see. I always start a round of applause.

Successfully managing a department starts with establishing, monitoring, and rewarding specific behavior. The truly successful manager is the one who continues the tedious task of daily requesting and reinforcing desirable behavior.

Be Consistent and Persistent

Don't expect what you don't inspect. A hard-fought and firmly-established behavior can be ruined in a few weeks of nonperformance while something great only needs to be ruined once to disappear. Daily diligence is necessary to keep everyone working at peak performance. Effective service management must be an ongoing, everyday process.

The service manager's (supervisor's) responsibility is to make sure that at 3:30 you know where your techs are and what they are doing. The field techs must also know that the service manager is still working and available to assist them if a problem arises in the field.

A successful service operation is driven by mutual respect and monitoring of every employee's responsibility of completing a full day's work. Instilling the need (through example and expectations) to utilize the entire workday is an essential factor in optimizing the service department's profitability.

Cell Phone Usage Policy

At a recent Business Technology Association-Southeast meeting and educational conference, Bob Goldberg, BTA's general counsel, spoke to the group on some of the "Potholes on the Superhighway to Success". During his presentation, Goldberg talked about several of the common legal problems that dealers must face.

One was the Americans with Disabilities Act. Goldberg related specific rules of the ADA that require dealers to have 36-inch wide entryways, clearly marked handicapped parking places, and ramps with clear access to the buildings. He discussed several lawsuits that unsuspecting dealers have been involved in resulting from deviations from the written law.

The attorney went into great detail about some potential patent infringement issues that can face dealers who use electronic commerce software. Some of the standard "shopping cart" type of purchasing software, thought to be in public domain by many, have been the focus of threatening letters. A number of dealers have received demands for software licensing payments in lieu of patent infringement lawsuits.

In most cases, the request for the software license fee is less than even one day of attorney's fees and court costs. Dealers are forced to choose between prudent business practices of paying a few thousand dollars of patent fees (which might appear as blackmail money) versus having to pay the cost of attorney's fees and court cases to prove the foolishness of the threatened patent infringement liabilities.

Driving Distractions

The portion of Goldberg's presentation that I found most compelling was his discussion of employee cellular telephone usage during the course of the regular business day. The attorney referenced a few lawsuits that ultimately required millions of dollars worth of settlements. In each case, the employer was found liable for the employee's accident while the employee was driving and using his or her cell phone.

Everyone listening to the presentation could directly relate to using their cell phone while driving. Even the most conscientious of drivers divert part of their attention from the process of driving to the process of dialing or talking on their cell phone.

In some cases, the errant driver sued their own company for making them talk on their cell phone while driving! The blame was shifted from the driver to the employer.

To avoid being named as the "cause" of driver distraction, businesses need to be proactive. Companies can protect themselves from potential lawsuits as well as providing their employees with a safer work environment by simply adding a page to their policy and procedure book, entitled "Sanctioned Usage of Cellular Phones."

Setting a Policy

By creating and enforcing a written company cell phone policy, you can help protect the dealership from liability if an employee does get into an accident while using either a personally-owned or company-provided cell phone during working hours.

It is vital that every dealership adds a written policy explaining to their employees that cell phone usage while driving is not allowed. Once documented, the policy naming the restriction is added to the company's policy and procedure book. Every employee should be given a copy of the page containing the new policy. Each employee should be asked to sign and date a copy of this page signifying knowledge and acceptance of the new company policy.

(SAMPLE)

Wireless Telephone Usage

While Operating A Motor Vehicle

This policy applies to the use of wireless (cellular) telephones by all employees during working hours.

Any employee who, in the course of performing his or her job functions, finds it necessary to use a wireless telephone must do so in a safe and prudent manner. If the employee is operating a motor vehicle, the vehicle must be stationary in a safe location, with the transmission in a "Park" position, before using any wireless communication device. Wireless telephone use is never permitted while operating a moving vehicle.

All necessary business phone calls must be made before leaving the previous location or after arriving at the next destination. In the event the employee must make or receive a call while driving, he or she must first find a safe place to stop the vehicle and put the transmission into a "Park" position before making or receiving a mobile telephone call. Business-only calls are permitted on wireless telephones that are provided to an employee by the company.

Violation of any part of this policy may result in disciplinary actions up to and including termination.

Signature ____ Date _____________

It is imperative that dealers take a proactive approach in monitoring the use of cellular phones. Not only is the health and safety of your company at risk; the life of your employees or other unsuspecting drivers or pedestrians must also be protected.

No-Call Beepers

In my own service department, we have taken cell phone usage safety one step farther. All of our technicians carry tone-only beepers. If we need to get in contact with a field tech, they are beeped. Because the beepers are "tone only" (no numbers are displayed) the field tech does not have to look at the beeper. They know if their beeper goes off, they are to call the office at the next safe and appropriate opportunity.

If they are driving, they can pull over when it is safe to make a call. If they are in a customer's office, they have been instructed to wait until an immediate conversation is completed. It may be appropriate to go outside or move to another area of the customer's office before calling the home office. If there is a special circumstance that requires getting in contact with the tech immediately, we beep them multiple times.

Dealers who have a written policy that specifically prohibits talking on a cell phone while driving establish an additional layer of protection if a lawsuit is placed against the company. Something as simple as adding one new page to your companies' policy and procedure manual can help protect your business from costly lawsuits and help maintain the safety of your employees.

Competition

The word "competition" itself can bring great excitement or deep fear to anyone who will soon be involved in the competing. Those who have a history of winning will find the challenge of competition exhilarating. Those who have never taken part in a contest or have a history of losing will shy away from the probability of defeat.

Companies, like individuals, have the same winner or loser attitude. Time out from your normal work duties to enter a contest may seem counterproductive. Objections range from "industry-focused competitions do not award monetary prizes" to "many contests actually require an entry fee" to "if you do win, there is some sort of expense necessary to receive the (non-monetary) prize."

Let me recap: extra work, no monetary gain, chance of failure. Why even bother? This sounds like a lose-lose situation. Aha! Herein lies the difference between winners and losers, excellers and get-byers.

In the office machine world, businesses are providing similar products. Customers choose to do business with one company rather than another for various and subtle reasons. One thing remains constant: It is human nature to want to be associated with a strong, secure, industry-approved company. The customers' security is tied to the servicing company's long-term viabilty.

Before a customer feels secure with signing a five-year purchase, supply, and servicing lease, the customer wants tangible assurances of the company's long-term success. While there are no guarantees for future success, a history of past accomplishments and company awards plays an important part in reassuring the customer.

Start-up companies can't invent a 20-year history of longevity. "Serving the community since 1965" is a claim that cannot be created in one week through extra diligence. New businesses have to work at creating an appearance of involvement and recognition. They can acquire a "history" within a couple of years by winning awards through competition.

Manufacturers, community organizations, industry associations, magazines, newspapers, charitable organizations all have regular awards to be earned. The key word here is earned. These awards are not just handed out.

Where to Look

The easiest way to earn an award is to find a worthy charity or educational institute in your area that distributes awards for contributions. For as little as $25 you can become a "Corporate Donor" to the local high school's scholarship fund. The YMCA, Boys and Girls Club, local religious organizations, are always raising money. Make your donation become an advertisement for your company's community involvement.

Once this tax-deductible contribution is made, use it as an advertising tool. Most newspaper are looking for community news items. Take a picture of a key company official handing your donation (check) to the worthy organization. Try to get your product and company name in the background of the photo. Send a nicely written article explaining a bit about your company and the charitable organization, along with the photo to local newspaper, business journals, community magazines, etc.

Also, be on the lookout for announcements of business competitions. If you see a story on the winners of a contest, look in the small print for information about the next such competition. Or, call the newspaper, magazine, or organization and ask about the procedures for entering next year's contest. You might be put on their mailing list or be able to have a timetable for your calendar about entry requirement deadlines.

Free Advertising

You will be surprised how easy it is to get free advertising. Once these news items are published, save copies to be included in the company scrapbook. Nicer articles can be framed or perma-plaqued and displayed in a prominent place in your company.

Within a few months, your company could establish its own history of positive community involvement. For less than the cost of running one paid advertisement in a newspaper, you can help the community and get positive free advertisement.

Once you have mastered the technique of achieving self-funded awards, you are ready to tackle the challenge of winning a real community-sponsored or industry-sponsored award. Don't expect to win the first time you enter. Don't wait until the last minute to work on and send your entry.

Awards can be proudly displayed in the reception area of your showroom. Smaller sales offices, away from corporate headquarters, can receive replicas of the original awards or copies of the newspaper or magazine articles announcing your victory. These can be framed and mounted or strategically left in the waiting room as reading material.

Many sponsoring companies will provide advertising "slicks" that can easily be added to your business cards, letterhead, Web page, or other advertising media. You can also request "originals" that can be used as envelope stuffers, handouts, or additions to your company's brochure. Articles discussing your company's being recognized as an industry or community leader are excellent forms of low-cost advertising.

As Always, It's the Deadlines

Most contest entry deadlines are the last day of the month. If your company is like mine, the last week of the month is a frantic time. Everything that hasn't been accomplished (closed) all month has to be concluded or carried over. Few employees have the time or the energy toward the end of the month to help write the winning entry. So plan ahead.

Have at least two people independently complete the entry form. Then pass around the "first drafts" for others to add information to or correct grammar and spelling. Have a few key people rewrite. Generally speaking, "less is more." Be concise. Be specific. Be original. It's usually OK to provide extra information on a separate piece of paper or send copies for those newspaper articles about all the wonderful, community-minded things your company does.

After the entire entry is completed, set it aside for a day or two. Then go back and re-read as if viewing it for the first time. Think in terms of the person who has to read dozens or hundreds of these entries. What will set your company apart? What will make your entry memorable? What will make your company be termed as a winner?

At this point, the non-winners in the group are saying, "Gee, this sounds like a lot of work with no guarantee of even winning."

A winning spirit will extend itself to your staff and customers. Those potential buyers who come from a winning organization strive to do business with other proven winners. Businesses who don't personally have a winning tradition are usually impressed with those who do.

Bragging Rights

If you do not participate, you will never win. Allocate a portion of your advertising budget to charity or education. Take part in industry sponsored events. Then brag about your accomplishments to the local press. Acknowledge your own good deeds in your showroom, letterhead and Web page.

Clean-Ups Improve Customer Impression

One Saturday morning I returned to work to pick up my laptop computer, which I had absent-mindedly forgotten. I was in a "weekend" state of mind as I pulled into the empty parking lot. That meant I actually looked at my office as an uninvolved third party might see it. I smiled inwardly and refocused on the quiet industrial area.

Our two-story building is quite attractive. But across the street is a vacant lot with waist-high weeds. A neighboring company had started parking semi-trailers on our street (which is posted 'no parking"). There were several pieces of trash in one corner of the now-empty parking lot.

The flowers to the left of the front door were still blooming late into the season, but I had never noticed all those weeds that surrounded the purple buds. And any customer who wanted to walk into our tastefully-decorated reception area had to walk past a three-foot-high ashtray full of dozens of cigarette butts.

At that moment, I resolved to take a fresh look at the office on Monday. When I normally arrive to work, my mind is already focused on the responsibilities of the day. I slip through a rear employee entrance and go up the back stairs into my corner office. I cannot remember the last time I looked at my business through a potential customer's eyes.

Look Again, Through New Eyes

Monday at about 10:30 a.m., I ventured outside with notebook in hand. I stood in the office driveway and pretended I was looking at this place of business for the first time. The parking lot was full except for two spaces reserved for visitors. That was a welcoming gesture.

I also saw two metal signs threatening dire consequences if you should park in these designated spaces. Each contained late-model foreign luxury cars with personalized license plates. Although practical, the restrictive signage was not very hospitable.

Trash that was apparent the previously Saturday was now hidden by parked cars. Our trash containers and loading area were not visible from the street. So far, so good.

I continued my scrutiny from the visitor's parking spaces. Those weeds in the flower beds were visible. That horrid ashtray now had smoldering cigarette butts. And the noxious fumes could be sniffed from 15 feet away. There was faded cellophane and a hardened piece of chewing gum nestled at the base of our front door's "welcome" mat.

The office windows were clean except for a perfect handprint about shoulder-high on the front door. There were overhanging cobwebs nested on the exterior corner of the balcony that sheltered the entrance.

I made a note to move the smoking area to the rear of the building. This would remove the unsightly ashtray by the front entrance. It might also help eliminate the trash, gum, and hand-printed window.

An Insider's View

The lobby holds four tastefully-upholstered chairs, two side tables, and a telephone for visitor use. A clean, functionally decorated unisex restroom was marred by a hand-scribbled note taped to the front door instructing "turn the light off." I removed the sign.

I spent the next 20 minutes walking around the office. actually examining the sights and sounds I normally take for granted. I made a list of concerns: Old phone books stacked in a corner; open file cabinets; a dead plant; two-year-old ads on the company bulletin board, and inappropriate posters in the warehouse.

We contacted the city zoning enforcement department to request that the weeds be removed from the vacant lot across the street. The police enforced the "no parking" zone after just one telephone call. The semi-trailers would no longer be parked on the street.

The Video Tour Tells All

I asked my service manager to take a critical look at the office and share his thoughts. A couple of days later, I found a videotape on my desk with a yellow Post-It note stating, "Watch this and weep."

The service manager had videotaped a tour around the office, including audio coverage of areas of concern. I felt as if Geraldo Rivera was doing an expose. The videotape was later presented to all the managers. The company now sponsors a fifteen-minute "spruce-up break" each Friday.

Businesses spend thousands of dollars on advertising trying to create the best possible image for their product and company. Those of us in service and sales management stress the need for a professional image in the field. We need to make sure that our professional image is extended to include our place of business.

Take time to walk a moment in your customer's shoes. Pay attention to the small details that will make a positive, if only subliminal, difference when a customer is ready to make the buying decision.

Selling Your Company – As A Potential Employer

First the good news: As I write, service, supply, and office equipment dealers are encountering record-breaking profits. Remanufacturing of used equipment is becoming highly profitable. Cartridge rechargers have gained credibility among the buying public. Small businesses have reorganized after the megadealers' buying frenzies. Business is truly booming.

Now the bad news: All those Baby Boomers of the '60s have smaller families. Millions of "Generation Xers" haven't gained the economical confidence to venture into parenthood. United States immigration regulations have lessened the stream of legal foreign workers into North America. What's a growing business to do?

The Pendulum Swing

For the first half of the 1990s, most entrepreneurs struggled to keep their organizations in business long enough to see their way out of the economical downturn. "Rightsizing" became the politically correct term for downsizing. Lay-offs, pay cuts, corporate relocations, and forced early retirements became commonplace. Unemployment levels soared.

Then the pendulum methodically swung the other way. The need for employees reached a decade-level high. Potential employees started being more selective when making the final decision on the company for which they chose to work.

Start-up or smaller companies with limited recruiting budgets, no health insurance or pension plans, had to become very creative in attracting good workers. Many "mom and pop" businesses literally ran out of kin to hire into the family enterprise.

Successful businesses began finding more and more of their strategic planning efforts being focused on hiring and retaining employees. All the emphasis on customer relations, response time, and instant product availability took its toll on companies' "people-power" requirements.

Keeping Employees

The days of second, third, and marathon interviews are gone. Many interviewers fear if they let a qualified candidate walk out the door, some other employer will hire the candidate before he or she has time to return for that second interview. If the job candidate meets the needed criteria, many employers will hire now and ask questions later.

The first impression a job candidate has of your company is significant in the candidate's decision process. Is this the type of atmosphere in which the candidate wants to spend up to a third of his or her life?

Selling your company to your current and future staff is every bit as important as closing the big deal with a paying customer. On the days I am interviewing for a job opening, it is vital that I dress and act as if I were the one being interviewed . . . because I am.

The type of vehicles in the parking lot reveals a bit of the social culture and pay scale of the company's work force. Has the company planned ahead to provide a convenient parking spot for a visitor?

How is the temperature, lighting, and noise level? Is there a break room, and refrigerator, and, are hot and cold drinks available?

Does the company provide free coffee, hot chocolate, juice or sodas? Will there be a window, comfortable chair, and a place to put my children's latest photo?

Increasingly, potential workers are looking at the big picture. Working atmosphere, ongoing training, 401K, flex time, profit sharing, health insurance, and college tuition are as important as the base wage.

Meeting the Family

Once it is decided that the interviewee may be worthy of a job offer, he or she must take the company tour. This is the time the candidate may be swayed to take the job.

I prepare my staff a day in advance. I tell them that tomorrow I will be interviewing. Immediately they know company's coming. Everyone will be expected to be on their best behavior. A cheerful smile and even a little wave is very effective in giving the applicant a comfortable feeling while receiving the company tour.

Introduce the applicant by name to a few key members of your staff. "Jim, this is Roger Magry. Roger just moved here from up north. We've been discussing the goals of our company."

Jim offers Roger a handshake. "Welcome. This is a great community in which to raise your family and work. I think you'll really enjoy living here."

If this sounds a little hokey, don't knock it until you try it. Changing jobs is considered to be one of the top three most stressful events in a person's life. A potential employee is usually looking for a secure working atmosphere. A smile and a friendly hello may be more instrumental in swaying an applicant's decision to work for you than an extra 50 cents per hour offered by another company.

When the good times roll, successful companies are focusing on the importance of selling the company to the potential employee. Managers are focusing on the business of hiring and retaining the employees who generate the products the business actually sells. No matter how good your product, it is the people who create the wealth.

Mystery . . .Unsolved

My frustration level has continued to escalate as I have had to deal with bogus end-of-lease charges that are being billed directly to our customers. It seems to be happening on a regular basis: trumped-up, end-of-lease, mysterious bills that multiple leasing companies are sending 30 to 90 days after a copier is returned off the lease.

The normal progression of these complaints begins with a mysterious, non-specific bill being sent directly to the end-user that had recently returned the copier. In all of these cases, as part of a new lease deal, our company has been responsible for picking up and returning the leased equipment to the designated wholesaler.

When the customer receives the after-the-fact bill from the leasing company, they immediately contact their sales person. Normally, the unexpected bill is faxed to the sales representative that recently sold the equipment. Invariably, the sales rep brings it into my office and asks me to look into it.

The Scenario

"Disc. meter . . . $400" was stated on the bill. I followed the regular procedure of calling the leasing company to make my inquiry. I encountered the normal voice mail prompts and waiting time before finally hearing a human voice. I recited my lease number.

"There is a $400 charge for 'disc. meter'. Can you explain that charge?"

"Yes, there is a reference to 'disc. meter' on this file." The leasing agent who identified herself as Maryanne passively agreed as she read from her computer screen.

"What does 'disc. meter' mean?" In my mind, I thought of disconnected meter, discounted meter, disgusting meter charges. "What does disc. meter stand for?" I repeated the question, for the second time.

Maryanne had no idea. Politely, she asked my name and telephone number. "Someone will call you back," she reassured me.

"How soon should I expect this call?" I queried.

Maryanne politely replied, "In two or three days someone should get back to you."

I finished our conversation by asking Maryanne for her last name and extension number. Maryanne quickly replied, "Any of our customer service reps can help you. Is there anything else I can help you with today? Have a nice day."

Repeat Performance

Two days later, another sales person brought me another bill one of her customers had just faxed. This one listed a missing sorter and a paper feed deck that was inoperable, plus the now infamous "disc. meter." The bill was for $450. It was from another leasing company.

I was familiar with this customer. It was the only company I have known who had leased an 85-copy- per-minute copier without a sorter. An innocent enough mistake, I thought. No one bothered to look carefully at the return documentation. They just took for granted that there should be a sorter. As for the inoperable paper feed section, I knew this copier was feeding properly when it was picked up.

Again, I saw "disc. meter." Maybe it is secret lease talk for unscrupulous dealers who set back or disconnected the meters. I knew we hadn't tampered with meters.

I dialed the 800 number on the bill. Shelia (the customer service representative) sounded a little more knowledgeable and authoritative than Maryanne had. She took my lease number (which I already had input through my touch tone dial pad) and matter-of-factly told me the sorter was missing and the paper feed section did not work.

"Look closely at your lease docs," I suggested. "There was no sorter included in the original lease."

"Well, it doesn't really matter." Shelia said, "The paper feed didn't work and then there is the meter issue. The base rate for problems is $450. It doesn't change the penalty fee because the sorter wasn't on the lease."

I masked my outrage with a matter-of-fact statement. I decided to deal with the issues one at a time. I told her, "I was involved in the installation of the replacement copier. I know the paper feeder was working 84 days ago when the equipment was picked up. The copier was shipped to a wholesaler's warehouse, which is less than 10 miles from the customer's location. I will send one of my factory trained technicians to repair this broken paper feed or we will provide any needed parts."

Shelia's tone did not change. "I will look into this." I had Shelia's name and phone number on the original billing that was sent to the customer. I knew who she was and how to get hold of her.

Next to No Response

Neither Maryanne nor Shelia had called me back. I called Maryanne's 800 number, which led to voice mail, follow prompt, voice mail, follow prompt, voice mail, input lease number. Then Jim asked me, "How can I help you?"

I told Jim that I was following up on a previous conversation with another customer service rep.

"It must be all taken care of, the account is clear. There is no outstanding balance," Jim stated with conviction.

"Is there any mention of the $400 billing and why it was charged and then credited?" I still wanted to get to the bottom of what "disc. meter" actually represented.

"There is no outstanding balance on this account. Is there anything else I can help you with today?" Jim asked in a polite robot-like manner.

I requested an e-mailed verification of this zero balance. "Thanks for your help Jim," I said and hung up. One small victory for our customer!

Back to Shelia

I would call Shelia again. I recited my lease number. Shelia instantly seemed to remember my case. No one had gotten back to her from the warehouse. "They have been very busy," she said, adding that she would follow up.

Three days later, Shelia called me. I was impressed. "The main gear was broken on the paper deck."

"Main gear," I replied. "That narrows it down to one of eight gears. Any chance of knowing a specific part number?"

"The main gear," she again stated.

"No problem," I said. I can play this game, too. "Where shall I send this main gear?"

Shelia gave me the warehouse address and contact. I UPS'ed the biggest gear I could find on the paper feed section.

A week later, I called back. I gave Shelia the lease number. I was still going have to deal with the "disc. meter" puzzle. As soon as Shelia pulled up the account, she quickly said, "The account was clear, no money is owed."

During the next two months, this scenario was replayed two additional times. The "disc. meter" charge continued to be referenced. Each time, the billing was credited when I follow up after my initial inquiry. I had yet to get an explanation.

Overage Reaction

I did finally receive a little insight when a leasing company clerk asked me to check directly with the wholesale facility when I questioned the "disc. meter" charges. The warehouse manager (who asked me not to reveal his name) explained, "For years, copier dealers took advantage of leasing companies. Half the equipment we received off lease didn't work. Boards were missing; entire feed and fuser sections had been removed before the copiers were shipped back.

"Now the leasing companies are tightening up our review procedures. We have to check out every machine. Paper has to feed through. A copy has to come out. Any copier that has over one million copies is being accessed an overage fee."

A light bulb flashed in my mind: "disc. meter." "How are you designating these high meter readings on your paper work?"

"We just note the meter count," he said. I was told the leasing companies started charging for excess copies. A lot of people complained. It was not legal. Nowhere in the lease is there a provision for additional excess copy charges. I was told that the leasing company's lawyers said the extra charges were illegal. But I know the practice has not stopped, because dealers are calling me all the time.

Anybody who complains gets the bill canceled. But I bet a lot of companies are just paying the invoice.

A Final Attempt

"What exactly does 'disc. meter' stand for. That abbreviation 'disc.' What does it stand for?" I was still trying to get an answer. I could almost see the warehouse manager remove his baseball cap and scratch his head.

"I honestly don't know. The meters aren't disconnected. I don't know what 'disc.' actually stands for. All I know is the leasing companies are charging the extra fee, dealers are complaining and the fee is credited," he said.

SCAM? Are leasing companies getting even with dealers who took advantage of the lease return system for years? Maybe everyone is just trying a little harder to make a profit in this digital, electronic business environment. I do not know any ultimate truth.

No one I spoke with would talk "for the record." I am only retelling my personal experience. Every additional, unwarranted charge was credited off. In each case, I requested and received e-mailed or faxed confirmation of a zero balance on the account.

In fairness to your customers, keep your eyes open. Encourage your customers to forward any after the lease return billings directly to the dealer, and follow up, follow up, follow up.

Raise Your Right Hand

There is a strong likelihood that one day your company will be sued. Lawsuits are part of the American culture. The climate for business today is infused with legalities and litigiousness. Rather than viewing this as a sad commentary on the state of American business, think of the probability of being sued as part of your overall business plan.

Every business needs a good working relationship with a lawyer they trust. This attorney needs to be well established in the legal community; you never know when you will need a referral for a great litigator or criminal attorney.

If you don't currently have a corporate legal counselor, start looking for someone you can trust before the need arises. A good source to find a legal counselor is to ask a friend or business associate for their recommendations.

I have spent a good part of a year as an expert witness in a very complicated lawsuit involving an office machine dealer, a leasing company, and an end user. I read more than 30,000 pages of depositions, testimony, and exhibits. I will use no names or specifics, to protect the guilty and innocent parties; but I would like to share some of the lessons I learned from this experience.

Questions to Ask Yourself Before the Fact

1. Have you checked your business insurance?
2. Do you have coverage that will help pay for some or all of a lengthy prosecution?
3. Does your multi-million-dollar umbrella include the cost of covering a long-term business lawsuit?
4. Have you checked on business interruption coverage as part of insurance policy updates?
5. Do you have a company policy in place that dictates how to deal with customers who double pay an invoice?
6. Do you send periodic account statements to customers that have credit balances?
7. Is this policy one that you would be proud to share with twelve strangers who have never run a business?

Other Scenarios

The IRS is not the only agency that may need to look through years of back business transactions. Suitable record-keeping within your business can help prove your innocence or re-enforce your guilt. Have you thought about the following:

1. Do you keep back-up documentation for all business transactions conducted over the past five to seven years?
2. Can you easily find a signed lease on a deal that was made 60 months ago?
3. How could you prove a customer agreed to a fair market buyout with the end user being responsible for the cost of the equipment return?

A Good Business Plan

The management of each company must decide what business conduct is appropriate in the overall context of a good business plan. Would you feel comfortable allowing a private investigator to make copies of hundreds of your business transactions? Would the honesty and integrity of your business practices be upheld when viewed by twelve impartial jurors?

Someone in a position of authority and knowledge must take responsibility for reviewing the business transactions your company represents. If the reviewer of sales or leases receives a direct bonus (monetary gain) from the deal, that person may not be viewed as an impartial judge to the correctness of the deal. Don't make the fox responsible for protecting the hen house.

No matter who in the company is the final reviewer, the employer is ultimately responsible for the deals that are written by an employee. Long after a rogue employee has quit and gone to work for a competitor, your company will be left with the responsibility of defending their actions. The company's owner will be the one proverbially holding the bag if the situation gets out of hand and winds up in court.

Good business practice dictates the need for careful inspection of each deal. Make sure all the terms of a lease have been completed: Length, buy-out, monthly charge, fees, insurance, taxes, penalties, etc. Does each part of the transaction make sense?

Too much profit can be just as suspicious as not having enough money in the deal. The simplest of office equipment deals can become very involved once it is scrutinized by the United States legal system. All that fine print on the back of the lease or sales order has a life of its own once a bailiff announces, "Court is in session."

Gathering Proper Information

Clarity will be vitally important if the big deal starts to unravel in the future. The more information that is clearly enumerated on a sales or lease document, the easier it is to prove your intentions. Consistently shoddy or incomplete filling out of sales or lease documents becomes a history of ambiguity by intent. Every line and box should be completely filled out or appropriately checked. If a problem appears, the faster you accept responsibility and take action, the easier and cheaper it will be to rectify the situation. Trying to cover-up or compound a problem usually makes the matter worse.

Lawyers, depositions, transcripts, expert witnesses, courier services, detectives, aggravation, and lots of working hours are far more expensive than righting the errant deal as soon as you realize the good deal has gone bad. Forgery or accepting signatures of inappropriate people will usually come back to haunt you.

Consistently dealing with the same person within the customer's office looks better in a court of law than having a half-dozen different people involved in the decision-making. If a document states, "Must be signed by a corporate officer," or the leasing company requires a "corporate resolution," it is the leaser's responsibility to follow the written rules. Normally, a lease is a binding legal document once it is signed. Once the deal is funded, greater complications come into play. A five-year lease allows 60 opportunities for a customer to realize something is not right.

Look at every deal from the standpoint of having to defend your actions in front of twelve Social Security recipients. Court is rarely an economical solution to any problem. Profit can be made in the office machine business without defrauding your customer. If a deal sounds too good to be true, it probably is.

In an ideal world, we all hope that each business transaction can stand on its own merits with integrity and fairness to both the buyer and seller. When a company lowers its standards of business ethics, allowing price gouging, used equipment being represented as new, improper servicing, double billing, or bait and switch, then no one wins.

Triple Loss

During this trial, I have witnessed three separate teams of lawyers diligently working for hundreds of hours on a case that ultimately proved that a lot of people did a lot of things that ultimately cost a great deal of money. The customer received no long-term value. The dealer lost a former good customer, forever. The leasing company had to conduct a long term, far-away investigation and trial. The over-crowded judicial system had to squeeze in another case. Twelve jurors spent two months of their life learning about CPCs, MAs, PMs buy-outs, upgrades, addendums, drums, toner, and developer.

There are such things as lose, lose, lose situations. An ounce of prevention is worth ten tons of cure when it comes to the legal system. I truly believe there will be no winners in this case. Dozens of people wasted hundreds of hours, spending thousands of dollars, to prove everyone shared in the guilt of not taking the responsibility necessary to following through on good business practices.

So much was wasted, so little achieved. None of this would have happened if one-tenth of the time and energy spent on proving innocence and guilt had been used to follow internally established rules of ethical business practices within the dealership, leasing company, and customer's business.

For over a year, I have tried to objectively view the past actions of others in the terms of 20/20 hindsight. I am glad I am not a lawyer, judge, court reporter, bailiff, jury member, court clerk, or parking attendant. I am proud to be an office equipment service manager.

This trial has emphasized my responsibility to always strive to do each part of my job in the most professionally ethical way possible. The diversity and daily challenges of running a business center on keeping our customer's expectations satisfied while creating a fair and ethical profit for our company. After one year of my life being involved with this court case, my personal beliefs of standards of the professional business ethics have been more sharply drawn.

Making the right decision is more than just an ethical judgment. Making the wrong business decision can have catastrophic repercussions. Make sure you are not guilty of endangering the reputation of your company or infringing upon the legal, moral, and ethical rights and expectations of your customers.

How to Handle the Customer Complaint

"I'm never doing business with your company again. Fax me a written quote of that outrageous price for repair you just gave me. I'll save it. I'll shove it in the face of the next salesman from your company who walks through my door asking for my business."

I have heard it all before. Upset, demanding, threatening, fire-breathing customers—some are a little more dramatic than others. This particular customer has threatened me for ten years. In the beginning, I accepted this office manager's words as truthful. But through the years I have come to realize that this is her way of bargaining with her vendors.

During our first encounter, she was rewarded for her demands and threats by a free $50-worth of toner. As I grew accustomed to her vitriol and her charges of being owed free products, I saw that she reacted the same, whether or not I gave in to her extortionist demands.

She continues to do business with our company, and she continues to find fault with everything we do.

The difference between the profitable, successful company and the want-to-be, struggling businesses is how they manage customers who take the time to express their concerns.

Any customer who writes a letter of complaint probably:

1) hit a roadblock when dealing face-to-face with your company's representative;
2) had their telephone calls ignored;
3) plans to take legal action and wants to have a paper trail;
4) has no power or status within their own company;
5) is a newly-hired manager who is trying to prove something to someone.

In each case, the complainer is requesting attention and validation of self-worth. The simplest way to make a customer happy and retain their repeat business is to refund their money, or give something away.

Face Up To Complaints

Paying off the complainer is usually not the best business decision. You have set yourself up to be extorted or blackmailed by your customer. You will teach your customers to find fault and look for loopholes in hopes of being rewarded for being a complainer.

A proactive manager must face complaints straight on. A problem that is viewed as an opportunity to increase revenue can be a seen as a warm call. The customer who complains is usually in need of something your company sells. Upgrading is the natural extension of a properly-handled complaint.

I find billable (time and material or charge call) customers always seem to complain more than our maintenance agreement (CPC) or prepaid customers. There seems to be an adversarial posturing from the onset of the chargeable service call. Out of self-protection, my staff has learned to over-estimate early on for the incessant complainer.

This gives us room to be able to give in to some of their demands for lower prices or additional service with no real additional cost to us.

When interacting with a complaining customer, I listen and listen and listen some more. I let the complainer have his or her say. During any pause that over three seconds (which is an eternity), I interject, "I can understand your concern." Normally the customer will repeat everything three times. It's just human nature. Three repetitions seem to clear the soul and lessen the animosity.

When the customer does have a legitimate concern, I treat their request with great importance and urgency. If I am not familiar with the problem, I always ask the customer for X amount of time to look into the situation. Promising a specific time in which someone will return the call, or asking what time the caller goes to lunch or goes home, sets a feeling of caring, as well as giving you a comfortable time for research before getting back with the customer.

If you have not managed to acquire the needed information at the appointed time for the return call, call back to let the customer know you are still working on the problem. Remember, the customer is really more concerned that you show them respect and concern than immediately fixing the perceived problem.

Two Way Communication

Whenever possible, ask the customer to electronically provide any pertinent information they have. This can save you hours of hunting for the backup information. Always preface this request with, "I will be better able to quickly track down a solution to your situation if you can fax (or email) me any information you have regarding your concern." If they don't have the needed information, make sure you fax the customer corroborating information once you have tracked it down.

Always ask for their fax number, with the explanation that you will send them the information for their files.

Customers love the reassurance of exchanging paperwork or e-mail. It is proof that reality is emerging from history, or that one of you is very organized. Always thank the customer for helping you solve their problem. Agree that your computer billing system is very difficult to understand. "We are updating our software to clear up any problems" is a universally-accepted answer for any computer shortcomings.

"I agree with you," always changes the tempo of a complainer's conversation. When you do realize a problem has occurred, take the full blame personally. Call the customer before they have a chance to call you. Follow up with a short note and your business card. End your conversation by restating your name and telephone number, and reassure that if they leave a voice mail, you will get back to them within X amount of time.

I change my voice mail each day to let people know of my current schedule. Customers feel more reassured when there are timelines attached to your voice mail.

Once the problem is identified and solved, use it as a learning situation. How can your employees be better trained to prevent this problem from happening in the first place? What internal company procedures need to be changed to guard against similar situations happening in the future?

Use the complaint letter as a guidepost for monitoring internal conditions that need to be improved. Every complaint is an opportunity to upgrade, sell a new product, extend a maintenance agreement, or provide additional supplies. A customer who takes the time to complain will stay with your company if the complaint is handled properly.

Avoid "Poison" Customers

The gun's barrel was pointed directly at my head. "You ain't leaving 'til the copier's fixed."

Was the guard kidding? Can you make a joke with a lethal weapon in your hand?

Forty-five minutes earlier, the presence of the armed prison guard escorting me to the non-functioning copier in the inmate-release office was a source of security. Now, the menacing grin on the guard's lips did not disguise the direct threat of his un-holstered pistol.

My pulse quickened. My chest was visibly rising and falling with each beat of my heart. I focused all my concentration on my hands, willing them not to shake.

How was I going to get out of here? This guard was not acting in a reasonable manner. I had entered this room as a copier technician. I was now being held captive at gunpoint in the city jail.

All the customer-relations training rules that say, "The customer is always right," echoed in my mind. This customer was NOT right. Nowhere in my field-tech job description was there any mention of having one's life threatened in the line of repairing a copier.

For a moment, I thought of diversionary tactics: "I have just the parts your copier needs in my car. Escort me to the parking lot and I'll have this fixed in no time." The minute I reached my car, I knew, I would never go back into this jail.

Lesson From a Gun Barrel

This gun-wielding guard is now only a memory of my technician days. But the incident taught me a lesson I have never forgotten. I have used it often since becoming a manager:

Customers are important, but employees are vital.

Mutual respect is needed on both sides. An abusive, disrespectful, threatening customer is not worth the fear and stress they cause your business.

As a manager, it is my responsibility to make my department profitable. Profitability depends upon employees who feel secure in performing their job. I must make sure my field service techs have a safe working environment--safe both emotionally and physically.

Do you provide and encourage–or require–the wearing of back supports, protective glasses, plastic gloves, or ear guards when the situation may warrant extra protection? When was the last time you did a safety check of your technician's vehicles? Are you sure all of your employees even have a valid driver's license or liability car insurance?

Ensure Emotional Safety

Emotional safety includes making sure my employees have the education, training, manuals, parts, supplies, and support that allow them to do their jobs effectively. An under-trained employee or one without the mental skills to properly repair a piece of equipment soon can soon become a frustrated or self-doubting worker.

Confidence, knowledge, and self-respect are the ingredients of successful field personnel. They rely upon the office staff to back them up with any necessary training, tools, parts, and support so that they can make decisions independently.

Equally essential for good business is to do business with customers who pay their bills promptly, treat employees with respect, and use common courtesy.

It takes an enormous amount of discipline to walk way from a customer, especially an established one. Sound business relationships require constant upkeep; that means re-evaluating relations with anyone who disrupts the workflow, threatens employee morale, or negatively affects your bank account.

On more than one occasion, I have called or written to complain about the actions of one of our customers. I have sent written complaints to city managers. I threatened to go to the board of supervisors with a formal complaint if our technicians were not treated in a more civilized manner while servicing the copiers under a three-year contract.

Customers to Avoid

After the guard pulled the gun, my manager quickly composed a formal letter of complaint, including our termination of any contractual obligations to service a copier in a life-threatening atmosphere. We continued servicing 68 other copiers under the county-wide contract, but none of our techs was asked to set foot in that jail again.

There is a fine line between valuing all customers and walking away from customers whose actions cause more problems than they are worth. Establishing the worth of a customer's business can be tricky.

The company who is always slow making payments, is repeatedly sent to collections, or has a history of bouncing payment checks, is not a customer. They are a business irritant. It takes a strong manager to walk away from potential profit. We all know those former customers who are not worth the time and energy your staff must expend to try to satisfy their one-sided needs.

Working It Out Takes Two

I recently dealt with a customer who was seven months past due on a payment for a rented copier. When they called for service on Monday, they were told there would be no service until the full balance on their account was paid. They called back with a check on Friday at 4:20 p.m., demanding we service them "now." When I told them that, due to the late hour, I could not service them that day, they demanded a week's credit for the time the rented copier had not been working.

Without missing a beat, I countered by demanding additional interest payments for the seven months of unpaid bills. The customer challenged my poor attitude. I retorted that my attitude was in direct ratio to their payment history.

My attitude may seem a little extreme. From time to time, we all deal with the downright no good, lying, offensive, threatening, and non-paying (want-to-be) customer. The business world must put these people on notice that working together is a two-way street. In order for both parties to benefit, each must require one another to function in a professional manner.

The next time an unreasonable customer puts a metaphoric gun to your head, stand your ground, look at the big picture, and do what is fair for your employees, company, and customers.

The Big Installation

Everyone is excited. Smiles all around. The bid has been won. All the paper work is signed. The purchase order has been issued. The sales department lets out a big sigh of relief. The dealer sales manager is thrilled. The leasing company has agreed to more than a dozen fine print changes. The company's quarterly rebate will be almost six figures.

I stand among the smiling facing and hide my apprehension and anticipated weariness. I express my congratulations. Now the enormous responsibility of the delivery and installation, and successfully connecting, scanning, e-mailing, faxing, and making all those private mailboxes work, falls on the shoulders of the service department.

Experience is the best teacher. I go to my files and pull out the checklist from the last big machine installation I supervised. The era of "digital solutions" multiplies the complexity of each installation. Today, we deal with at least a one-half dozen individual line items of necessary equipment to make one connected solution. Hours of telephone time, e-mails, and on-site inspections will be logged before any equipment arrives.

I am confident enough in the network literacy of the service department to be able to boldly tell the sales department, "You sell it, we will get it connected." The moment of truth has arrived. They did sell it.

Now, the service department must step up to the plate and deliver the grand slam home run.

It now becomes the sole responsibility of the service department to contact the customer's IT department, do the site surveys, run extra drops, order the proper configuration for each main frame, assemble, prepare, install, do the key operator training, and make it all happen. *Solution* takes on an entire new meaning.

If It's the Big One . . .

The concept of "a large installation" is relative to the size of your technical staff. Two pieces of equipment can place a burden on a one-tech operation. A large manufacturer-owned dealership might easily handle a 500-piece placement without missing a beat. Any time you deliver as many pieces of equipment as you have techs, it is a "large installation."

Before you place your equipment order with your wholesaler, physically record on paper or spreadsheet the complete configuration of each piece of equipment. Make sure you include all the accessories, print systems, duplex units, extra memory, drawers, stands or spacers, copy management devices, surge suppressors, extension cords, interface harnesses, modem hookup cords, supplies (including enough for the customer to have an initial supply on hand), software, drivers, user manuals, and the main piece of equipment being ordered. It is helpful to differentiate which items will be serialized, which must be ordered from the manufacturer, and what items can or must be outsourced from other vendors.

At some point, a decision must be made on how and when all the equipment will be assembled and delivered. Or delivered and assembled. Items to consider when making this decision must include cost, space, and labor availability.

The cost of transporting items in a sealed container is always less than "blanket wrap" transporting of equipment that is already set up. The potential for damage during transportation is greater when the equipment is already put together.

Control of serial numbers, equipment received, quality control, technical help if the new equipment will not work, labor hours, control or safety hazards, trash removal, availability of forgotten items, needed supplies and facility control is always better at *your* office location.

Back-up checking of the compatibility of operating systems and software functions with the hardware is more easily controlled from your network test lab than in the customer's business environment.

It is imperative that someone with facilities management authority and someone from the technical side of the both companies spend some time together discussing mutual needs and limitations.

Back It Up

I use the backward method of time management to plan labor needs. It goes like this: Make a list of everything that you will need to accomplish. Include the potential need of training current technicians on new products or hiring additional staff. Make sure that the *proper* equipment is ordered. Calculate how much time will be needed to unpack, set up, test, and prepare for delivery, wrap, accurately inventory, and stage for delivery. Just unboxing and disposing of hundreds of square yards of packaging material can cause unanticipated grief. You may actually have to order an extra trash container or more frequent refuse pickups.

Order enough extra supplies, paper, staples, surge suppressors, etc., to accommodate the initial install and the first 30 days of anticipated customer usage. Check with the customer to see where they plan to store extra supplies. Will it be centralized or in several different locations? Is the customer on a prepaid supply program or do you need to receive a separate purchase order? Their answers will affect the amount of supplies you will need to provide.

Make sure no one has made unrealistic delivery promises to the end user. Nothing is worse than starting a long-term relationship with unfulfilled promises. Sales people historically try to rush deliveries in order to "lock in the sale" or guarantee their commission being paid as soon as possible. "Feel out" the end user. You may find that an extended delivery date, or a trickle delivery, is preferable.

At some point before the actual delivery, an on-site inspection is a must. If YOU are in charge, YOU should not delegate this one task. A seasoned professional will intrinsically see those little tell-tale clues that can spell disaster, delay, or need for some quick explanation of why the installation is not proceeding smoothly. An ounce of prevention is worth a ton of customer complaints.

Inspect Before You Move

When you are doing the pre-installation site survey, take your time. Look at EVERYTHING. The road in, parking availability, the ground surface, curbs, the size of doorways, elevator availability, the size of the stairwells, even the flooring in the building (marble tiles and plush carpets can cause havoc) must be inspected. If you do your inspection with a clipboard in hand and take notes, the current office workers will usually make a point of finding out what you are doing. This is your opening to ask if they know of any situations that will affect your installation. You will be surprised at the information that will be volunteered.

If you are replacing similar equipment, don't be lulled into a false sense of security. Check the footprint (actual size including room needed for clearing jams, adding paper, and servicing). Make sure YOUR equipment's electrical cord is long enough to reach the electrical outlet. Carefully inspect all outlets. Is it loose, the wrong amperage, or connected to the company refrigerator and microwave? The new customer may be forgiving of their old (now being replaced) equipment's shortcomings. Your new equipment will be expected to work flawlessly.

Connectivity can be a simple as handing the customer's IT department the new equipment's drivers to weeks of trial and error trying to connect one-half dozen different operating systems to dozens of work stations. Make sure there is a predetermined (written) scope of work that has been included in the original sales agreement. It is very easy to slip into the role of surrogate IT department for the customer. A systematic signoff sheet, as each piece of equipment is successfully connected, will help establish a finality of your responsibility.

And All The Rest

Up until now we haven't even discussed the overtime labor that may be necessary for unpacking, set-up, testing, loading, delivering, re-set-up, training (retraining), and initial hand-holding of your newest "most important" customer. All the while, you must keep the rest of your service department running at its regular 100% efficiency.

This need for massive overtime should be discussed with your owner, office manager, controller, and payroll clerk. Keep the other members of your company apprised on the hidden cost of this type of installation.

Make sure you share the excitement and overall worth of this large order with your service staff. Thank them in advance for the extra hours that everyone will have to contribute to the successful completion of this operation. Spend a few moments sharing how each worker will spend the extra money they will earn from this project.

Now I'll go congratulate the sales staff for a job well done. I'll grin ear to ear, shake a lot of hands, and tell everyone how excited and happy I am. I deserve an Academy Award!

Knowledge Is Power

I read recently that Hewlett-Packard spends in excess of 250 million dollars for employee training. Yes, they are big and successful. They understand the power and value of knowledge. I often read about companies who are on the leading edge of the explosive information age.

Every company on the ascending edge of success has an aggressive employee educational philosophy. Curiosity is company-sanctioned. Change is viewed as a desirable trait. Mentoring is encouraged. Successful companies have a history of encouraging their employees' mental, physical and philosophical (spiritual) growth.

Education Creates Growth

Company-sponsored education should be your firm's second most important responsibility. Just as a business plan, fiscal budget and policy and procedure book are planned in advance and updated, so must your ongoing employee educational philosophy be nurtured.

Where to begin? Make a commitment. Take some baby steps. Offer one hour of time off each week in exchange for a simple written report on an hour's worth of industry-related outside learning. A person who leads an independently researched mini in-house training session (presented during your regularly scheduled departmental meetings) can also earn this bonus hour off.

Set up a climate for personal and professional growth. Every new employee should be assigned a mentor. The word "mentor" dates back to the time of the famous Greek wanderer Odysseus and his son Telemachus, written about by Homer in *The Odyssey*. Before Odysseus's wanderings, Mentor was a friend and counselor. Thus, the actions of Mentor hundreds of years ago have led to his name becoming our word to describe the nurturing of raw talent.

Assigning a mentor to a new employee will be a temporary pairing. Within six months, the new employee should be encouraged to find someone of his or her own choosing to help along the corporate path. This mentor may be a vendor, a manufacturer's representative, an outside trainer, or someone within your own company. The acknowledged need to have a mentor is vital to personal and corporate growth.

Within the service department, a mentor allows a newer tech to feel comfortable asking those "dumb questions" of a trusted friend. Within the computer world, a mentor is a necessity. When your computer is locked up or a file is lost, a knowing friend is a lifesaver.

Common Schedules

Employers can regularly sponsor learning groups. Establish scheduled learning times where employees can eat together (outside of business hours) to share knowledge.

Having a monthly lunchtime forum helps stimulate thought and potential mentor-mentored matching. Sometimes I will pay the group leader or offer "comp" time, but everyone else is attending on a voluntary basis.

I used to offer to pay techs for after-hour training. Even this was greeted negatively and with a "I have to work Saturday morning" mentality. Now that outside learning is voluntary, a new positive attitude abounds.

Voluntary learning is an amazing concept. The eager, self-motivated employees will take advantage of these off-hour learning opportunities. Education becomes an added employment benefit.

An in-house lending library can lead to positive growth. You can include books, magazines, audio and videotapes, software, CDs, training courses, etc. Encourage employees to donate items they have "intellectually outgrown" or are willing to share with other employees.

Personal comments can be attached to donated items: "Great book and easy to understand;" "heavy reading, don't take to bed;" "too advanced for most, read with a MCSE in attendance." The sharing of information can become contagious.

Design for Self-Motivation

Each employee should have a self-written learning plan. These can be self-monitored and adjusted as needed. A schematic for ongoing education is vital. Plan for success.

Set expectations for ongoing personal growth. Focus your time, energy, and resources on those who are willing to make a personal commitment and share the time and expense of learning.

Start every service meeting with a "brag time." Encourage sharing of positive things that recently happened. Set up an atmosphere for achievement. Allow your employees to be proud of their own accomplishments. By sharing current victories, other employees see an on going path to success.

Some employees will learn without your guidance. Others will never advance. But a vast majority of your employees will grow beyond your expectations with a little creative pushing. Establish a company atmosphere of mentoring. Everyone will take the next step toward excellence.

Turn Summertime Blues to Green

The good old summertime, lazy days of summer, or the summer doldrums . . . whatever you call it, the time comes every year when equipment sales and incoming service calls seem to take a well-needed vacation. We have time to take a deep breath, to get off a little early and spend some time with the family.

There is a big difference between taking a deep breath and kicking back for the rest of the summer. Summer is the time for management to be more creative than ever with your labor force. Even when the workload is down, the hourly cost of doing business remains the same.

How do we maximize the use of our summer labor force while allowing a bit of a mental rest to recharge everyone's spirits?

The worst thing you can do is to start letting everyone go home early. This will breed discontent when you have to reinstate the 40-hour week. Summer is the time to look around the office for those important projects that always lose out to the urgent matters of the day.

Creative Productivity

Establish a sign-up sheet for "volunteers." Find out which technicians want to spend a couple of days in the shop, in grubby clothes, being offered company-purchased pizza, while they:

1. Reorganize your in-house parts manuals.
2. Paint the showroom.
3. Clean out the warehouse.
4. Update the network in the demo room.
5. Throw away 48 boxes of stored paper records that date back longer than any IRS auditor will require.
6. Actually get rental machines ready for placement before they are needed.
7. Remove, categorize, and store all the usable parts off those junk machines.
8. Throw away the stripped carcasses of those junk machines.
9. Establish a secondary parts tracking system (numbers) for those (re) usable parts.
10. Clean up the shop.
11. Rearrange your work areas for maximum efficiency.
12. Clean up the exterior of the building.
13. Wash and wax the company truck.
14. Clean out the company refrigerator.
15. Have every used piece of equipment ready for placement.

After a few days of manual labor and in-house camaraderie, most technicians will be happy to get back into the field or work on more cerebral activities.

The Less-Physical Challenge

For those who do not volunteer for the physical labor:

16. Have your supervisors ride with each tech once a week.
17. Do an accurate car stock inventory.

18. Set up an in-house lending library of audiotapes, training CD's, shareware, technical books, and manufacturer's modifications.
19. Set up some peer-to-peer training, techs sharing with techs their own expertise.
20. Challenge everyone to reduce their car stock by 10% without negatively affecting their first-call completion rate.
21. Advertise half-price Friday service rates for your billable customers.
22. Offer a bonus to technicians next winter for all the "perfect PM's" that are performed this summer. (Machines that do not have any service calls until the next PM is due.)
23. Send your techs to manufacturer-sponsored training.
24. Have a tech and dispatcher swap places for a day.
25. Make up some new in-house forms to help techs in the field.
26. Write a group thank-you letter to your best customers.
27. Take some extra time to train your worst customers.
28. Organize a company sponsored picnic or evening outing.
30. PM the equipment in your own office that is always neglected.
29. Create an in-house training seminar for your customers.
30. Establish a new employee mentoring program.
31. Redesign your service order forms to reflect the new charges that are necessary when working on connected products.
32. Create a flyer or envelope stuffer that explains the new technical services that are being offered by your company.

When all else fails . . . offer bonus vacation time. Use one week vacation time on, get a sixth day for free. Or work 8 a.m. to 2 p.m. and use one vacation hour to complete an eight-hour day.

Slow Down, But Don't Stop

You get the idea. Don't waste this slow time of summer. A great manager leads his or her people into creative, fun, useful summer activities. A complacent (non)manager will kick back, allowing everyone to moan about how hard we all had to work last winter. This type of compliance attitude will again require a great deal of catch-up work next autumn.

Challenge your techs to come up with two special projects they can accomplish. Offer a stay-home day that will result in the task of their choosing being accomplished. Establish a timeline for completing the task. Rotate days in the shop or at home to finalize the project. If a tech stays at home for the day and does not complete the project, that "work day" becomes a "vacation day."

The manager who can create a simulating change of pace can refresh their employee's spirit while creating a productive synergy that will establish a foundation for continued smooth sailing in the hectic months that are just around the corner.

Ben Franklin's Business Sense

"The rules of business are changing. Everything is dynamic. History is no longer useful in helping to plan the future. The computer, the Internet, and the dot-com world have changed everything."

I disagree with those sentiments. So does Dr. Blaine McCormick, author of *Ben Franklin's 12 Rules of Management*. The business world has changed, and digital is quickly replacing analog. However, the evolution of human nature occurs at a much slower pace.

Tattoos, multiple piercings, and spiked hair may be the rage. Nevertheless, the basic interpersonal and business skills valued by Ben Franklin over 200 years ago are still good business traits three centuries later.

Ben Franklin's Rules of Management — a summary and commentary.

1. "Finish better than you begin." Maintaining the status quo is not good enough. A business requires growth to stay prosperous. Through natural attrition, the average business will lose 25% of its customer base each year. To achieve a desired annual growth of 10 percent, a business must increase its customer base by 35 percent.

2. "All education is self-education." Others may try to teach you. But only you can actually learn. You are ultimately responsible for your own knowledge and progression. If you are not willing to make the effort, no one else can force you to learn.

3. "Seek first to manage your self, then to manage others." A consistent, positive example is the most effective memo ever written. A mirror is more reflective than e-mail.

4. "Influence is more important than victory." The building of business (and inter-personal) relationships is more productive than destroying the (imagined) enemy. Today's subordinate may be your superior tomorrow.

5. "Work hard and watch your cost." A million pennies saved is $10,000 earned. Venture capitalists prefer actual value over large tax write-offs. The rise and fall of dot.com high rollers has become an eye-opening commentary on the value of free spenders.

6. "Everyone wants to appear reasonable." Harmony is a more productive product, in the work place, than is coercion. Even the hard-nosed drill sergeant uses reasonable duress in his actions. Make sure the causes and effects of your actions are understandable to the onlooker. To be a successful manager, others must buy into your plan.

7. "Create your own set of values to guide your actions." Consistency works with the human spirit. A known standard helps others work more productively. Inconsistency plays havoc in the work place. If you make a mistake, acknowledge the erroneous behavior quickly. Take full personal responsibility for the blunder and move on.

8. "Incentive is everything." Reward is the manager's most valuable tool. Money is the least long-acting of any available incentive. The same incentive given too often becomes expected. Ultimately when a long-given incentive is withdrawn, negative repercussions will occur. Be creative and vary your incentive programs. Acknowledgment and simple verbal praise of a job well done are very powerful incentives.

9. "Create solutions for seemingly impossible problems." A successful worker is in the business of problem solving. If you can economically solve another's problems, you will create a customer. When you bring a problem to your superior, be prepared to recommended two or three viable solutions to the situation. A manager's job is creating paths around the daily roadblocks we all encounter.

10. "Become a revolutionary for experimentation and change." The successful manager is a catalyst for change. Convincing others to follow along an untrodden path requires creativity, motivation, and leadership. If it's not broken, you need to look for something other than fixing it. A successful leader is one who can get average people to consistently achieve extraordinary results.

11. "Sometimes it is better to do 1,001 small things right than only one large thing right." Hoping for one great idea to keep your company in business is as foolish as depending on your lottery winnings to finance next week's payroll. Consistency of effective work habits will prove to be the winning plan. Imagine how much can be accomplished if each employee did one thing better today than was done yesterday. The mighty ocean and vast deserts are made up of drops of water and grains of sand. There is superior strength by linking small bits of success.

12. "Deliberately cultivate your reputation and legacy." Learn to consistently and conservatively advertise your achievements. A reputation of ethical winning is your greatest competitive advantage. Be involved in your industry and community. Give back more than you take. Ultimately people do business with people. The Internet may be faceless, but it is not nameless. Ultimately, your reputation is your greatest product.

The more things change, the more they stay the same. Human nature and good business habits work hand in hand in for lasting success.

* McCormick, Blaine. Ben Franklin 12 Rules of Management: The Founding Father of American Business Solves Your Toughest Problems. Entrepreneur Media Inc., 2000.

Chapter 6

Taking The Next Step:

Personal Growth

Self-Motivated Learning Is Now a Job Necessity

Writing allows me the potential for frequent interchange of ideas with the readers of my words. I continue to learn from each e-mail, voice mail, letter, or personal interaction that I receive.

The knowledge shared by those who respond never ceases to amaze me. It re-stimulates my own thought process.

A recent service management seminar I taught reinforced my commitment to teaching and writing. The level of knowledge apparent in our meeting room was inspirational. Those who make the commitment for lifelong learning are on the leading, profitable edge of our industry.

There were several attendees at this seminar whose involvement with the office equipment industry spanned more than a quarter of a century. They truly had forgotten more than the youngsters in the room had yet learned. The consensus of opinion was that much of our past knowledge can be deleted from our personal cranial hard drive.

It was generally agreed that the less we use the past as a barometer for future actions, the better off we will be. Using the status you gained by your past technical knowledge as a yardstick for the future is normally detrimental to attaining 22nd-century productivity.

The star technician of the 1980's is but a remnant of the past. A major universal truth embraced by all attendees was, "Ongoing, out-of-

office, self-education is vital to anyone who wants to succeed in our business."

Go Outside to Learn

Employees can no longer expect their employers to provide 100% of the knowledge they require to stay employed. An industrious office equipment worker can no longer expect that all needed education will be supplied by the employer during paid working hours. The era of attending a few training classes, reading the manufacturer's updates, and doing your job is no longer adequate for long-term employment.

In the past, the sales staff could learn equipment functions and features and familiarize themselves with the show room equipment. Keeping current on lease rates and commission bonus programs was all that was necessary to earn a respectable living.

Now everything has changed. Success requires continuous learning on your own time. Each time the industrious employee accomplishes a learning goal, the plateau moves up one notch. Ongoing, forever, seems to be our fate.

I remember straining to learn the computer word processing program "MultiMate." Looking back, I see that "MultiMate" was more of an application than a program. But I was not computer savvy enough at that point to know the difference. Many times, in frustration, I returned to my then state-of-the-art electric typewriter. When I was ready to take a major step forward, I struggled whether to advance to Word Perfect or Word. Having once owned a Sony Betamax (the forerunner to the current VCR) I was not sure if I could trust my own judgment.

After asking around, thankfully, I choose to learn Word. I struggled through the nuances of Word 3.1. The knowledge I gained was a nice platform for future learning. But this knowledge by itself would have left me far behind the needed information to be an effective service manager in the 21st Century.

Learn More, Be More

Ongoing, self-motivated training is necessary for long-term, well-paying employment. The younger generation may not have the experience of the older generation, but they don't need it. No one can earn a living with e-stat and treated paper fax mentality. Being a great analog service or sales representative will greatly reduce your earning capabilities.

The academic phrase of "publish or perish" can be extended to the office equipment industry. Computerize or economize. Learn or yearn (for a new vocation).

Sales and service personnel alike must make a personal commitment. Self-motivated, at-home learning is a necessity. Ongoing learning cannot be accomplished by occasional cramming or attending a weekend workshop. The key word is ongoing. Success is a by-product of an active, personalized after-hours training regiment.

Successful long-term employment will hinge upon a personal familiarization with the structural change of global information transfer. You must embrace the change and have it work for you. Insightful workers realize their employer cannot afford to train, pay, and promote workers for showing up for work without providing a personal commitment to ongoing learning outside of business hours.

In many companies, embracing the digital era has been the focus of the service department. Now that your company is technically competent to connect the equipment, an increased emphasis has been placed on educating the hardware sales department.

An advanced level of sophistication is necessary to communicate to the buying public exactly what it is that your sophisticated, digitally connected, solution-providing equipment can do. It has become increasingly difficult for sales reps to walk the walk of their solution talk.

For those who have not stepped up to the plate of self-motivated learning, the longer you wait, the farther behind you will be. The soonest you can start learning is now. So, if you have read this, consider it part of your first lesson. You now have officially started your customized personal learning program. Congratulations. Continue to focus on YOUR FUTURE. Your joy of learning has begun.

Watch, Learn, and Become a Leader

Leaders are separated from followers by how well they invest their time outside of regular working hours. What happens after 5 p.m. and before 8 a.m. makes the real difference in what you are able to accomplish from 8 a.m. to 5 p.m. Those who make a personal commitment to learn something new every day are the ones who arrive in front. Winning rarely happens by accident.

Much of what a service department offers customers is KNOWLEDGE. In order to be part of a great service department, you must remain on the cutting edge of the information revolution. This quest for knowledge does not have to be expensive or encompass every spare minute of your time. However, ongoing education does take a conscious desire to be the best you can be.

Part of my responsibility as a service manager is to instill this quest for knowledge in my technicians. Just as I must be aware of cost of the goods we buy to resell, I must guide my staff to the most economical way for them to increase their personal educational opportunities.

The need for ongoing education is more important now than ever before in the office equipment industry. Sales, service, supplies, support, research and development . . . every aspect of what we do requires constant upgrading of our personally acquired professional skill. Employees must take the initiative to continually educate themselves outside of normal working hours.

In the past, our company "sold copiers and provided service to our customers." Currently, I am "enrolling end-users into solutions." Often these solutions are accomplished through the sale of equipment that is so new the patents are still pending. Instruction manuals are not available. My techs haven't been certified. The sales brochures haven't arrived. Advertisements for the mystery equipment are already generating customers' inquiries.

What is a self-respecting service professional to do?

Relentlessly push yourself to learn, read, explore, question, seek, listen, and watch. Take advantage of every bit of free information that is made available to you. Subscribe to the sources of free industry publications. Use manufacturer help lines. Take advantage of corporate-sponsored training. Encourage your employees and customers to enroll in community-college classes and publicly-funded vocational schools.

The library is still free. Librarians are paid to share knowledge. For those who aren't ready to make the financial commitment needed to go online at home, the library is an effective stepping stone. Most public libraries offer free access to the Internet. Not only will the librarians answer your questions, but fellow library patrons are often very helpful. I have found there is a real sense of sharing and friendly helpfulness among fellow computer users.

My favorite form of self-learning is still the audiotape or CD. I also find great bargains on Ebay or buying used on Amazon. It's a very easy way to feed my mind while I am driving, exercising, working in the yard or around the house. I usually borrow these tapes from the library or professional organizations. This way I am allowed more freedom to experiment with audioforms I would not be willing to buy or rent. I have been able to stretch my comfort zone of topics using the resources of the public library.

For those of you who haven't been to a bookstore lately, the entire atmosphere encourages testing the product before you buy. Most bookstores have comfortable chairs and sofas. Many bookstores have coffee shops, cafes, and piano bars attached to their reading areas. Book signings and reading groups abound. Bookstores have become social meeting places for the self-achievers. Stand in front of the computer self-help book section for a few moments. It's a great way to recruit future employees who are actively interested in learning.

Another great place to acquire free education is at a computer reseller. Large and small computer stores are great places to listen and learn, ask and share. Watching the ads in the newspaper allows you to see what is on the leading edge as well as what is on the way out. Just by scanning the daily newspaper, you can keep abreast of many of the trends in our business.

The business section of your local newspaper should be a "must" look each day. I emphasize the word look. You don't need to read every article. It is important to be aware of the big picture. Watch the industry's words of change. They are terms that you need to drop into your everyday conversation to increase your own creditability.

In today's business atmosphere, keeping up is not good enough. To be a leader, you must do more. Encourage yourself and those around you to help make history, not just watch it go by.

Human Networking

I remember when networking meant making professional contacts. We went to Chamber of Commerce mixers, Rotary Club meetings, and Toastmasters sessions to make personal connections that could extend to the business world.

Then the term networking upgraded itself to mean LANs and connectivity, digital, Novell versus NT, and something to do with the World Wide Web and surfing that had nothing to do with spiders or Malibu.

As a long-time traditional copier and fax dealer, I am forced to use my networking skills (making friends) to find other businesses that can allow me to sell their networking skills (hooking up digital things) to my customers.

Should I spend a great deal of time and money getting and keeping our employees cross-trained on ever-changing digital products, or spend time and energy making new professional friends?

The handwriting—or should I say the HP laser writing—is on the wall. I am networking to find the proper networkers.

I decided to identify the people and organizations who could do for me that which I was unable or unwilling to learn. If a customer needs cabling, I sub-contract to a qualified cabling company. This cabling issue brings to mind a special problem that smaller companies encounter.

Customers sometimes lose faith in a company that appears too small. Take, for instance, the highly-effective employee who can go out on Monday and make the sale. On Tuesday, they do all the clerical work of ordering and take up the details of lease acceptance. On Saturday, they show up in Levi's and baseball cap to do the cabling in the attic. The following Monday the same person is back to do the equipment delivery and the installation. Super employee then returns on Tuesday for on-line testing, followed on Wednesday by doing the in-house training.

Customers enjoy the security of having a key person to contact when dealing with a vendor. But a little strength in the backfield is also very reassuring. By outsourcing the cabling and delivery, the appearance of strength in numbers reassures the customer of your viability as a company.

Share the Work

Often, smaller companies can actually trade functions, expertise, or leads. Integrity plays a large role in this process. I have a group of about two dozen other businesses that I know I can trust with the well-being of my loyal customers. We have a verbal commitment among ourselves to never take away the core business from the originating dealer.

If the customer is in need of products or services I do not offer, I will give the customer the name and telephone number of the referral company. But if there is a concern about what products and services I am willing to share with one of my trusted fellow business people, I always make the initial call to the other business for my customer. I clearly outline, verbally or in writing, what my relationship is with the customer. Sometimes the referral is done for a lead fee or for on-going remuneration. Other times it is just an on-going process of sharing referrals that helps both companies and the customer.

When I do a favor or ask a favor of another vendor, I always end the conversation with a "You owe me for this one." Or "I owe you for this one, thanks." I keep a little file of favors and referrals. When a deal is tight and I need a favor from another vendor, I can refer back to a specific good deed or deal from the past. This helps to keep the balance of favors equal. Partnering with other companies must be mutually advantageous to both you and the customer.

When attending technical, sales, dealer, or organization meetings, make a point of meeting, exchanging business cards, and keeping in contact with those that can help your business prosper. Many computer and software companies present seminars at no charge throughout the USA. These are ideal occasions to network with businesses that are focused on learning new state-of-the-art skills.

Advertisers in business newspapers and magazines are also an excellent starting point when seeking a new networking contract. Writers, columnists, and those featured in articles are excellent sources for networking with quality people within our industry.

Old-fashioned networking requires ongoing integrity, record-keeping, and the genuine belief that who you know (and trust) is just as important as what you know.

Feel Better About Work and Life

If you want to achieve true success, sometimes it will take an attitude adjustment. We hear all the time:

"Take it easy."

"Don't work too hard."

"Thank goodness it's Friday."

"Let's take a break."

Whatever happened to the work ethic? Shouldn't we be saying:

"Work a little smarter."

"I love Mondays."

"I'll meet you in the conference room."

The Mule and the Ox

I remember the story of the farmer who had a mule and an ox. Both were plow pullers. The mule was a steady worker who did his job with no complaints. The ox was a tad lazy and decided to lie down and feign illness when the farmer arrived to harness the two workers.

When the mule returned from the day's plowing, the ox asked the equine, "How did things go?"

"The farmer and I had to work harder, but we managed to get the job done," brayed the mule.

The next day the ox decided that staying in the pasture was much better than working, so he again appeared too weak to pull the plow. At the end of the day, the ox again asked the mule if the farmer had said anything about the sickly bovine.

"Not to me," the mule replied, "but I did overhear the farmer asking the butcher how much a pound he was paying for ox meat."

The difference between an ox and mule's mentality is that mules have the pure determination (stubbornness) to get the job done. It is very easy to blame others for your boring or stressful life. Those who don't have the gumption to exercise, educate, and motivate themselves usually spend an enormous amount of effort figuring out how to get out of work or blame someone else for their own shortcomings.

A good manager is the key to focusing a worker's effort toward producing revenue rather than on figuring out a way to avoid working until the end of the workday.

Managerial Greatness

Too often, workers forget that we each must generate worth within our company if we are to be paid. A good manager can inspire average people to achieve extraordinary results.

I recently asked a group of people to write down the memorable characteristics of a great manager they have known.

In each case, the great manager was always willing to go the extra mile for their workers and the company.

A great manager never has the excuse of having a bad day, or expressing that work done on Monday and Friday does not need to be of equal quality to the work achieved on Tuesday, Wednesday, and Thursday.

A great manger is subconsciously thinking about better ways to get things done most of the time.

I came into work early Saturday morning to work on a special project. I instinctively checked my voice mail; I found a message left by a field supervisor at 4:45 a.m. as he sat in a golf course parking lot waiting for his 6:00 tee time. He was silently reviewing the happenings of the past week and had come up with a couple of new ideas for a special project we had been discussing.

His Saturday morning sharing of thoughts brought a wide smile to my face. Even in times of leisure, his free-flowing thoughts were helping improve our work place.

Working to Live or Vice Versa?

There is a fine line between living to work, and working to live. The better you feel about yourself, the better you will perform at work. And the better you feel about work, the better you will feel about your life. It is a true circle of success.

After a recent service meeting, one of my Hispanic workers approached me to share his newly-awarded United States Citizenship papers. He told of his final interview with the naturalization officers. "I did just what you have taught us to do when we are talking to a customer. I looked professional, then offered a handshake and my business card. I looked directly at them in a pleasant, attentive way. I listened to their questions and answered clearly. I made sure I arrived on time, was well dressed, and sat in the front row. I was the second person selected (out of over 100 applicants) for the interview.

An integral part of training a technician to be a good employee is helping them understand the importance of being a complete and balanced person. Never underestimate the power of ongoing management practices that help your employees be good people. This includes being a good spouse, parent, or child.

Take the time to praise and groom those worker-mules in your company. Good managers set an example of dedicated, conscientious work with an emphasis of helping their fellow workers lead balanced, successful lives.

Lessons in Leadership

Leadership is one of those great words that encourage you to stand a little taller, hold your head erect, and straighten both shoulders. No matter what position you hold in your company, community, or family, leadership is a lofty goal.

As I was poring over piles of receipts, struggling with the April 15th tax deadline, I came upon some notes I had taken several years ago. I had the privilege of being part of the audience listening to (then newly retired) General Colin Powell speak.

Years later, reading my notes, I felt goose bumps ripple on my arms. The hair stood up on the back of my neck. This man has charisma. While listening to General Powell speak, I understood why he is a multi-star general. After listening to this leader, I would follow him into battle or anywhere else he would choose to lead me.

Regardless of your political persuasion, the General and later Secretary of State Colin Powell is a man of substance. The speech I listened to that day showed humility and pride, humor and steadfastness. His speech that day addressed Leadership. General Powell is the personification of a leader.

I share with you a few notes I jotted down while listening to General Powell's speech.

Lesson 1:
Being responsible sometimes means getting people upset. Trying to get everyone to like you is a sign of mediocrity.

Lesson 2:
The day a soldier stops bringing you his problems is the day you stop being their leader. Do not treat those who ask for help as weak. Show concern for the challenges faced by others.

Lesson 3:
Don't be buffaloed by experts and the elite. Experts often possess more data than judgment.

Lesson 4:
Don't be afraid to challenge the pros, even in their own backyard. Leadership never emerges from blind obedience.

Lesson 5:
Never neglect details. Good leaders delegate and empower others liberally

Lesson 6:
You don't know what you can get away with until you try. Be prudent, not reckless. It is easier to ask for forgiveness than permission.

Lesson 7:
Keep looking below surface appearances. If it ain't broke, go find a better product that will work more effectively.

Lesson 8:
Organizations, plans, and theories don't accomplish anything. People make things happen. Only by attracting and keeping the best people can you accomplish great deeds.

Lesson 9:
Organizational charts and fancy titles count for next to nothing. Titles mean little in terms of real power. The capacity to influence and inspire is more powerful than any written title.

Lesson 10:
Never let your ego get so close to your position that when your position goes, your ego goes with it. Real leaders understand all jobs are continually becoming obsolete. A person's long-term worth is in their willingness to continually learn new skills and grab new responsibilities.

Lesson 11:
Fit no stereotypes. Don't chase the newest management fads. Flitting from fad to fad creates team confusion, reduces the leader's credibility, and drains organizational coffers.

Lesson 12:
Perpetual optimism is a force multiplier. The ripple effect of a leader's enthusiasm is awesome. Equally is the impact of cynicism and pessimism.

Lesson 13:
"Powell's Rules for picking people." Look for intelligence, judgment, a capacity to anticipate, and the ability to see around corners. Look for loyalty, integrity, high energy, balanced ego, and the desire to get things done.

Lesson 14:
Great leaders are usually great simplifiers. They can cut through arguments, debate, and doubt to offer a solution everybody can understand. Make your visions lean and compelling, not cluttered and buzzword laden.

Lesson 15:
Use the formula P@ 40 to 70 ratio. P equals probability of success. The other number indicates the percentage of information acquired. Once the information is in the 40 to 70 range, go with your gut.

Lesson 16:
The field commander is always right and the rear echelon is wrong, unless proven otherwise. Shift the power and financial responsibility to the folks who bring in the beans.

Lesson 17:
Have fun in your command. Don't always run at a breakneck pace. Take leave when you earn it. Spend time with your families. Surround yourself with those who take their work, but not themselves, seriously. It is best to work hard and play hard.

Lesson 18:
Command is lonely. Harry Truman was right, the buck must stop here. Leadership is the ability and willingness to make the tough, unambiguous choices that directly impact the fate of the organization.

I am going to keep this list in my desk drawer, handy for future reference. I thoroughly acknowledge his leadership skills.

Training Means Servicing the Brain

Today's office equipment service department is selling and implementing knowledge as its number one product. The term "solution" has become synonymous with the word "training," as technicians must learn to put into practice new ways accomplish procedures. Service employees must understand the equipment and the network it is attached to, but they also must enable customers to use products. A department's selling and training methods must match the learning styles of both employees and customers.

Training is a constant of any successful business. The perceptive service professional must realize that no two people learn in the same manner; training techniques must be flexible enough to allow for individual learning personalities.

Think for a moment about the great variety of external features of people, the diversity of their physical appearances—tall, short, male, female, blond, bald, etc. Even greater than these obvious differences is the difference in the way each of their brains perceives the world.

Before venturing into any company-sponsored training, whether of employees or customers, the trainer should understand how these differences affect learning styles and anticipate the diversity of learning avenues. Learning first how the brain learns is vital to selling, managing, training, and keeping a positive working atmosphere.

Brain connections grow when there is an enriched environment, stimulation, and challenging activities. Exposure to new ideas, problem-solving, pattern-seeking, challenges, novelty, and physical activities all help to create brain enrichment. The "Need to Know" will help stimulate attention, engage the thinking process, and ultimately produce learning.

Cognitive dissonance takes place when the brain does not understand a stimulus. The brain's attention will stay with the confusing thought, trying to make sense of the incomprehensible. As the brain stays concentrated on the non-understood issue, all other information is blocked out. Understanding the meaning of previous information is essential to be able to process the incoming data.

The Brain and Thermostats

The average adult brain can listen passively for 15-25 minutes. The brain must rest before the learning process can be optimized. The adult brain can only concentrate on one item at a time. However, the brain can address up to 16 different items per second. While trying to connect meaning to information presented, the brain switches back and forth between receiving and processing new information.

The brain learns by connecting new information to old information. When the pattern of incoming information doesn't make sense, it cannot be processed into the brain's memory. We must communicate in ways that the brain can make connections from past connections.

If a teaching environment is too hot, too cold, or too noisy, the brain cannot process information properly; it is too busy processing the irritation to be able to process the learning. If people are afraid or concerned for their emotional safety, the flight mode is always at the front of their consciousness. They will not be able to listen. A relaxed, comfortable level is much more conducive to learning or making decisions.

The old saying, "Let me sleep on that before I give you a decision," easily explains the way the brain works. When we sleep, newly gathered information is processed and stored into our long-term memory. Therefore, sleep is vital to long-term knowledge. Learning requires periodic ongoing processing. Most of us have heard horror stories related to technical employees that have been sent off to a two-week training school. Too much information is presented in too short of a time. The attendee cannot comprehend all the information in such a short length of time.

What does all this information about the human brain have to do with the digital, network, solution, scanning, document-storage, facility-management, copier, printer, processor, software-selling former old-time copier sales company?

It is vital to understand that our selling and training methods must match the learning styles of our customers. We must be able to identify and change our styles to bend to their needs. Our effectiveness must be structured around the way the brain captures and processes information. The human brain retains (captures and processes) information in the following proportions. Within three days of first being exposed to a new idea or concept the percent of retention is:

Read-only, silently--10%

Hear-only, what someone says or reads aloud--20%

See-only, information in e-mailed PowerPoint or proposal--30%

See and hear--50%

Say aloud, personal understanding of the information--70%

See process done, followed by doing it personally--90%

It is easier to learn something right the first time than to try to change deeply entrenched habits. Think and plan before you teach. When you teach new concepts correctly the first time, thousands of costly mistakes will never happen.

Trainers and sellers must realize that emotion drives attention and attention drives learning. Acknowledge the five senses of learning: sight, sound, touch, smell, and taste. Each of these areas can be a direct link to greater individualized learning.

Tune In to Learning Styles

In a training environment, everyone should be encouraged to learn at their own optimum level. Say it, see it, write it, hear it, feel it, smell it, taste it. Ask questions, take it apart, break it, repair it, look at a diagram, touch the surface of a photograph. Make up jingles that use the first letter of all the needed information.

Trainers must stay intimately attuned to the feedback of their students. Subtle mode shifts must be acknowledged. Ask questions that are learning tools. Ask a question; praise the person who answers, even if the given response is not the one you were anticipating.

"Explain to me how you reached that conclusion" is preferable to "Wrong, who has a better idea?" The student who logically explains an incorrect response will help the instructor be able to understand the student's line of thinking.

A creative instructor will skillfully ask a chain of individual questions. This will enable the students to positively rethink their own logic. The ability to construct their own personalized path toward success is the desired learning process.

Interactive training must encourage each individual to have the freedom to learn at their personal optimum level. Tools of learning include flip charts, white boards, dissection tables, manuals, multicolored highlighters, crayons, tracing paper, file cards, chairs, flashlights, tape recorders, cameras, non-judgmental thinking, curiosity, camaraderie, and a little comic relief.

Anything that is worth learning needs to be repeated at least twice. "This is important, write it down," is a common instructing phrase. But it might be equally prudent to request it to be spoken aloud, or sung in a catchy verse.

Other methods that stimulate learning and help processing:

- Sharing Real Life experiences (demo, field trial, tour of company)
- Immersion: tell a story that creates a word picture and/or moral or real life experience the listener can visualize and believe.
- Interactive concrete activities: hands-on participation in whatever is being taught. Using a new scanning or email product.
- Interactive abstract: computer training or interactions showing the desired learning process. Self-directed animated PowerPoint of product being sold or taught
- Field independent activities: get customer or student away from their area of familiarity to see what is happening in person. This can be an in-house demo, or visiting another customer who is currently using the product.

There are no dumb questions. A trainer must never chide or downgrade anyone who politely asks a relevant question. (Trainers must creatively divert anyone who constantly interrupts or "tells war stories" under the guise of questions.)

The road to success is always under construction. The only way to never fail is to never try. The fastest way to succeed is to learn from each failure. The learning process must be narrowly focused on the wide variety of needs that must be met in order to optimize each person's learning ability.

Job Descriptions

Occupation: ______________________________

When is the last time you had to fill out some type of form that asked you to list your occupation? Did you automatically have an acceptable answer? Perhaps you can easily identify yourself as an owner, sales representative, service manager, or technician; but this occupation question always makes me pause.

When I write "Service Manager," I always envision a car dealership. The service manager's office is always just to the right of the parts department. The service manager's office is always empty. I imagine the service manager is away from the office dealing with an irate customer, talking with the warranty claims national representative or looking into the computer sensing device under the hood of a vehicle.

For the office equipment dealership owner to write "Owner" or "President" is rather ambiguous. Owner or president of what? Might you be confused with the U.S. Chief of State? If you write "Sales Representative," you are sales rep of what? Are you the checkout clerk at Wal-Mart or the seller of billion dollar jets at Boeing?

This occupation question can, indeed, be perplexing.

In today's business environment, we all must strive to be coaches, mentors, educators, entrepreneurs, controllers, electricity usage monitors, students, governmental rule followers, and customer relation representatives. The old song lyrics say it best: My job is "taking care of business," which encompasses an entire gamut of duties and responsibilities.

What Do *You* Do?

As everyone's tasks within the business community continue to evolve, the understanding of each employee's work responsibilities continues to change. The age- old, employer-furnished "Job Description" has fallen into decline as workplace duties evolve at a breakneck pace.

A former dot-com executive once told of his roller-coaster job history: "In less than six months I went from pizza delivery man (my last college job), to graphic designer, to programmer, to Web Master, to C.O.O., to being unemployed. Before I could figure out what my job responsibilities were, I was standing in the unemployment line."

The quickly changing status of the business world reinforced my need to re-examine the long ignored job descriptions within my service department. I found two sets. One was written with very general language encompassing large categories of duties. It has held up pretty well with the test of time. The second was much more detailed and focused on specific tasks and responsibilities. Its language was archaic. Voice and e-mail, cellular phones and digital networking were not addressed. While the basic structure was usable, the language and scope needed generous revisions.

If you do not have formalized job descriptions, or if they have not been reviewed for a while, it is time to revisit these documents. When the workload tends to slow down during the summer is a great time to work on this project.

One of the easiest ways to start your quest for appropriate, up-to-date job descriptions is to ask your employees to make a list of the tasks they do. Rather than have everyone sit down and write up what they think they do, have it be a month-long project. In some cases, it may be appropriate to have this list compiled over a fiscal quarter or to include a year-end closing.

Assign each employee the responsibility of listing all the little tasks they do on a daily basis. Over the course of a month (or quarter), a very detailed list of duties will be compiled. Once the "what-I-do" list is completed, the "how I do this" documents can be made.

A Perpetual Guide

This specific list of duties can be used as a basis for the job description. It will also provide an accurate job or "desk" work guide.

The transitive nature of employment often finds one employee leaving before the replacement can be fully trained or hired. Cross training of jobs and duties can be simplified when preparations have been made in advance.

Sample job descriptions can be found on the Internet on various Web sites. There are also many books on the subject. The want ads in your local newspaper can spark your imagination on items you need to list.

Here are some items to be considered when writing your job descriptions:

- ✔ Job Title
- ✔ Functions of the Job
- ✔ Major Duties: can be very general or extremely specific
- ✔ Working Relationships: Who do you report to; who reports to you; general chain of command
- ✔ Ongoing Learning: how this is going to be accomplished; whose responsibility

- ✔ General: Follow all local, state, regional and federal laws. This includes immediately notifying a supervisor or manager of any on the job injuries, sexual harassment, health hazards, on the job accidents, inappropriate on-the-job actions or any other situation the employee finds offensive.
- ✔ Privacy Issues and Proprietary Information
- ✔ E-mail, Voice mail and Cell Phone Usage limitations
- ✔ Safety: "Always follow safe work procedures and habits. Safety is the number one priority."
- ✔ Reaffirm mandatory compliance to all the rules and regulations in the Policy and Procedure book.
- ✔ An open statement of personal learning commitment might be appropriate. "Ongoing training and familiarization with industry progress, outside of paid work hours, is essential for advancement and continuing employment."

If the employee drives their own car on the job or a company vehicle is provided, reference to their responsibilities can be included in the Job Description. Appropriate references may include:

- ✔ Always follow safe driving habits.
- ✔ Report any on the job accidents or out of the ordinary incidents.
- ✔ Current state issued drivers license and active vehicle registration and insurance on any vehicle used for transportation during work hours is mandatory.

Always include the phrase, "And any other duties or responsibilities that are assigned by management" in the text of the job description. "Including, but not limited to" is another great catch phrase that can be used.

If appropriate recourse for employee wrongdoings is mentioned, refer to more than one person who can be contacted in case of sexual harassment or other infringements of an employee's rights. This provides the employee with another person to contact if their supervisor is the alleged wrongdoer.

There may be many overlaps between the requirements listed in your Policy and Procedure Manual and the items included in the Job Description. Just make sure that the two documents agree. Important issues can be stated in both documents. Generally, individual job descriptions will be more detailed.

Variations of Job Titles

Many organizations are using a *desk task list*. This encompasses a list of jobs that are assigned to a *desk* or work group. It can be compared to a field service territory. Different people may be assigned to do specific jobs, as needed. Rather than cover for an absent person, the duties of the *desk* can be reassigned. Physiologically, socially, and politically speaking, work place psychologists believe it is easier to shuffle workers from *desk* to *desk* than to substitute for a missing worker.

Some companies use multi-page, very specific Job Descriptions. Others use a simpler, one-page outline format. Job descriptions can be as varied as the positions and companies they represent.

Part of management's responsibility is to have the structure and framework that encourages employees to achieve to expectations. If management is not willing to do their job (provide appropriate job descriptions), chances are employees will emulate that example. Be professional, be proactive: update or create Job Descriptions.

Exposition/Convention Etiquette

I was standing in line at the base of the ski bowl waiting for my turn on the ski gondola. Out of the corner of my eye I spied the strangest sight. There stood a man wearing a snorkel, mask, 24-inch-long swim fins, and a pair of Speedo swim trunks.

Goose bumps were erupting out of his zinc oxide-coated arms, because the temperature at the base of this ski run was hovering in the teens. He looked very uncomfortable. I couldn't imagine what strange set of circumstances had brought him so unprepared for the ski slopes.

I have encountered this same sense of perplexity when viewing convention-goers who attend yearly events equally ill prepared. Wearing three-inch high heels, hard-soled dress shoes, or tight-fitting, uncomfortable clothes is inappropriate. These same people bring two business cards, no pen, and forget their reading glasses. They arrive 45 minutes before the show closes and have no plan for optimizing their time spent on the floor.

In order to take full advantage of your next conference opportunity, here are a few tips to demystify the experience.

Most conferences offer educational presentations. Carefully read the catalog of topics and speakers. Be bold. Attend an educational seminar that you know nothing about. You will have nothing to lose but your own ignorance. As quickly as industries change, you need to take advantage of the ability to share an hour of your time with an industry expert.

Panel discussions and question-and-answer periods are often offered in many programs. Be a participant. The questions you have formed in your own mind will probably be of interest to others. When a panelist uses a term or acronym you don't understand, make a note to find out what it means.

Upon completion of each presentation, take time to fill out the comment cards. Your candid comments will help the convention-planners better accommodate your needs and concerns in the future,

Register and Hit the Floor

Before entering the convention floor, you must be registered. Read the overhead signs carefully before you choose a line. There is no need to waste precious time waiting in the wrong line.

Display your name (admission) badge for easy visibility. You will be able to move in and out of the convention floor without being stopped by the door attendants. You also will allow the vendors to respond to your needs and location more easily.

Speaking of vendors — they want you to come into their booth. The only reason their companies have paid thousands of dollars for that little checkerboard space is to entice you into their domain. You might find it intimidating to walk into a booth void of any attendees. Be bold. The lone exhibitors you see are waiting just for you.

It is acceptable convention etiquette to visit the booth of a vendor you know nothing about, even if you have no need for the advertised product right now. Every vendor is looking for new customers. Most dealers are attending the convention to gain new ways to improve their business. Meeting new vendors is a vital part of convention attendance.

Many vendors will offer free giveaways or contests. If you want their prize, be prepared to listen to a little bit about their product. Most vendors will request you give them a business card or allow them to "swipe" your registration card.

It is also acceptable to walk into a vendor's booth and eavesdrop on a conversation that is in progress. You also can ask questions in the middle of someone else's demo or conversation. It's like a big old-fashioned party line. All for one; one for all.

Once in a booth, if you meet another attendee who is of interest to you, talk to him or her. If the conversation is going to be prolonged or if the vendor's booth is too crowded, the two of you should move to another area to continue your conversation.

Plan Ahead

It is socially acceptable to exchange business cards. Bring four times more business cards than you think you will need. The most repeated statement I hear at the convention is, "I ran out of business cards," followed closely by, "Do you have a pen?"

When you are on the convention floor, have a plan. Even if you plan to wander aimlessly wander in a systematic pattern. Otherwise, it is easy to miss entire areas of the show. Or, you see the same areas repeatedly. Check out the hours the convention floor is open.

Look at the convention coverage before arriving on the floor, to view the list of exhibitors, sponsors, educational events, a time schedule, detailed layout of the convention floor, and location of all exhibits. You should also take note of the locations of the telephones, food areas, restrooms and sign-up areas.

I hope you will mark out a few vendors (booths) that are on your must-see list. Many of the vendors will have presentations at specific posted times. Make note of the times for the programs you want to attend. Many vendors have theater-style seating in their booths. Show up a little before Showtime to get a good seat. Your feet will appreciate the rest.

Speaking of feet, wear shoes that are appropriate for a 5K run. Fashion must take a back seat to comfort. Clothes that are loose-fitting with multiple pockets are ideal for the task at hand. Just as the prudent vacationer plans ahead, so must the far-sighted business person plan to make the most out of his or her convention experience.

We're Responsible for Learning

As I stand on the convention floor watching refurbishing specialists teaching the on-lookers the profit-making tricks of their trade, I'm reminded of my own initiation into the servicing world.

I remember my first technical-training school. Upon successfully completing the class, I still had no idea how I was going to fix the equipment I had just spent two weeks dissecting. I had been taught how to install it and identify all of its components and switches. I could recite the PM cycles and the sequence of operation. I soon discovered that customers do not pay for these cerebral activities. I needed to know how to fix broken copiers in order to earn a living.

I was very fearful. The manufacturer's trainer had not taught me the facts and skills that my boss and our customers expected me to know. They had failed me.

After this rude awakening, I became acutely convinced of my task when attending any training course, lecture, or seminar. I was brutally made aware of the need to take responsibility for my own learning. It is my responsibility to make sure I arrive prepared to absorb that which I am taught. Additionally, I must make sure I ask appropriate (respectful) questions. These inquiries will fill the gap between what I am told and the information I need to bring back from the learning experience.

Whether you are attending a one-hour lecture or a four-week certification school, you are ultimately responsible for the amount of learning you receive.

The Art of Learning

Learning is more of an art than science. Each person must enter upon the journey of learning from a practical and personal point of view.

As a manager, trainer, lecturer, and person who hires, I am constantly amazed at how unprepared some people are for success. People will travel a long distance and pay money to attend a learning event (or job interview), but they will forget to bring along their tool case for learning.

The minimal physical tools for learning are: showing up, having something to write with, and having something to write on. Achievers often show up 15 minutes early with mini-recorder, laptop computer, spiral notebook, highlighters, multiple writing tools, a light jacket, mints, gum, candy, and caffeinated liquid.

Once your body appears with pen and paper, the important points of learning become apparent. Why are you attending? Have you actually taken the time and effort to think about what you expect to receive in exchange for the time (and money) you are investing?

The success of any learning experience has more to do with your actions than the trainer (sponsor) of the meeting. Learning takes active participation. You must make the decision about whether you are going to attend as an observer or an active participant.

If you choose to make the optimum use of your time, make sure your tool case for learning is properly stocked.

- Eat enough to keep your stomach quiet and your eyes active.
- Be on time.
- Sit up front. The closer you sit to the front of the room, the more you will learn.
- Get an appropriate amount of sleep the previous night.
- Jot down questions you hope will be answered.
- Make notes on the handouts. Take them back to the office. Use them.
- Talk to the presenter before and/or after the presentation.
- Fill out (turn in) the post-seminar questionnaire honestly.
- Seek out an on-site seminar official and express your feelings.
- Take away three ideas that will help you or your business.
- Implement the use of these new ideas within one week.
- Be courageous; attend a seminar on a new technology.
- Meet new people. Group meetings are made for networking.
- Talk to people between sessions. Ask meaningful questions.
- Exchange business cards with other attendees and speakers.
- Follow up with a phone call or note to anyone you think you may be able to do business with in the future.
- Have some fun. Laugh out loud.

For those of you who are reading this at a conference, put these ideas to work today. For those reading from the comfort of your home or office, slip this article in your suitcase. The next time you have to travel for business, it will be there to remind you of your responsibilities. Bring an open mind and a full tool case for learning.

Taking the Next Step Forward— It's Up to You

The Internet, executive retreats, newspapers, magazines, television, and trade journals often guide service managers and business officers on how to become more effective in the work place.

How can the non-managerial employee take the next step? What actions can be taken by a sales representative, technician, dispatcher, supervisor, administrative or warehouse worker to improve their own position within the company and community?

The old adage, "actions speak louder than words," still holds true. To be noticed, appreciated, and ultimately rewarded takes patience and persistence.

Start your quest for advancement by having an untarnished work history of reliability. Come to work every day, on time. Contribute a full eight hours of work each day. Do more than what is asked of you. Always answer "Yes" to any reasonable request made by a superior or fellow worker. Volunteer for any new project. Better yet, volunteer to be on the planning committee of the company's open house, work session, or holiday party.

Yes, this will take extra time and effort. Managers are required to do more on a regular basis. Dependability is essential, and showing up matters. Having a reputation for being five minutes early rather than always being a few minutes late makes a difference. This requires that you have a dependable car, money for gas, an alarm clock that works, and an unbending commitment to self-respect.

Making Practical Choices

You can attain leadership status without management issuing you a new title on a business card. Fellow workers will look up to and instinctively follow a person who displays ongoing leadership qualities. Emotional and intellectual trust is earned one action at a time.

When a problem develops at work, be a problem solver rather than a blame pointer. Rather than complaining about the problem, develop a strategy. When appropriate, present a written synopsis of the problem with one or two possible solutions. If an economic expenditure is part of the solution, present a sample budget explaining how much money will be required to complete the required changes. Explain the positive monetary outcome, once the problem is resolved.

If management does not implement your suggestions, move on. Do not dwell on your unfulfilled suggestions. Keep an open mind and positive attitude. Attend company functions. Always be attentive. Take notes when appropriate. Offer to share the information with others.

When you are attending an off-hours company function, act as if you are still at work. Dress conservatively for the function. Make a point of meeting new employees and their families. Ask questions about the work they do within the company. Be cautious with what you say. You never know whose spouse may overhear an indiscrete comment.

A bad manager need not ruin a good employee. But a good employee can rise above a lackluster superior. How can quiet, hard-working employees make sure they are not overlooked? How do you get a non-responsive boss to react to your ideas?

Make a conscious habit of dressing to the next level of achievement. Continually self- educate yourself to the changes within your industry. Keep abreast of trends in the national and world economic markets.

Put your ideas into writing. Make suggestions. Prepare a needed form or work sheet. Give one copy to your manager. Ask if it's OK to pass out your newly created form to other employees at the next (service) meeting.

It is acceptable computer etiquette to put a file name at the bottom of your form. Make sure your name is part of the file name. Soon other workers will be asking you for a copy of that form. This is a perfect way to quietly advertise your extra effort and leadership qualities.

Many workers who spend a great deal of time in their car listen to "books on tape." Volunteer to organize a lending library of educational and entertaining tapes for fellow field employees to share. You will help yourself as well as showing leadership ability to your peers.

Share Knowledge, Rise to the Top

When you find an easier way to do something, take the extra effort to share the knowledge in the form of a short memo. The use of a digital picture or hand-drawn sketch is helpful. Again, give a copy to your manager and ask to share time (cost) saving tips with the other techs at the next service meeting.

If you have service bulletin board, post your cost-saving tip on the board for all to see. Eventually other people (including the owner) in the company will see your extra effort.

A clean car, an organized tool case or work area, always being early, wearing clean, ironed clothes and polished shoes, exhibiting a confident attitude, make a statement for all to see.

Often technicians do not get the opportunity to interface with other employees from their company. When you run into one of your sales people in the field (doing a demo), make sure you introduce yourself. Shake hands and say your name slowly. Thank the sales person for increasing the company's customer base.

If you do everything perfectly, it may take two or three years for the appropriate people to see your leadership characteristics. Even the best of cream takes time to rise to the top of a glass of unpasteurized milk.

A forward-thinking manager realizes that the only way to be promoted is to train (mentor) someone to do the job. A good manager is always looking for those who show the ability to move up to a more responsible position.

A more productive employee can eclipse a bad manager. If your immediate supervisor is not a star performer, his or her job may be up for serious review.

The manager who is afraid to allow employees to grow will stagnate not only his or her own career, but also the career of others and the growth of the company. A good leader will grow to meet the challenges of other employees, pushing the envelope of their mutual growth.

If you follow these steps and are not rewarded with advancement within your own company, you will have prepared yourself for being able to move on to a new company.

Exhibiting leadership characteristics, confidence, sharing new ideas with other workers, and continuing your education will help you in any future endeavor. Making the effort to improve your job performance will ultimately allow you to improve your own talents and grow your career possibilities.

Credits and Acknowledgements

These six chapters comprise articles written and copyrighted by Ronelle Ingram over the past several years. All of the articles have appeared in various publications, both print and electronic, starting in the early 1990s. Asay Publishing Network and the author would like to acknowledge the work of the editors and staff of publications in which Ronelle Ingram's articles have been featured: *ENX* Magazine and ENX Online; *ImageSource* Magazine and ImageSource Online; Repair, Service, and Remarketing (RS&R) News and RSRNews Online, 1995-2004.

Asay Publishing Network appreciates the kind and able assistance of many people who have participated in making this book happen. The company relied upon the expertise of Brenda Tidd, Asay's graphics specialist and production manager, for designing the cover and pages; photographer Anamaria Brandt, Tustin, CA, for providing quality photographs of the author; Rebecca Kanan for editing the collection; and Roger Asay, owner and publisher at Asay Publishing Co., for generating enthusiasm, resources, and support for the publication. And, of course, we thank Ronelle Ingram for continuing to do what she does so well—always offering service with her indomitable smile.

Index

Comments

"You learn and are entertained in every seminar led by Ronelle Ingram, and the'Service with a Smile'articles bring her savvy to book form. Every office machines professional will glean service tips and advice from this book by Ronelle, who also brands her seminars and writing with a sense of humor."

--Neal McChristy, former Repair, Service, and Remarketing News editor at Asay Publishing Network, currently a freelance writer for the imaging industry.

Comments Ronelle Ingram has received:

"It was raining money. Our only regret was it took so long to implement the ideas you presented in the seminar we attended. We generated $14,000 of revenue the first month we used your"End of Warranty"form. Thanks for sharing your knowledge and increasing our bottom line."

--Tom Skerl, V.P. Sales, North Coast Business Systems, Cleveland, Ohio

"Your knowledge is universal. Thanks from all your Australian friends. We learn and profit (from) and enjoy your humor and sweet rewards. Your hands-on, been there-done that approach saves all of us the frustration of trying to reinvent the wheel."

--David Kyle, Executive Director, BTA Australia

"I finished reading your article this morning. I fell asleep with you in my arms last night. My wife is getting jealous. Thanks for providing practical, proven, ready to implement ideas I can start using today."

--Noel Jago, Managing Director, Office Equipment Solution Center, Townsville, Australia

"Your University of Service Management Program helps us all master the science of dealing with field service employees. I never understood the nuances of dealing with "out of sight"employees. Thanks for opening my eyes to the subtle management changes I need to use to motivate my outside techs."

--J. W. Bowman, V.P. Service, Alta Office Systems, Salt Lake City, UT

"Your articles read like a Diary of Success. Whenever things are going good or bad, I know I can use your writings as a reference. When I forget to plan the agenda for a service or sales meeting, I just turn to your writings and I sound like a genius who spent hours planning a motivation program. Thanks for making me look so smart."

--John Wisniewski, Owner, Central Business Equipment, Saratoga, N.Y.

"You have always been my role model. A female who had done it all: Field Service Tech, Technical Manager, Director of Supply Sales, Writer, Speaker, Humorist, BTA FIX instructor, BTA Volunteer of the Year, Champion Equestrian and dog trainer. Thanks for breaking the ground for all those who have followed your path of success."

--Paige Davison, Owner, South East Solutions, Key West, FL

About the Author

Ronelle Ingram started her involvement in the office equipment industry as a tool case carrying copier field service technician. She was the first female to ever graduate Savin's full line copier technical school in 1972. Through the years she has worked for a major copier equipment manufacturer, a start-up copier dealer and established dealerships. Her natural speaking, writing and leadership abilities led to her involvement in NOMDA's (now BTA) dealer training programs. As her reputation as a national trainer and speaker grew, requests for written explanations of her training programs and service management philosophies expanded into her writing career.

Through the years she has been recognized by her peers by winning: BTA National Volunteer of the Year, Pat Merritt Spirit Award (for the BTA instructor that best exemplifies professionalism in training), NOMDA's National Train-the-Trainers Speak-off Champion, Manager of the Year (at multi-companies), Presidents Club, Mita's Technical Proficiency Test (multiple year winner), BTA Western Region Educator of the Year and Volunteer of the Year (both multiple year winner).

Ronelle has served as a Member of the BTA's International Board of Directors, BTA Western Region President, Southern California BTA President, Member of ITEX Advisory board, spoken for National Dealer meetings including Mita, Katun, AIMED (Assoc. of Independent

Mailing Equipment Dealers), Time Clock Dealers Assoc., International Business Products Inc, BPCA (Business Products Council Association), BTA Australia, and BTA Canada.

All the while, Ronelle has worked fulltime as a technical service director. Ronelle has remained on the cutting edge of the industry. She actually goes to work each day and manages a service department. Ronelle writes and speaks about her day to day trials and tribulations of what it takes to create and sustain a profitable office equipment service department.

Ronelle lives on mini-ranch in Orange County, California, with her family, including three dogs and two Icelandic horses. As an accomplished equestrian, she has won multiple regional, state, and national English and Western horseback riding awards and year-end championships.